CINDY PAWLCYN

WITH BRIGID CALLINAN

Ten Speed Press
Box 7123
Berkeley, California 94707
www.tenspeed.com

Distributed in Australia by Simon & Schuster Australia, in Canada by Ten Speed Press Canada, in New Zealand by Southern Publishers Group, in South Africa by Real Books, in Southeast Asia by Berkeley Books, and in the United Kingdom and Europe by Airlift Book Company.

Cover and book design: Marianne Agnew
Design assistance: Toni Tajima
Book production: Betsy Stromberg
Copyediting: Sharon Silva
Manuscript development: Jackie Wan
Mustard illustrations: Marianne Agnew
Principal food and location photography: Laurie Smith
Additional location photography (pages ii, viii [Condiments], ix, x, 75, 99, 103 [left], 126, 127, 131, 142–43, 158 [top right], 159 [top left & right, bottom right], 221, 230): Jonathan Chester
Food and prop styling: Wesley Martin

Library of Congress Cataloging-in-Publication Data

Pawlcyn, Cindy.
  [Mustards Grill cookbook]
  Mustards Grill Napa Valley Cookbook
Valley / Cindy Pawlcyn with Brigid Callinan ; photography by Laurie
Smith.
      p. cm.
Includes index.
  ISBN 1-58008-045-6
  1. Cookery, American--California style. 2. Mustards Grill. I. Title:
Mustards Grill cookbook. II. Callanan, Brigid. III. Title.

  641.59794--dc21

                        2001000927

Printed in Hong Kong
First printing, 2001

1 2 3 4 5 6 7 8 9 10 — 06 05 04 03 02 01

Acknowledgments

Tons of gratitude to all of the recipe testers, especially Lois Lee, Yvonne Moody, Elizabeth Owen, Michael Wolf, David Graham, Nickie and Peter Zeller, and Aimee Newberry. And to all of their eaters as well.

What can I say about Brigid Callinan, other than she's one of my favorite sugar, butter, and chocolate magicians. The chapter on desserts is her handiwork. I don't think she'll ever forgive me for getting her into this project, but I hope she'll be proud of it.

Thanks to Marianne Agnew for eating at Mustards ever since the beginning and for making the book look like the real place.

Thank you to Jackie Wan, who made English out of my writing, and to everyone at Ten Speed for their support, especially publisher Kirsty Melville; editor Lorena Jones; and designer Toni Tajima. Many thanks also to photographer Laurie Smith and food stylist Wesley Martin.

A million, zillion thanks to Sherry Fournier, without whom my part of the book would never have gotten done.

And to my husband, Murdo Laird, a rabid fish hater who let me cook fish in our house when I was testing the recipes, as long as I'd make him the ham-and-cheese sandwiches he loves so much. He also read and reread the manuscript, and helped unscramble my words into terms others could understand. Much love always, m'dear.

The biggest thank-you of all

goes to my mom, Dorothy Jane Pawlcyn, the woman who taught me how to cook (or at least how to get out of doing the dishes). This book is dedicated to you, Mom. . . . XOX

Way Too Many Wines

Introduction

Appetizers

Soups

Salads

From the Smoker & Grill

Out o' the Pan

Sandwiches

Sides

Condiments

Oddities

Desserts

I was out of town the night Mustards Grill opened, but I certainly heard about it when I returned. It was 1983 and the event was widely (and wildly) discussed all over Napa Valley. The three partners—Cindy, Bill, and Bill— had expected a modest turnout. Instead, they were over-whelmed by eager customers from the moment they opened the doors. At some point, I learned later, batteries of kitchen helpers and friends had to be dispatched to several local markets to buy additional groceries.

My first visit was a few days after that legendary opening night. For me, it was love at first sight— the start of a romantic affair that continues today. I was struck by the creative genius that went into the restaurant: the playful tongue-in-cheek exterior signs, the colorful descriptions on the menu, the lighthearted way the local wines were offered. The food was inventive and tasty, served by a staff both professional and fun loving. It was easy to get caught up in the charm.

The Napa Valley didn't have many restaurants in the early 1980s, and most of those in the business seemed almost oblivious to the emerging international interest in the local wines. Mustards obviously wasn't a restaurant in which you'd expect to see an encyclopedic wine list chained to the table, but it was clear that the place was wine friendly and willing to experiment. This attitude set the stage for the future.

The first list included twenty wines, all local. I suspect that many had been selected as much for their availability and price as for their quality. As the area's vintners grew increasingly comfortable with the place, however, it became a matter of great personal pride to have one's wines represented at Mustards. What better way to secure a spot on the wine list than to offer the restaurant something rare, something sure to impress a visitor? Soon the list was packed with scarce wines, many of them from older vintages long sold out. Without actually meaning to, Mustards had become a sort of wine geek's paradise. It was about this time that I learned about Manzanilla and a little more in the process.

A restaurant critic visiting from Los Angeles invited my wife and me to join him at Mustards for dinner one night. His knowledge of food and wine was extensive, and I was eager to spend an evening out with him. At the same time, I wanted to impress him with the sophistication of my latest restaurant discovery. As he sat down and I handed him the wine list, I was certain he would be bowled over by the extensive selection of rare and valuable choices. He quickly turned the list back to the waiter, asked if

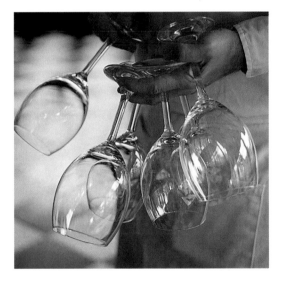

the Manzanilla was fresh, which it was, and chilled, which it also was, and ordered us each a glass. "This place is great," he remarked. "It's rare to find a restaurant that knows how to serve Manzanilla properly." I had never even looked at that section of the list. And so it was that I learned a valuable lesson in dining out. I also learned a valuable lesson about Mustards Grill and the people who own it, and I haven't underestimated it since.

A few years later, Michael Ouelette became the restaurant's manager, and not long after, a partner. His zeal for wine led Mustards into the golden age of wine service that it enjoys today. At one point, there were probably as many fine French wines on the wine list at Mustards as there are at all but a handful of the top French restaurants in Manhattan. Every table enjoyed its wine in glass made of the finest crystal. All wines—red, white, even the occasional rosé—were decanted, a simple act that enormously improved the quality of what was served and introduced a practice now common at many restaurants. Michael developed a program for wines available by the glass that is also widely copied. One can, for example, enjoy a glass each of four widely different Zinfandels with baby back ribs, or a glass each of four different styles of Chardonnay with Chinese chicken salad. Reliable French champagne was made available by the glass, just as at, say, Taillevent. The bar had been raised, and the raising had happened in my own backyard.

Lately, Mustards has struck out in new directions, focusing on wines of the New World, once again staying a bit ahead of the curve. The enthusiasm for wines has never wavered, and the energy necessary to seek out the best remains high. Mustards's open-mindedness is as refreshing today as it was eighteen years ago. After all these years, the excitement of discovering the next new thing is a natural part of any meal at Mustards, and the restaurant is still a required stop for any out-of-town wine enthusiast. It's rare for a wine celebrity or tradesman to travel to the Napa Valley today without Mustards on the itinerary, and has become a sort of local party game to drop in and see just who is in town dining with whom. Mustards has become the wine-trade equivalent of Toot Shor's, but with better food.

A great wine list is hard to find, but a restaurant with an enduring fondness for their customers will create one. Today, I look forward to my periodic visits to Mustards the way I look forward to a meal at the home of an old friend. I know I'll be welcome and comfortable. I know I'll eat and drink well. I know I'll relax, and I'll probably see someone I want to see or learn something I need to learn. Most importantly, though, I know I'll start the meal off with a glass of fresh, chilled Manzanilla.

—Bruce Neyers
Napa, 2000

Introduction

This book has been a very long time in coming—eighteen years in fact. I've been through a lot of silly, fun, and painful stuff creating Mustards and keeping it going, some of which I could have lived without. I've opened and sold maybe a dozen other restaurants in those years, more than I ever would have dreamed of when I first started out. Today, Mustards is still alive and well, and what more could a girl ask for? All I ever wanted was a restaurant.

This book is about the best part, all the good times of the last eighteen years, some of the people who have helped me out along the way, and the food, of course. (Actually, these are only the recipes that have stood the test of time and that I can remember. I wish I were better at taking notes!)

Throughout the years, many chefs, cooks, and dishwashers have worked at the restaurant, and each could probably add a chapter to this book, if not several volumes. To them I owe my deepest respect, not to mention my reputation, for a chef is nothing but a reflection of the people who work alongside her. I could not have managed without their expertise, imagination, and just plain hard work.

This is not a collection of our fancy recipes, but ones that people have asked for and others that I think people would like to try making in their own kitchens. It is not my intention to wow fellow chefs. I want to enhance the experience of the home cook and allow the wonderful people who have eaten at Mustards to take a bit of the place home with them.

I hate to follow recipes—it's a pain in the ass. But it's the only way I have found to keep things somewhat consistent, so we follow them as best as we can at the restaurant. Feel free to make substitutions as you see fit, though, for personal taste or to eliminate a trip to the store. Think of these recipes as a collection of kitchen maps to get you headed in the right direction.

So go cook. It's good for the belly and the soul, and your family and friends will love you for it.

Appetizers

When I eat out, I'll often order two or three appetizers, split the main course with a friend, or maybe even skip it, and go straight on to dessert. That way I get to taste a little bit of a lot more dishes.

We do a lot of fish and shellfish appetizers at Mustards. It's a wonderful way to take advantage of the bounty of our coastal California waters, and it also allows us flexibility, which is important, as availability varies from day to day. We call our fish purveyor the first thing in the morning to see what we're going to get (as opposed to what we thought we were getting), and then we decide what seafood appetizers will go on the specials board for the day.

The most difficult thing about appetizers is keeping them small. Shellfish, in particular, is rich, so don't get carried away when you're serving clams or crab as starters, unless, of course, you want to serve any of these appetizers as main dishes, which is easy enough to do. In most cases, you only need to double the recipes and add a side dish or two.

Depending on the rest of your meal, you might want a simple appetizer, like grilled asparagus or leeks served with a vinaigrette or aioli, or maybe some grilled polenta. Or try something completely different and experiment with strong flavors, exotic combinations, and some complex dishes. Appetizers are one of the best ways to introduce people to something they have never tried before. Often we will do sweetbreads, sardines, or whitebait (aka fries with eyes) as appetizers because people are more apt to try them, knowing they'll be followed by something "safe," like a platter of ribs or a steak. This is my theory, in any case, and I'm sticking to it, even though in fifteen years of marriage I've never gotten my husband to try any of the above.

Whole Roasted Garlic with Croutons

Serves 6

This dish has been on our menu since the day we opened. You can bake the garlic earlier in the day, set it aside at room temperature, and reheat it on the grill just before serving. That last step adds a great smoky flavor to the garlic. Save the oil from the garlic to use on the croutons.

For a casual get-together with a grilled main course, set the garlic out with roasted peppers, olives, cherry tomatoes, and bread or croutons. People can help themselves while you cook the main course. With a bottle of Napa Valley wine, it makes a light lunch or supper.

6 very large heads garlic
³/₄ cup extra virgin olive oil
2 or 3 bay leaves (fresh, if you can find them)
3 or 4 thyme sprigs
¹/₄ teaspoon salt
Freshly ground black pepper

1 baguette

To make the roasted garlic, preheat the oven to 300°. Cut a thin slice off the very top of each head of garlic to expose the tops of all the cloves. Set the garlic heads in a 9- to 10-inch-wide shallow baking dish. (For best results, use a terra-cotta dish that will hold the heads together snugly.) Pour the oil slowly over and into each head, distributing it as equally as possible. Scatter the bay leaves and thyme over the garlic, and season with the salt and pepper to taste. Cover the pan with aluminum foil and bake for 1³/₄ hours, until the garlic is very soft and tender. Don't rush it; older garlic may take longer. Drain and reserve the oil, and set the garlic aside. Discard the bay leaves and thyme.

To make the croutons, preheat the oven to 375°. Cut the baguette at a severe angle. You need 12 slices each about ¹/₄ inch thick. Brush one side of the slices with the reserved oil from the garlic, and bake oil-side down for 5 to 7 minutes, until crisp and golden. You can also grill the bread slices over coals.

If you've roasted your garlic ahead, reheat it either in a 375° oven or on the grill. Put 2 crisp croutons and a head of garlic on each serving plate. People can use the tip of a knife to fish the roasted garlic out of the individual cloves and smear it on their bread, or they can, as we do it in the restaurant, grab the whole head with a napkin and squeeze all the garlic out into one luscious pile, then smear it liberally onto their croutons.

Curry Chicken Skewers with Eggplant Relish and Tomato Chutney Vinaigrette

Serves 6

My husband really only likes pota-toes, well-done steak, cheeseburgers, and boneless, skinless chicken breasts. So when we dine at Mustards, he'll order these chicken skewers (if he doesn't have a side of mashed potatoes for an appetizer, that is). You can marinate the meat and arrange it on the skewers the day before, if you like. We have found that 8-inch bamboo skewers, presoaked in water for 30 minutes, work best. Make the relish and the vinaigrette ahead, too, and you'll be all set.

1¼ pounds boneless, skinless chicken breasts
1 tablespoon curry paste, homemade (page 213) or purchased
1½ teaspoons rice vinegar
1½ teaspoons extra virgin olive oil
¾ teaspoon soy sauce
Pinch of salt
Pinch of freshly ground black pepper

TOMATO CHUTNEY VINAIGRETTE
1 tablespoon golden raisins
3 tablespoons Tomato Chutney (page 204)
2 tablespoons rice vinegar
Salt and freshly ground black pepper
6 tablespoons extra virgin olive oil

EGGPLANT RELISH (PAGE 207)
6 tablespoons Lime Crème Fraîche (page 196) or plain yogurt
6 cilantro sprigs or fresh mint leaves

To marinate the chicken, cut the chicken breasts crosswise into 36 equal-sized strips about 2 inches long by ½ inch wide. Whisk together the curry paste, vinegar, olive oil, soy sauce, salt, and pepper in a container large enough to hold all the chicken. Toss in the chicken strips, stir to make sure they're well coated with the marinade, cover, refrigerate, and allow to marinate for at least 1 hour, or for as long as overnight. To prepare the skewers, weave 3 strips of chicken lengthwise onto each 8-inch skewer. Refrigerate again until ready to grill.

To make the vinaigrette, whisk together the raisins, chutney, vinegar, and salt and pepper to taste in a small bowl until the salt is dissolved. Gradually whisk in the olive oil, and continue to whisk until fully emulsified.

When you're ready to serve, place the skewers on the grill rack and grill for 2 minutes. Turn the skewers and grill for 1 to 2 minutes more, until cooked through.

To serve, place a mound of relish on each plate and crisscross two skewers over the relish. Drizzle with the vinaigrette and a little crème fraîche. Garnish with cilantro.

Grilled Figs with Pancetta, Balsamic Vinaigrette, and Walnuts

Serves 6 to 8

In Napa, we are blessed with two fig seasons, one early in June and the other at the end of August. Figs prepared this way—wrapped in pancetta, threaded onto skewers, and grilled—make delightful mouthfuls on their own or as an accompaniment to grilled meats and poultry. We have discovered at Mustards that when figs are not available, ripe peaches, pears, or plums make great substitutes. Just remember to pit them first. Have your butcher slice the pancetta as thinly as possible. The strips will be slightly curved, but that's okay because you want to wrap them only once around the fruit. You can also use applewood-smoked bacon in place of pancetta.

24 large Black Mission figs or green Adriatic figs
24 very thinly sliced strips pancetta

VINAIGRETTE
2 tablespoons balsamic vinegar
2 tablespoons sherry vinegar
$^1/_2$ teaspoon salt
$^1/_4$ teaspoon freshly ground black pepper
$^3/_4$ cup extra virgin olive oil
1 tablespoon finely shredded fresh basil leaves
1 tablespoon finely shredded fresh mint leaves
1 tablespoon finely minced fresh chives

Extra virgin olive oil for the figs
Salt and freshly ground black pepper
2 cups walnut pieces, almonds, or pistachios, toasted
$^1/_4$ cup thinly sliced scallions, white parts plus 2 inches of green (cut on the diagonal)
Fresh mint leaves for garnish

Wrap each fig in a strip of pancetta, and thread 3 or 4 figs together onto an 8-inch-long bamboo skewer, securing the pancetta with the skewer. If the figs are large, use 2 skewers, placed parallel to each other. Prepare the skewers several hours ahead of time, and refrigerate them on a baking sheet. They handle better when chilled.

To prepare the vinaigrette, whisk together the balsamic and sherry vinegars, salt, and pepper in a small bowl, until the salt dissolves. Gradually whisk in the olive oil, continue to whisk until fully emulsified, then whisk in the basil, mint, and chives.

When you're ready to serve, brush the figs with olive oil and sprinkle with salt and pepper. Grill until the fat on the pancetta is rendered and the figs are heated through.

Drizzle the figs with the vinaigrette, sprinkle the walnuts and scallions around, garnish with the mint leaves, and enjoy.

Crab Cakes with Red Beet and Horseradish Rémoulade

Serves 6

Believe it or not, the secret ingredient in these crab cakes is grated baked potatoes. Most recipes call for a lot of bread crumbs, which makes for very dry crab cakes, but we've found that substituting potatoes for part of the bread crumbs keeps the cakes nice and moist. We use yellow Finns, but if you can't find them, use any small, creamy potato or even a russet type. We have made these crab cakes with our local Dungeness crab, which works well, but we like the East Coast blue crab better. It has a sweeter flavor and a better texture for this dish. Other decisions to make: The crab cakes can be deep-fried or sautéed in a nonstick skillet, and you can make them any size. I like appetizer-sized crab cakes, but Brigid loves them so big you could make sandwiches with them.

RED BEET AND HORSERADISH RÉMOULADE
1 bunch small beets
Extra virgin olive oil for coating if baking plus ¼ cup
1 tablespoon rice or champagne vinegar
2 tablespoons Dijon mustard
2 to 3 tablespoons freshly grated horseradish
¼ teaspoon freshly ground black pepper

¾ to 1 pound yellow Finn potatoes
1 pound fresh blue-crab meat, picked clean
1 red bell pepper, roasted, peeled, seeded, and minced
3 scallions, white part only, minced
3 tablespoons minced fresh parsley
½ jalapeño, seeded and minced
1 egg
6 to 7 tablespoons mayonnaise
2 teaspoons salt
¼ teaspoon freshly ground black pepper
½ to ¾ cup fresh toasted bread crumbs
Peanut oil for frying
Red Beet and Horseradish Rémoulade (recipe follows)
Lemon wedges for garnish
Chervil or tarragon sprigs for garnish

To make the rémoulade, bake or steam the beets. To bake the beets, trim them, leaving 1 inch of the stem intact, but do not peel. Lightly coat with olive oil and put them in a roasting pan or baking sheet. Bake at 375° until fork tender. This should take 30 to 50 minutes, depending on their size and age. To steam the beets, trim as directed but do not rub with oil. Place on a steamer rack over boiling water, cover, and steam for 15 to 25 minutes, until tender. Allow the beets to cool, then peel and grate enough to measure 1 cup. Save any leftover beets for salads.

Whisk together the vinegar, mustard, and ¼ cup oil in a bowl, until emulsified. Stir in the 1 cup beets, the horseradish to taste, and the pepper. Cover and refrigerate until serving.

Preheat the oven to 375°. Bake the potatoes for 15 to 20 minutes for small ones and up to 1 hour if they're very large, until tender. Allow them to cool, then peel and finely grate.

To make the crab mixture, combine the crabmeat, potatoes, bell pepper, scallions, parsley, jalapeño, egg, 6 tablespoons mayonnaise, salt, and pepper in a large bowl. Mix gently. Add the remaining 1 tablespoon mayonnaise if the mixture seems too dry. Sprinkle ½ cup of the bread crumbs over the

continued from page 9

mixture and combine gently, adding more bread crumbs, as necessary, until the mixture just holds together. (If you are going to panfry the crab cakes, the mixture can be looser.) Cover and refrigerate for at least 20 minutes (or for as long as several hours).

When the crab mixture is well chilled, form the cakes. Make 12 small ones or 6 large ones, depending on your preference, making each one an equal thickness at least $^3/_8$-inch thick. To deep-fry the crab cakes, pour the oil to a depth of 2 inches into a deep, heavy saucepan and heat to 375° on a deep-frying thermometer. Working in batches, add the crab cakes and fry until golden brown and warm through. This should take 4 to 6 minutes, depending on how cold they are when they go in. Do not crowd the pan, and turn the cakes over if they float. Using tongs or a wire skimmer, transfer the cakes to paper towels to drain briefly and keep warm in a low oven while you fry the remaining crab cakes.

To panfry the crab cakes, use just enough oil to coat the surface on a nonstick skillet. Place over medium-high heat, and when hot, add the crab cakes, again being careful not to crowd the pan. Cook for about 7 minutes, until golden brown and crisp on one side. Turn the crab cakes over and cook on the second side for about 5 minutes until browned. Place on a platter in a low oven while you cook the remaining crab cakes.

To serve, divide the crab cakes among serving plates and top each with a small dollop of the rémoulade. Garnish with lemon wedges and chervil sprigs and serve at once.

Cornmeal Pancakes with Caviar and Crème Fraîche

Serves 6

We've always called these pancakes, but they're really crepes. You'll have enough batter for 11 or 12 crepes, so you'll have 5 or 6 extra ones. Cooked crepes hold well if you cool them, then stack them with waxed paper in between to keep them from sticking to one another, and wrap up the whole stack. The batter keeps well for a day, too, so you could refrigerate the extra batter for breakfast the next morning. Just be sure to stir it up well before using it.

When you can splurge on this recipe and use beluga or osetra caviar, you should. Paula Upson, my former partner's wife, loves this dish, so when I know she's coming, I like to run it for her.

CORNMEAL PANCAKES
2 tablespoons plus 2 teaspoons cornmeal
1/3 cup all-purpose flour
4 eggs
1 1/2 cups milk
1 1/2 tablespoons brandy
1 1/2 tablespoons extra virgin olive oil
Pinch of salt
Butter for cooking pancakes

1/2 cup crème fraîche
2 shallots, minced
3 ounces caviar
Minced fresh chives
Freshly ground black pepper

To make the pancakes, combine the cornmeal, flour, eggs, milk, brandy, olive oil, and salt in a bowl and mix well until smooth. Strain through a medium-mesh sieve into a clean bowl. Allow the batter to rest for at least 1 hour before using. Even overnight is okay, but the batter should be refrigerated for that period of time.

To cook the pancakes, heat a crepe pan or 8-inch nonstick skillet over medium-high heat. Add a small amount of butter to the pan. (I unwrap one end of a stick of butter and lightly "paint" the surface of the pan with it.) Stir the pancake batter well, ladle 2 to 3 tablespoons of it into the hot pan, and tilt the pan to spread it evenly. Cook for about 1 1/2 minutes until golden brown on the underside. Flip the pancake with a spatula and cook it for about 1 1/2 minutes more on the second side. Don't worry if the first one isn't perfect. No matter how many times I've made pancakes, more often than not the first one doesn't come out. Slide the pancake to a sheet of waxed paper or parchment paper, then repeat the process, starting with buttering the pan and stirring the batter, until all the batter is used up. Stack the pancakes as they are finished, always separating them with a piece of waxed paper or parchment.

When you're ready to serve, preheat the oven to 375°. Spoon a dollop of crème fraîche on each pancake, sprinkle the crème fraîche with the shallots, and fold the pancakes in half. Place them in individual gratin dishes or in one large, shallow dish, and bake until the edges are golden brown and the filling is warm, about 5 minutes. Dollop with more crème fraîche, spoon on some caviar, and sprinkle with chives and pepper. Serve immediately.

Artichokes with James Beard's Beer Batter and Tarragon Aioli

Serves 6

These artichokes were on our first menu, but I had to take them off because we just couldn't keep up with the demand. Yes, it takes a little extra time to prepare them, but they are well worth the effort. It's probably a good idea to plan a light meal after this appetizer, as it's quite filling. You might want to sprinkle the artichokes with some chopped tarragon or parsley just before serving, and you should definitely put out lots of lemon wedges. The batter is good with all kinds of vegetables and is also excellent with shrimp, snapper, and chicken.

Sherry Fournier, my pottery teacher, served these beauties in her handcrafted cobalt blue bowls with the lemon and the aioli, and they looked spectacular. If you're not in the mood to fry the chokes, just grill and serve with the aioli. To grill, cut the artichokes in half lengthwise, brush the cut sides with olive oil, and season with salt and pepper. Put the halves on the hot grill, cut-side down, and grill until the edges are caramelized and the chokes are hot throughout.

6 large or 12 small artichokes
3 or 4 lemons, cut into wedges
1½ cups dry white wine
Juice of 1½ lemons
3 bay leaves
2 teaspoons flour
1½ teaspoons black peppercorns
1½ teaspoons coriander seeds
1 tablespoon salt plus additional salt
    for sprinkling

TARRAGON AIOLI
2 egg yolks
1 tablespoon minced garlic
1 teaspoon tarragon or white wine vinegar
Pinch of salt
Pinch of freshly ground black pepper
1⅓ cups extra virgin olive oil
1 tablespoon minced fresh tarragon
1 tablespoon ice water

JAMES BEARD'S BEER BATTER
1 cup all-purpose flour
1 teaspoon baking powder
1½ teaspoons salt
1 cup beer
1 tablespoon extra virgin olive oil
½ teaspoon Tabasco sauce
Peanut oil or sunflower oil for frying

To prepare the artichokes, remove the outer leaves until you reach the tender, inner light green leaves, leaving 1 to 1½ inches of the stem intact. Peel the stem. Trim off the tops, down to about 2 inches above the base of the heart. As each artichoke is trimmed, rub all the cut surfaces with a lemon wedge before going on to the next artichoke (you should have some lemon wedges left over to use for garnish). Put the artichokes in a large pot along with the wine, lemon juice, bay leaves, flour, peppercorns, coriander seeds, and 1 tablespoon salt. Add water to cover the artichokes, and weight them down with a plate.

Bring the water to a boil and reduce the heat to a simmer. Cook the artichokes for 20 to 25 minutes, until a knife inserted into the bases comes out. Drain the artichokes and allow them to cool. Remove the purple choke with a spoon and quarter the artichokes lengthwise. This can be done up to a day ahead, if desired. Cover and refrigerate until needed.

To prepare the aioli, put the egg yolks, garlic, vinegar, salt, and pepper in a food processor or blender and pulse to combine. With the motor running, add the olive oil in a thin stream until the aioli thickens. Turn off the processor, add the tarragon and ice water, and pulse briefly to combine. Cover and refrigerate until needed.

To make up the batter, whisk the flour, baking powder, and salt in a medium mixing bowl. In a separate bowl, combine the beer, olive oil, and Tabasco sauce. Gradually whisk the wet ingredients into the dry ingredients, mixing until the batter is free of lumps. If lumps persist, strain the batter through a sieve.

When you are ready to serve, preheat the oven to 325°. Pour the oil to a depth of 3 inches into a deep saucepan and heat to 370° on a deep-frying thermometer. As you are frying the artichokes, use the thermometer to monitor the oil temperature, watching carefully that the oil doesn't burn and allowing the oil to come back up to temperature between batches. Have ready the artichokes, the beer batter, an artichoke trawling device (a slotted spoon or skimmer), and 2 plates lined with paper towels or fine-mesh cooling racks placed over a baking sheet.

Dip an artichoke piece into the beer batter and carefully place it in the hot oil. Repeat with 2 or 3 more artichoke pieces, depending on the size of your pot, watching that the oil temperature is high enough. (It will cool down with each addition, but it should come back up quickly if you don't overload the pot.) Fry the artichokes, turning them as necessary, for about 3 minutes, until they are golden brown and delectably crispy. Remove the artichokes, allow to drain briefly over the pan, place on the paper-lined plate or on the rack, and sprinkle lightly with additional salt. Hold the fried artichokes in the preheated oven on the paper towels until you're done.

Serve the artichokes immediately with the aioli and the remaining lemon wedges on the side.

Stuffed Squash Blossoms with Cherry Tomato Salsa

Serves 6

I hadn't made these stuffed blossoms in years when I decided to include them in the book. I was looking for something a little unusual, and this came to mind. Since I was trying to find squash blossoms a little ahead of the season, it took the produce guys forever to find me some for testing. By the time they finally arrived, I was anxious to see if they were as good as I remembered them. They were, and after tasting them, I had our gardener start planting zucchinis. Previously, I had always told him no zucchinis because you always end up with way too much. But not if you harvest the blossoms before they become fruit! Your best chance for finding squash blossoms, other than in your garden, are farmers' markets.

Queso fresco is a mild cow's milk cheese that is common in Mexico. You may be able to find it in markets that specialize in Latin foods. If not, substitute a mild goat cheese or a soft Monterey Jack.

SQUASH BLOSSOM STUFFING
1 tablespoon extra virgin olive oil
1 cup finely diced zucchini or summer or
    pattypan squash
1 teaspoon minced garlic
1 teaspoon minced fresh epazote, oregano,
    or sage
$1/4$ teaspoon salt, plus more to taste
$1/8$ teaspoon freshly ground black pepper,
    plus a pinch
$1/2$ teaspoon chopped fresh cilantro or
    flat-leaf parsley
2 cups crumbled *queso fresco* or
    fresh goat cheese or finely shredded
    Monterey Jack (a mixture of all three is nice)

CHERRY TOMATO SALSA
2 tablespoons champagne vinegar
6 tablespoons extra virgin olive oil
3 tablespoons pure olive oil
Salt and freshly ground black pepper
1 cup red cherry tomatoes, stemmed and halved
1 cup gold cherry tomatoes, stemmed and halved
3 scallions, white parts and 2 inches of green, minced
2 teaspoons chopped fresh parsley
2 teaspoons chopped fresh cilantro

18 to 21 large squash blossoms (allows extra for
    breakage during stuffing)
Peanut oil for frying
$1/2$ to $3/4$ cup buttermilk
Mustards' Secret Coating (page 214)
Salt
Cilantro sprigs for garnish
1 to 2 limes, cut into wedges

To make the stuffing, heat the olive oil in a sauté pan over medium heat. Add the squash and sauté for 2 minutes. Do not allow it to brown. Add the garlic and cook for 1 minute more. Add the epazote and continue to cook for about 2 to 3 minutes, just until the squash is crisp-tender. Remove from the heat, season with $1/4$ teaspoon salt and $1/8$ teaspoon pepper, and stir in the chopped cilantro. Spread the mixture out on a large plate and let it cool quickly in the refrigerator. This will keep it from getting mushy. When it has cooled, stir in the cheese and a pinch more pepper. Taste for seasoning, and add more salt if necessary (you may not need any if the cheese is on the salty side).

To make the salsa, whisk together the vinegar and olive oils in a small bowl and season to taste with salt and pepper. Put the tomatoes, scallions, parsley, and cilantro in a bowl. Add just enough of the vinaigrette to coat, stirring gingerly to avoid breaking up the tomatoes. Taste and adjust the seasonings with salt and pepper.

To prepare the blossoms, gently open up each flower and, holding it gently by the stem, remove the stamen and pistil and the prickly points on the outside of the blossom. Place 2 tablespoons of stuffing into each blossom, and gently fold the petal tips together. Refrigerate the blossoms to chill thoroughly before proceeding.

Pour the peanut oil to a depth of about 2 inches into a heavy, straight-sided pot and heat to 365° to 370° on a deep-frying thermometer. Have ready the blossoms, the buttermilk, the coating, a wire skimmer, and cooling racks placed over a baking sheet. Working in batches, dip the stuffed squash blossoms into buttermilk, drain off the excess, then dip them into the coating. Gently place the blossoms into the hot oil and fry for about 2½ minutes, until crisp and golden brown on all sides. You don't want them to touch each other as you're frying them, so don't crowd the pan. Remove with the skimmer, allow to drain briefly over the pan, place on the rack and let drain for a moment, then sprinkle with salt. Repeat with the remaining blossoms, allowing the oil to come back up to temperature between batches.

To serve, place a spoonful of the salsa on each plate and arrange 3 squash blossoms around the salsa. Garnish with cilantro sprigs and place a wedge or two of lime on each plate.

Goat Cheese from the Very Beginning

Serves 6

*My best friend, Laura Chenel, was
one of the first people I met when I
moved to the Napa Valley in 1980.
She's the person responsible for my
love of goats and goat cheese. She was
a pioneer, one of the first people to
make French-style goat cheeses commercially in the United States. Now
many varieties are available, from
very mild, creamy fresh cheeses to
tangier aged ones. The best cheese
stores allow you to taste the cheeses
before buying them. It's a good way
to learn what you like.*

*We always offer a couple of goat
cheese items at Mustards. This recipe
was on our first menu, and it's still
my favorite. If you don't have time to
make Those Nuts, use toated almonds
instead.*

$^{1}/_{4}$ cup chopped Those Nuts made with almonds (page 212), or almonds toasted for 7 minutes at 375°
$^{1}/_{4}$ cup toasted bread crumbs
2 to 3 tablespoons extra virgin olive oil
4 ounces goat cheese logs, cut into 6 rounds

VINAIGRETTE
1 tablespoon red wine vinegar
1 shallot, minced
$^{1}/_{8}$ teaspoon salt
$^{1}/_{4}$ teaspoon freshly cracked black pepper
$^{1}/_{3}$ cup walnut, almond, or olive oil
2 cups frisée, radicchio, escarole, or other bitter greens

6 oil-packed sundried tomatoes, cut lengthwise into strips
12 to 18 croutons (page 212)

Combine the almonds and crumbs on a plate. Pour the olive oil onto a second plate. One at a time, dip the goat cheese rounds in the olive oil and then in the crumb mixture, coating them evenly, and place them on a baking sheet. If you do not plan to serve them immediately, cover and refrigerate.

To make the vinaigrette, whisk together the vinegar, shallot, salt, and pepper in a small bowl until the salt is dissolved. Gradually whisk in the walnut oil, and continue to whisk until fully emulsified. Taste and adjust the seasoning.

When you are ready to serve, preheat the oven to 400°. Wash and spin dry the greens, and tear them into bite-sized pieces. In a large bowl, toss the greens with just enough of the vinaigrette to coat them. To serve, put the cheese in the oven for 3 to 4 minutes, until warm and slightly soft to the touch (be sure not to melt the cheese). Put a mound of greens on each plate, and top each with a round of goat cheese. Arrange several strips of sundried tomato on the cheese. Accompany each serving with 3 or 4 croutons.

Smoked Trout with Warm Sweet Potato Salad and Horseradish Cream

Serves 6

If you ever have a day when the trout are practically jumping into your boat, and you're tired of eating them grilled or panfried, try brining and smoking them for a nice change of pace. Fillet the fish, leaving the skin on, cure them in a brine, and smoke them. (I've given recipes for both a maple syrup cure and a ginger brine—I couldn't pick a clear winner during the testing.) This works well with salmon and sturgeon, too. Since you're firing up the smoker for the trout, you might as well smoke some chicken wings, tomatoes, ducks, or ribs, too, to make the best use of the fire. Of course, you could buy smoked trout to make this salad, but then you'd miss out on all the fun. Allow 8 to 16 hours to cure the fish. Cook the sweet potatoes just before you want to serve the dish, but everything else can be made ahead.

I have made this potato salad with new red potatoes, creamy German butter potatoes, yams, and sweet potatoes, all with good results. The sweet potato version is nice for a

3 or 4 trout

GINGER BRINE
$^1/_4$ cup firmly packed brown sugar
$^1/_4$ cup salt
2 tablespoons peeled and grated fresh ginger
2 cups water

MAPLE CURE
$^1/_4$ cup salt
$^1/_4$ cup maple syrup

WARM SWEET POTATO SALAD
2 large sweet potatoes (about $1^1/_2$ pounds total)
2 shallots, minced, plus 2 shallots thinly sliced
$^1/_4$ cup balsamic vinegar
$^1/_4$ cup coarse-grain mustard
Pinch of salt
Pinch of freshly ground black pepper
$^3/_4$ cup extra virgin olive oil
3 tablespoons chopped fresh parsley
2 tablespoons capers

HORSERADISH CREAM
$^1/_2$ cup sour cream
2 tablespoons freshly grated or prepared horseradish
1 tablespoon heavy whipping cream or plain yogurt
Pinch of salt
Pinch of freshly ground black pepper
2 to 3 tablespoons water

1 head Belgian endive, thinly sliced lengthwise
1 head butter lettuce, torn into bite-sized pieces
1 head frisée, white and light green parts only, torn into bite-sized pieces
Caramelized Onions (page 200)
Thin slices rye bread, toasted

Fillet the trout and carefully remove any tiny bones remaining along the center of the fish. If the fillets are more than 1 inch thick, score the skin to allow the cure to permeate the flesh faster.

Select the ginger brine or maple cure. To make the ginger brine, put the sugar, salt, ginger, and water in a nonreactive container just large enough to hold the fish, and stir until the sugar and salt are dissolved. (Often I'll heat 1 cup water, dissolve the salt and sugar in it, then cool it back down with a cup of iced water.) Submerge the fillets in the brine.

To make the maple cure, sprinkle the salt evenly on the flesh side of the trout, drizzle evenly with maple syrup, and then rub the salt and syrup into the flesh.

With either cure, cover the fish and refrigerate for 4 hours if the fillets are $^1/_4$ to $^1/_3$ inch thick, 6 to 8 hours if they are $^1/_2$ to 1 inch thick. Then, rinse the fillets, place them on a rack, and allow them to dry uncovered in the refrigerator for an additional 4 to 8 hours. This sets the surface so the fish will absorb the smoke better.

To make the potato salad, place the sweet potatoes in a saucepan with salted water to cover, bring to a boil, and cook until tender when pierced with a fork.

change of pace and seems right for
this dish. Good for your eyes, too!
Dress the sweet potatoes while they
are still warm, and serve the salad
soon after it is made.

Meanwhile, make the vinaigrette. Whisk together the minced shallots, vinegar, mustard, salt, and pepper in a small bowl, until the salt is dissolved. Gradually whisk in the olive oil, and continue to whisk until fully emulsified.

When the sweet potatoes are done, drain them. When they are cool enough to handle, peel and cut them into thick wedges or $1/2$-inch-thick slices and place in a bowl. Add the sliced shallots, parsley, capers, and just enough of the vinaigrette to coat the sweet potatoes liberally. You may need to add a bit more later, depending on how much vinaigrette they absorb, but be sure to reserve some of the dressing for the greens.

To make the horseradish cream, combine the sour cream, horseradish, heavy cream, salt, and pepper in a small bowl. Mix well, adding water as needed to thin to a drizzling consistency.

The fish will smoke quickly, so add quite a few soaked chips to the heat source to get a nice smoky atmosphere inside the smoking chamber before the fish is put inside. Place the trout in the smoker as far from the heat source as possible and smoke for 20 to 25 minutes. Remove from the smoker and chill. The flesh will feel firm and flake easily.

About 30 minutes before serving, prepare the sweet potato salad. Wash and spin dry all the greens, and, using leftover vinaigrette from the sweet potato salad, dress the greens lightly, coating them without drowning them. Remove the skin from the fish, and flake the meat into nice-sized pieces. Prepare the Horseradish Cream.

To serve, place the greens in the middle of a large oval platter, and surround them with small mounds of the potato salad. Top the greens with the trout, and drizzle the fish with the Horseradish Cream. Serve with several rings of Pickled Onions and rye bread.

Morel Mushroom and Goat Cheese Toasts

Serves 6

Morel mushrooms are smallish, look like cone-shaped sponges, and have honeycomblike caps that suck up sauces and pan juices wonderfully. They are fairly plentiful in spring, at least in certain areas, such as the Midwest and parts of the Northwest. Always buy dry, clean-looking morels, and when you get them home, look for hidden insects and shake out any forest debris. Do not wash them, however. If you can't find morels, you can use other wild mushrooms—porcini in the fall and chanterelles later in the year—or if all else fails, purchase a nice combination of cultivated mushrooms, such as button mushrooms, shiitakes, and portobellos, from the market. A combination of dried and fresh mushrooms also works well. Figure on one-eighth to one-fourth the weight of the fresh mushrooms when computing the amount of dried mushrooms.

2 tablespoons extra virgin olive oil
4 teaspoons butter
2 shallots, thinly sliced into rounds
4 cups fresh morel mushrooms, quartered lengthwise and carefully cleaned
Salt and freshly ground black pepper
2 teaspoons chopped fresh thyme
1/4 cup Calvados, Madeira, or Cognac
1/4 pound fresh goat cheese
2 tablespoons heavy whipping cream or half-and-half
6 slices rustic country bread, each 1/3-inch thick
1/4 cup chopped fresh parsley

Heat the olive oil and 2 teaspoons of the butter in a sauté pan over medium heat. Add the shallots and cook, stirring, for 3 to 5 minutes, until they begin to caramelize. Add the morels and sauté, stirring occasionally for 8 to 10 minutes, until tender. Sprinkle to taste with salt and pepper. When the mushrooms start to caramelize and give off their juices, add the thyme and sauté for 1 minute more. Then stir in the Calvados and the remaining 2 teaspoons butter and keep warm over low heat until you are ready to serve.

In a bowl, mix the goat cheese together with the whipping cream to make it spreadable. Toast or grill the bread, smear each slice with a nice layer of the creamy goat cheese and place on serving plates. Pour the mushroom sauce over, sprinkle with parsley, and serve at once.

Morel Mushroom and Green Corn Tamales

Serves 6 (2 to 3 tamales per person)

We call these "green" tamales because they are made from fresh uncooked corn thickened with grits (or you could use polenta) rather than masa harina dough. And we wrap them in fresh husks right off the corn, which are easier to use than the dried husks you buy at Latin markets. They are a beautiful light green when done. When I tested this recipe at home, I used button mushrooms at a ratio of 3 to 1 with dried morels, and that worked out nicely. If you use dried mushrooms, save the soaking water to cook the filling in or to substitute for part of the cream in the filling. Serve these with any kind of salsa you like or have on hand. We use Avocado and Pumpkin Seed Salsa.

I learned to make this filling from Mary Sue Milliken and Susan Feniger of the Border Grill in Santa Monica when I caught them on a cooking show. The filling has since become one of my husband's favorites, and I am forever in their debt. We use the stuffing in tamales at Mustards, and in pasilla chiles in the

TAMALE FILLING
3 ears of corn, preferably white, husked
1¹/₂ teaspoons butter
1¹/₂ shallots, minced
1 clove garlic, minced
1¹/₂ cups milk
¹/₂ cup heavy whipping cream
Dash of Tabasco sauce
Pinch of freshly grated nutmeg
¹/₂ teaspoon salt
Pinch of freshly ground black pepper
¹/₂ cup instant grits or polenta
³/₄ cup grated sharp white Cheddar cheese
³/₄ cup grated Asiago cheese

2 tablespoons butter
1 shallot, minced
2 cloves garlic, minced
1 pound fresh morel mushrooms or other favorite mushroom, carefully cleaned and sliced
2 tablespoons minced fresh epazote, or a mixture of fresh basil and oregano
Salt and freshly ground black pepper
15 to 20 green or dried corn husks
Lime Crème Fraîche (page 196)
Avocado and Pumpkin Seed Salsa (page 202)

To make the tamale filling, grate the ears of corn over your largest bowl, using the large holes on a handheld grater. Melt the butter in a large sauté pan over medium heat. Add the shallots and garlic and sweat for 1 to 3 minutes, until soft but not caramelized. Add the grated corn, including all the liquids, the milk, cream, Tabasco sauce, nutmeg, salt, and pepper. Bring it to a boil, reduce the heat to medium, then gradually stir in the grits and cook, stirring frequently, for 15 to 20 minutes if you are planning to stuff tamales or for 20 to 25 minutes if you are planning to stuff chiles. The grits should be thickened, creamy, and no longer "gritty." The shorter time is okay for tamales, as the grits will cook further when the tamales are steamed. The longer time is necessary for the chiles, as the grains must be fully tender since they are not cooked again. You may need to add more water if the grits dry out before they are tender.

Remove the pan from the heat and stir in the cheeses. Pour the grits into a shallow pan to cool, or over an ice bath if you're in a hurry, then use as directed in the individual recipes.

To make the mushroom mixture, melt the butter in a sauté pan over medium-high heat. Add the shallot and garlic and sauté for 3 to 5 minutes, until soft. Add the morels and cook for 5 to 6 minutes, until tender. Stir in the epazote, season with salt and pepper, and remove from the heat.

To assemble the tamales, place the green or dried corn husks in a large pot with water to cover. Bring to a boil and cook for 1 minute, or until pliable for the dried husks, then turn off the heat but leave the husks in the hot water. Remove 2 husks and shake off the water. Place them together lengthwise side by side, overlapping them by ¹/₄ to ¹/₃ inch, with the inside of the husk facing toward you and the wide end at the bottom. It works best to do this in the palm of one hand. Place 2 tablespoons of the filling about two-thirds of the way down the husk, leaving a ¹/₂-inch edge on either side. Place 1¹/₂ to 2 tablespoons of the mushroom mixture on top of the filling mixture. Fold

recipe that follows, but it is good in Hungarian gypsy peppers or other sweet peppers, too. It's even delicious on its own, as you will find out if you sample a spoonful. I have also steamed it in buttered 3-ounce custard dishes and served it nestled in Cherry Tomato Salsa (page 14).

Once you've mastered the basics of making tamales, you can experiment a little. Try chicken, shrimp, or duck, in place of the mushrooms. Or, if you want to impress someone you love, make lobster tamales: Tuck a nice big chunk of lobster in the middle of each tamale, and serve a tomatillo salsa (page 40) on the side.

the bottom of the husk up over the fillings, then fold in the sides, then fold the top down to cover the filling completely. Don't overfill the tamales or fold them too tightly, as the filling will swell as it steams. You should end up with a bundle about 1½ inches wide by 2½ inches long. Tie each tamale with a long strip torn from a softened corn husk or with kitchen string, if desired, although this isn't necessary if you carefully place the tamales in the steamer. The tamales can be made as much as a day ahead, covered, and refrigerated, and then steamed when needed.

Gently place the tamales seam side down in any kind of steamer basket, or you can improvise, using a colander set on custard cups in a large pot. Just make sure you have a tight-fitting lid for whatever vessel you use. The tamales can be stacked. Put 1½ to 2 inches of water in the bottom of the steamer or pot and place the basket in it. Cover the top with a moist towel and put the lid in place. Bring the water to a boil, reduce the heat to a strong simmer, and then set your timer. Steam the tamales for 20 to 30 minutes, until they are firm and hot all the way through. Keep an eye on the steamer, adding more water as necessary to keep the original level. After 30 minutes, remove and unwrap one tamale to test for doneness.

When the tamales are ready, remove them from the steamer and wrap them in a cloth napkin for up to 30 minutes, to keep them warm until serving. Serve with lots of the crème fraîche and salsa.

Grilled Quail with Sesame Dressing and Papaya-Lime Relish

Serves 6

Quail are tiny game birds, so tiny that the only sensible way to eat them is to pick them up and start nibbling. They are now being farm-raised all across the country, so butchers who don't regularly carry them can easily special-order them for you. Because their meat is mild, quail are a great introduction to game birds for the uninitiated. Their size also makes them less intimidating: You need to serve two birds per person as an entrée. Some of the testers couldn't find quail and substituted Cornish game hens, and they were very happy with the results. If you can't find bok choy or other Asian-style greens, spinach and baby green beans make a great alternative. These birds are first blanched in a Chinese-style poaching liquid that both flavors and colors them.

The relish makes a great finish to any grilled poultry dish. In place of the papayas, you can easily substitute mango, pineapple, pear, or whatever fruit is ripe, the key word being ripe. For the grilled quail, I prefer tropical

6 quail

PAPAYA-LIME RELISH
1 large papaya, peeled, halved, seeded, and diced
Pinch of red chile flakes
$1/4$ to $1/2$ jalapeño chile, seeded and finely minced
Grated zest and juice of 1 lime
Pinch of freshly ground white pepper
Pinch of salt

POACHING LIQUID
$1^2/3$ cups soy sauce
1 cup tamari soy sauce
2 tablespoons five-spice powder
$2/3$ cup Chinese rice wine or sake
2 tablespoons sugar

SESAME DRESSING
$1/2$ cup sugar
$3/4$ cup freshly squeezed lime juice
3 red Fresno or other hot green or red chiles, seeded and finely minced
2 tablespoons peeled and grated fresh ginger
$1^1/4$ teaspoons chopped garlic
3 tablespoons soy sauce
2 tablespoons poaching liquid (above)
$1/4$ cup peanut oil or pure olive oil
2 tablespoons sesame oil

VEGETABLES
1 to 2 tablespoons peanut oil
3 to 4 heads baby bok choy, cut on the diagonal
$1/4$ pound Chinese long beans, trimmed, cut into 2-inch lengths, and blanched

Trim off the tips and the first joint of the wings from each quail, and reserve them for stock. Trim off the neck, if necessary. Set the quail aside.

To make the relish, gently mix all the ingredients together in a bowl. Cover and refrigerate until needed.

To make the poaching liquid, combine all the ingredients in a saucepan just big enough to hold one quail, and set aside 2 tablespoons of the mixture for the sesame dressing. Bring the remaining liquid to a boil. One by one, blanch the quail in the poaching liquid while you count to 8, then remove and drain well. Repeat this step one more time. Split each quail in half so that each half has a half breast, leg, and thigh. If you are not cooking immediately, refrigerate until you are ready to grill. The poaching liquid may be frozen and used again. Be sure to bring it to a full rolling boil before beginning.

To make the dressing, whisk together the sugar, lime juice, chiles, ginger, garlic, soy sauce, and the 2 tablespoons poaching liquid in a bowl, until the sugar is dissolved. Gradually whisk in the oils, and continue to whisk until fully emulsified.

Grill the quail bone-side down first, turning them when they're almost done. Leave them on the grill just long enough to heat them through and caramelize the skin. This should take about 3 to 4 minutes. The birds may be kept warm and held, as the vegetables take just a moment to cook.

fruits, as they marry well with ginger and other Asian flavors. Of course, this relish pairs well with Latin American dishes, too. Any leftovers would be great on a duck, chicken, or even a vegetarian tostada. The relish may be made several hours ahead.

To prepare the vegetables, heat the peanut oil in a sauté pan over medium-high heat. Add the bok choy and long beans and quickly stir-fry for 1 minute. Add enough sesame dressing to coat the vegetables lightly, and cook until just tender yet still somewhat crisp.

Place the vegetables on a large serving plate. Top with the grilled quail and some of the relish. Drizzle a bit of the remaining sesame dressing all around. Serve the extra relish alongside.

Smoked Salmon, Pasilla Corn Cakes, and Crème Fraîche

Serves 6

With this recipe, the secret to success is to have everything lined up and ready to go before you make the corn cakes, which should be done at the very last minute. So do everything in advance that can possibly be done. You can even measure out the dry ingredients for the batter and set them aside in one bowl, and do the same for the wet ingredients.

For our appetizer plates, we make 2-inch corn cakes, and serve 3 per serving. For cocktail parties, though, we've often made 1-inch corn cakes, topped them with small pieces of smoked salmon, and served them as individual canapés. You can use a high-quality Scottish or other smoked salmon or smoked whitefish or trout. The bits of pasilla chiles add a bright green to the corn cakes and just the right amount of spiciness. If you end up with extra chiles, sprinkle some on soups or tuck some into a burger for a little zip.

PASILLA CORN CAKES
$^2/_3$ cup cornmeal
$^1/_3$ cup all-purpose flour
$^1/_2$ teaspoon baking powder
$^1/_4$ teaspoon baking soda
2 teaspoons sugar
$^1/_2$ teaspoon salt
$^1/_3$ cup buttermilk plus 1 to 2 tablespoons more, if needed
1 egg
$^1/_2$ cup white corn kernels
2 tablespoons roasted, peeled, and diced pasilla chile, or 1 tablespoon peeled and minced roasted jalapeño chile
2 tablespoons butter, melted, plus butter for cooking corn cakes

$^1/_2$ cup crème fraîche
12 to 18 thin slices smoked salmon
2 tablespoons extra virgin olive oil
2 tablespoons minced fresh dill, fennel tops, chervil, or tarragon
2 tablespoons minced fresh chives
2 tablespoons minced shallots
1 to 2 tablespoons freshly cracked black pepper

To make the corn cakes, combine the cornmeal, flour, baking powder, baking soda, sugar, and salt in a bowl and set it aside. Beat the $^1/_3$ cup buttermilk and the egg together in another bowl and set it aside. Just before you are going to cook the cakes, combine the dry and wet ingredients, and the corn, chile, and melted butter. If the batter seems too thick, add 1 to 2 tablespoons more buttermilk as needed. Add it cautiously. You don't want the batter too thin or you will end up with crepes.

Preheat a griddle to 350° or heat to medium-high, and butter it liberally. Ladle the batter onto the griddle, allowing 2 tablespoons per cake. When the cakes are golden brown on the bottom and bubbles are rising to the surface, after about 1 minute, flip them over and cook on the second side. At home I use a flat griddle that fits over 2 burners, and I can make 6 to 8 corn cakes at a time. Keep the finished corn cakes warm in a low oven while you cook the rest. You should have 18 cakes in all.

To serve, stir the crème fraîche, adding a few drops of cold water, if necessary, to thin it to a drizzling consistency. Place 3 corn cakes on each serving plate, and arrange 2 or 3 salmon slices around and partially over them. Drizzle with crème fraîche and then the olive oil, and sprinkle with dill, chives, shallots, and pepper.

Coconut Curried Mussels

You can make the sauce ahead and then just return it to a boil when you are ready to cook the mussels. Clams, lobster, and crab also taste great finished in this broth. Traditionally, the sauce is made with red or yellow prepared Thai curry paste, but I have found it to be good made with Indian-style curry pastes, too. If you have some curry powder, you can easily make your own curry paste: Just heat some neutral-flavored oil in a sauté pan, and cook the powder in it until it is aromatic. Each tablespoon of curry powder will make a tablespoon of paste (see page 213).

2 pounds (about 4 dozen) mussels

2 tablespoons peanut oil

⅓ cup sliced shallots

3 tablespoons sliced garlic

2 to 3 teaspoons minced lemongrass, from bulb end only (optional)

3 tablespoons sake

Finely grated zest and juice of 1 lime

1 (13½-ounce) can coconut milk

⅔ cup fish stock (page 221), vegetable stock (page 215), or chicken stock (page 218)

1 tablespoon curry paste, homemade (page 213) or purchased

1 teaspoon fish sauce

1 red Fresno or jalapeño chile, julienned

2 teaspoons peeled and minced fresh ginger

GARNISHES

3 tablespoons minced fresh cilantro

3 scallions, white and light green parts, thinly sliced

2 tablespoons fresh mint leaves, finely shredded

Trim the beards off the mussels, then scrub them thoroughly under cool running water. Set aside.

Heat the oil in a sauté pan over medium-high heat. Add the shallots, garlic, and lemongrass and sauté for 1 minute. Add the sake, lime zest and juice, coconut milk, stock, curry paste, fish sauce, chile, and ginger and cook for 8 to 10 minutes to develop the flavors. Add the mussels, cover, and cook over medium heat until the mussels open, shaking the pan occasionally to keep them from sticking. This step should take 3 to 5 minutes.

Uncover and spoon the opened mussels into serving bowls. Cook any unopened mussels for 1 to 2 minutes longer, transfer the opened ones to bowls, and discard any that haven't opened by this time. Reduce the sauce slightly and pour it over the mussels. Garnish with the cilantro, scallions, and mint and serve.

Grilled Pasilla Chiles with Tamale Stuffing and Salsa Ranchera

Serves 6

These stuffed chiles have been on our menu for some time, with the salsa and other garnishes changing season- ally. This particular combination is one of my favorites. Stuffed chiles are usually made with Anaheims, but they are little too mild for my taste, and too narrow, too. So I use poblanos, or what we in California more often see labeled as pasillas, as they have good flavor and are the per- fect size and shape for stuffing. (Pasillas are dried chiles everywhere else.) You could substitute small, fresh sweet chiles, if you prefer, maybe adding a little minced serrano or jalapeño to the filling to spice things up.

You can prepare the chiles and the stuffing as much as a day ahead— even stuff the chiles, if you want. Refrigerate them, but pull them out early enough so that they are not refrigerator-cold when you grill them.

6 pasilla chiles
Tamale Filling (page 24), plus 1 to 2 stemmed, seeded,
    and minced serrano or jalapeño chiles (extra chiles optional)
$^1/_4$ cup pumpkin seeds
Salsa Ranchera (page 197)
$^1/_2$ cup Lime Crème Fraîche (page 196)
Cilantro sprigs for garnish

To prepare the chiles for stuffing, core each chile, leaving the stem intact by cutting around the stem at the top of the chile. Carefully pull the stem out (most of the seeds will come away with it too). Cut off the string of seeds, leaving a neat cap with the stem attached. Set the caps aside for later use. Trim any remaining seeds and membrane out of the chiles. Blanch the chiles in boiling water for 1 to 2 minutes. Plunge them into ice water to stop the cooking, then drain well.

Prepare the filling, cooking it for 20 to 25 minutes and add the minced serrano or jalapeño if you want more zip.

Stuff each chile with $^1/_3$ to $^1/_2$ cup of the filling, ensuring it reaches down to the very tip of the chile. Replace the stem tops, pressing each one into the filling to hold it in place. Press the chiles gently to flatten them slightly, which will make them easier to grill.

Toast the pumpkin seeds in a dry skillet over medium-high heat, shaking the pan often, for 3 to 6 minutes, until they begin to pop and smell nice and toasty. Alternatively, you may roast the seeds in a 375° oven, shaking the pan occasionally for 7 to 10 minutes, until done. Set aside.

Just before serving, grill the chiles, turning them gently to keep the stuffing from falling out, for about 2 to 3 minutes on each side. You want nice grill marks on the chiles, and the stuffing should be heated through.

To serve, pour a small pool of the salsa on each plate and top with a chile. Drizzle with the crème fraîche, sprinkle with the pumpkin seeds, and garnish with cilantro sprigs.

Crispy Calamari with Curried Slaw

Serves 6

Our good friends Bill Jenkins and Kathy Dennett eat with my husband and I every other week at the restaurant. Bill likes this appetizer so much that he orders it almost every time. Once in a while I can get a small forkful of it, but usually not. Calamari, which is the name most American restaurants use for squid, is sold in two forms, the large squid "steaks," and the small whole squid, which are 6 to 8 inches long, complete with tentacles. Buy the small ones for this dish. You can usually get them already cleaned at a good fish market.

CURRY VINAIGRETTE
2 tablespoons curry paste, homemade
   (page 213) or purchased
1 tablespoon Dijon mustard
2 tablespoons freshly squeezed lemon juice
2 tablespoons rice vinegar
1 teaspoon salt
$3/4$ teaspoon freshly ground black pepper
$1/4$ cup pure olive oil
2 tablespoon extra virgin olive oil

3 pounds whole fresh calamari,
   or 2 pounds frozen, cleaned squid
$1/3$ head green cabbage, thinly sliced
1 carrot, peeled and grated
1 red Fresno or jalapeño chile, seeded and
   thinly sliced, plus 3 more for garnish
Peanut oil or canola oil for frying
1 cup buttermilk
Mustards' Secret Coating (page 214)
Fresh cilantro leaves for garnish
12 scallions, white and light green parts,
   thinly sliced on the diagonal

To make the vinaigrette, whisk together the curry paste, mustard, lemon juice, vinegar, salt, and pepper in a small bowl until the salt is dissolved. This will take about 30 seconds. Gradually whisk in the olive oils, and continue to whisk until fully emulsified. Set aside.

Clean the calamari, if necessary, removing the beak and snipping off the eyes. Cut the bodies into $1/2$-inch-wide rings and cut off the tentacles, leaving the small clusters of tentacles whole and halving the large ones. This can be done ahead and the squid refrigerated until needed.

To make the slaw, toss the cabbage, carrot, and the 1 chile together in a large bowl. Cover and refrigerate until needed.

To deep-fry the calamari, pour the peanut oil to a depth of 3 to 4 inches into a deep, heavy saucepan and heat to 375° on a deep-frying thermometer. While the oil is heating, get the first batch of calamari ready. Put the buttermilk in one bowl, and the coating in another larger bowl. Dip the calamari in the buttermilk, drain it, and toss it in the seafood coating. Place the calamari in a sieve, and shake off the excess coating, separating any pieces that stick together and dusting them with coating again. (You could also shake the calamari and the coating together in a paper bag, then shake off the excess coating in a sieve.) Working in batches, carefully slip the calamari into the hot oil and fry for 2 to 3 minutes, until just golden. Be careful not to crowd the pan, planning on four or five batches. Using a wire skimmer, transfer to paper towels to drain. Allow the oil to come back up to the temperature between batches.

To serve, give the curry vinaigrette a stir, and toss the slaw together with just enough of it to coat lightly. Arrange the slaw on a large platter. Put the calamari on the bed of slaw, and sprinkle with the remaining chiles, cilantro leaves, and scallions. Serve any remaining vinaigrette on the side.

Seared Ahi Tuna on Sesame Crackers with Wasabi Cream

Serves 6

I think the homemade sesame crackers are what makes this our hands-down most popular appetizer. Everything can be prepared ahead of time—the tuna, crackers, wasabi cream, dipping sauce—and assembled at the last minute. If you make the crackers ahead, keep them tightly covered and out of sight (otherwise they will quickly disappear). Try to get a nice, thick triangular cut of tuna so the center stays rare when the outside is seared. Wasabi, also known as Japanese horseradish, is a spicy green condiment. You can buy small cans of wasabi powder in Asian markets.

This cracker recipe will make 2 to 3 dozen, which is more than you will need for this appetizer. Any extras can be used to liven up a tomato soup or a tuna salad, or you can eat them solo for a midnight nibble. If you have a bread machine, you could probably make the dough in it on the dough-only setting. Check Asian markets and gourmet ingredient retailers for black sesame seeds, or, if preferred, use all white.

CRISPY SESAME CRACKERS
1½ teaspoons active dried yeast
1 teaspoon sugar
⅓ cup warm water
⅓ cup plus 1 teaspoon cold water
2 cups all-purpose flour, or more as needed
1 tablespoon butter, cut up
2 teaspoons salt
1 egg
2 tablespoons sesame seeds, preferably a mix of
    black and white

1 pound best-quality ahi tuna loin
½ teaspoon salt
3 tablespoons white sesame seeds
3 tablespoons black sesame seeds
1½ tablespoons poppyseeds
2 teaspoons freshly cracked black pepper
1 tablespoon peanut oil

TAMARI DIPPING SAUCE
2 tablespoons mirin or sake
2 tablespoons tamari soy sauce
2 tablespoons rice vinegar

WASABI CREAM
3 tablespoons wasabi powder
2 tablespoons water
¼ cup sour cream
2 tablespoons half-and-half, or as needed

To make the crackers, combine the yeast, sugar, and warm water together in the bowl of an electric mixer or a large bowl. Let rest for 8 to 10 minutes, until it becomes foamy. Add the ⅓ cup cold water, then add the flour, butter, and salt. Mix to combine with the dough hook or knead with a wooden spoon. If using a mixer, mix the dough on medium speed until smooth and elastic, pulling the dough down off the hook if it climbs it. If mixing by hand, turn the shaggy dough mass out onto a cutting board and knead for 5 to 8 minutes, until the dough is smooth and elastic. If the dough is sticky, add a little more flour. Gather into a ball, place the dough in an oiled bowl, turn to coat lightly, cover, and set it aside in a warm place to rise until doubled in size, 1 to 1½ hours.

Preheat the oven to 350°. The easiest way to make very thin crackers is to pass the dough through a pasta machine. If you don't have one, take manageable-sized pieces of dough and, on a lightly floured surface, roll them out as thinly as possible into 6-inch-wide, 3- or 4-inch-long strips. The goal is for the crackers to be almost paper-thin. I have found that it helps to roll out strips of dough, let them rest for 5 or 6 minutes, and then roll them out again. Sometimes I repeat again if necessary. Lay the strips of dough on a nonstick baking sheet or a baking sheet lined with parchment paper. Beat together the egg and the 1 teaspoon cold water, and brush the crackers with the egg wash. Sprinkle with the sesame seeds, then score the strips of dough to make triangular shapes (they'll break apart into individual crackers when they bake).

Turning the crackers as necessary, bake for 7 to 10 minutes, until they are a deep gold. Remove to a rack to cool, then store in an airtight container for up to 1 week (or less, if humidity is high).

To prepare the tuna, cut away the blood line, then cut the tuna lengthwise into 3 triangular bars each about 2 inches on each side. Season the tuna with the salt. Combine the sesame seeds, poppyseeds, and pepper in a shallow bowl. One at a time, roll the tuna pieces in the seed mixture.

Select a sauté pan large enough to hold the tuna flat and heat the pan over high heat until almost smoking hot. Carefully sear each side of each piece of tuna in the peanut oil. You only want the meat to cook through about $1/4$ inch, leaving the interior rare and very red. Transfer the tuna to a plate and chill it in the refrigerator until cold.

To make the dipping sauce, combine the mirin, tamari, and rice vinegar in a small bowl and set it aside.

To make the wasabi cream, stir together the wasabi and water in a small bowl until smooth. Whisk in the sour cream and 2 tablespoons half-and-half, adding more half-and-half if the mixture is too thick. You should be able to drizzle it. Cover and refrigerate until ready to assemble the dish.

To serve, place 2 or 3 crackers on each plate. With a sharp, thin knife, slice the tuna crosswise into as many thin slices as you have crackers. Place a slice on each cracker. Drizzle the dipping sauce on the tuna, then the wasabi cream. Arrange the cilantro, chile strips, and scallions across the tuna and crackers, and serve immediately.

Steamed Manila Clams or Mussels

Serves 4

I usually go into Mustards' garden and decide which herb we have too much of and then build this dish around that herb. You have plenty of flexibility in picking which herb to use, but it's important to feature just one herb. The only herbs I would not use are sage and lavender.

Verjus is an acidic wine product that's not fermented. It is often used instead of lemon juice in wine-growing regions where lemons are not in season or able to grow.

This dish is wonderful as an entrée on its own, in which case you would want to double the recipe. But my idea of a super meal is to serve the clams or mussels as appetizers, and follow them with some grilled sausages, and a tossed green salad. Whatever you do, serve the clams with rustic country bread brushed with olive oil, rubbed with garlic, and quickly grilled. It is especially good for dunking in the broth. My friend Nickie Zeller, who tested this recipe with Hog Island Sweetwater Manila clams, said, "I'm sure it is the best clam dish I've ever had! Very easy and quick to make."

36 Manila clams or mussels (fewer if using green lip mussels)
4 thick slices rustic country bread
Extra virgin olive oil from roasted garlic (page 5)
1 tablespoon olive oil, plus extra for bread
10 cloves garlic, sliced, plus extra for bread
$1^{1}/_{2}$ to 2 tablespoons peeled and grated fresh ginger
Finely grated zest and juice of 1 orange
3 tomatoes, peeled, seeded, and minced
$^{1}/_{2}$ cup dry white wine or verjus
$^{1}/_{4}$ cup butter
3 tablespoons chopped fresh basil, dill, chervil, tarragon, mint, thyme, savory, or chives
$^{1}/_{2}$ teaspoon salt
$^{1}/_{4}$ teaspoon freshly ground black pepper
Pinch of red chile flakes

Scrub the shellfish thoroughly under cool running water. If you're using mussels, trim away any beards.

Preheat a grill. Brush one side of the bread with garlic oil and grill, oil-side down, until nice grill marks appear.

Heat the 1 tablespoon olive oil in a large, deep sauté pan with a cover over high heat. (Use 2 pans if you don't have one large enough to hold all the shellfish at once.) Add the garlic and ginger and sauté for 30 seconds. Add the clams or mussels, and toss for 2 minutes more. Add the orange juice, tomatoes, and wine. Cover and cook over medium-high heat for 6 to 8 minutes until the clams or mussels open. Uncover, raise the heat, and add the butter, basil, orange zest, salt, pepper, and chile flakes. Cook until the butter is melted and the juices have thickened somewhat.

Transfer the shellfish to a plate, discarding any that have still not opened, and reduce the broth over high heat a bit more, if desired. Pour the broth over the shellfish. Serve with the grilled bread.

Mustards' BBQ Smoked Chicken Wings

Serves 6

This is quintessential football-watching food. You have a lot of options here: First, if you don't have a smoker, just grill the wings, covered, over a low fire, lowering the grate to crisp the skin when they're done. Or, you can use a conventional oven. Not all of our recipe testers had smokers and some didn't feel like starting up their grills in the middle of a Minnesota winter, so they did these in the oven (350° for 15 minutes), finished them under the broiler, and still enjoyed them. I like them just as they are, but you could serve them with additional BBQ marinade or hot sauce for dipping. The Chinese-Style Mustard Sauce (page 196) works great as well. You can smoke the wings a day ahead, then crisp them up and heat them through on the grill when you want to serve them.

3 pounds chicken wings
3 tablespoons Dijon mustard
$^1/_2$ teaspoon Worcestershire sauce
1 tablespoon honey
1 scant cup BBQ sauce for ribs (page 112) or a nonsmoky commercial BBQ sauce

To marinate the wings, trim off the tips of the wings, reserving them for stock. If desired, cut each wing in half at the joint. Combine the mustard, Worcestershire sauce, honey, and BBQ sauce in a container large enough to hold all the wings. Toss the wings into the marinade, stir to make sure they're well coated with the marinade, cover, and marinate in the refrigerator for at least 1 hour, or for as long as overnight.

To cook the wings, spread them on a rack in the smoker, and smoke them for 1 hour, adding soaked chips as you see the smoke dying down. (We added more chips three times during the hour the wings were smoking.) When the wings are done, remove the water pan, lower the rack as close to the coals as possible, and crisp the wings over the hot fire. These are best served hot but they are also good at room temperature.

Chinese-Style Chicken Wings

Serves 6 to 8

These can be cooked directly on a slow grill, but I like them better if they're smoked first, as this renders out more of the fat and makes the skin crispier. Either way, serve the wings with a drizzle of the mustard sauce, some cilantro, and scallions tossed about, with toasted sesame seeds sprinkled liberally over all—my idea of finger-lickin' good. The wings are good hot, at room temperature, or even cold (leftovers taste great at midnight when you raid the refriger- ator in your pajamas and slippers).

3 pounds chicken wings
2 tablespoons peanut oil
$^1/_3$ cup dark soy sauce
2 tablespoons honey
2 tablespoons dry sherry
1 clove garlic, minced
1 teaspoon peeled and grated fresh ginger
Minced fresh cilantro for garnish
Minced scallions for garnish
Toasted sesame seeds for garnish
Chinese-Style Mustard Sauce (page 196)

To marinate the wings, trim off the tips of the wings, reserving them for stock. Cut each wing in half at the joint. Whisk together the oil, soy sauce, honey, sherry, garlic, and ginger in a container large enough to hold all the wings. Toss in the wings, stir to make sure they're well coated with the marinade, cover, and allow to marinate in the refrigerator for at least 2 hours, or for as long as overnight.

To grill the wings, cook them over a medium-high fire, turning often, for 10 to 15 minutes, until they are well browned, crisp, and cooked through. To smoke them, place the wings on the racks and smoke for 1 hour, adding soaked chips or green fruitwood as you see the smoke dying down. (We added soaked wood chips three times during the hour, and felt the amount of smoke absorbed was great.) If you want to serve the wings right away, remove the water pan, lower the rack as close to the coals as possible, and crisp the skin over the hot fire. Because there is honey in the marinade, you need to watch them carefully to make sure they don't burn. If you're serving the wings later, remove them when they are done and then toss them on the grill briefly or pop them under the broiler to reheat them, turning them once to crisp the skin.

To serve, place the wings on a platter and sprinkle with cilantro, scallions, and sesame seeds. Driz- zle with the mustard sauce or offer it on the side for dipping.

Duck Carnitas Tostadas with Ancho Chile Salsa and Tomatillo Salsa

Serves 6 to 8

These tostadas of shredded duck piled on a crispy tortilla, topped with two salsas, a mild slaw, and some crumbled goat cheese, are definitely upscale. The idea came to me when we had some leftover duck confit— not really enough to run for a menu addition, but too much to throw out. I shredded the meat, and it made me think of pork carnitas, and this dish came out of it. (Carnitas is pork that has been slowly cooked in its own fat, then shredded, and usually served in tacos or on tostadas.) We serve them with two salsas, which might seem a little excessive, but I've always felt that people deserve a little extra when they come to the restaurant to eat. The duck, the salsas, and the dressing can be done ahead and the tostadas assembled when desired.

DUCK CARNITAS
1 tablespoon extra virgin olive oil
4 to 6 whole bone-in duck legs
1/2 onion, thinly sliced
3 cloves garlic, crushed
1/4 teaspoon salt
4 marjoram or oregano sprigs
4 thyme sprigs
1 large orange, cut into chunks
1 cup milk
2 or 3 bay leaves
1/2 teaspoon freshly ground black pepper

TOMATILLO SALSA
6 to 8 tomatillos, papery husks removed and quartered
2 scallions, white and light green parts
2 to 3 cloves garlic, unpeeled
1/4 red onion, thickly sliced
1/2 jalapeño chile
Juice of 1/2 lime
1 1/2 tablespoons chopped fresh cilantro
1 1/2 tablespoons extra virgin olive oil
Leaves from 3 mint sprigs
Salt and freshly ground black pepper

ANCHO CHILE SALSA
2 or 3 ancho chiles, stemmed and seeded
2 tablespoons white wine, sweeter rather than dry
Finely grated zest and juice of 2 oranges or tangerines
1/4 cup extra virgin olive oil
1 to 1 1/2 teaspoons peeled and grated fresh ginger
1 tablespoon sherry vinegar
1 tablespoon brown sugar
1/8 teaspoon freshly ground black pepper
1 teaspoon salt

CABBAGE-RADISH SLAW
1 1/2 cups very thinly sliced green cabbage
4 or 5 large radishes, thinly sliced into rounds
2 tablespoons minced fresh cilantro
3 or 4 fresh mint leaves, finely shredded
1/2 pasilla chile, stemmed, seeded, and julienned
1/4 red onion, very thinly sliced
1 tablespoon rice vinegar
1 1/2 tablespoons freshly squeezed lime juice
1 tablespoon Dijon mustard
1 shallot, minced
Pinch of salt
Pinch of freshly ground black pepper
1/2 cup plus 1 tablespoon olive oil

6 to 8 (6-inch) corn tortillas
Peanut oil or safflower oil for frying
Salt
1/2 cup sour cream
Cilantro sprigs for garnish

To prepare the duck carnitas, heat the olive oil in a large, heavy skillet or pot over medium-high heat. Add the duck legs and cook, turning as necessary, for 8 to 10 minutes, until browned on both sides. Add the onion and garlic and cook, stirring occasionally, for 8 to 10 minutes, until brown. Add the salt, marjoram, thyme, orange, milk, bay leaves to taste, and pepper and stir well. Bring to a simmer, cover, and cook for 30 minutes, until the duck begins to get tender. Uncover and cook for 20 to 30 minutes more, until the liquid has completely evaporated and the duck is very tender. Remove from the heat, allow the duck to cool, then remove the skin and bones and shred the duck into bite-sized pieces.

To make the tomatillo salsa, heat a heavy skillet or griddle (cast iron is perfect) without any fat or oil over medium-high to high heat. Add the tomatillos, scallions, garlic, onion, and jalapeño and roast, shaking and turning often to keep them from burning, for 10 to 12 minutes, until they are dark golden brown. Take your time, going a minute more rather than less, as this is the step that develops all the flavors.

Peel the garlic and put it in a blender with all the other roasted ingredients. Add the lime juice, cilantro, olive oil, mint, and salt and pepper to taste. Purée until the salsa is the consistency you like. Some people (me, for instance) like it a bit chunky; others prefer it quite smooth. Taste and adjust the seasoning.

To make the ancho chile salsa, toast the chiles in a dry pan over medium-high heat for 1 to 2 minutes, until fragrant and slightly darker. Put the chiles in a small saucepan along with the wine and enough water to cover, bring to a simmer, and simmer for 5 minutes. Put the chiles and their cooking liquid in a blender, add all the remaining ingredients, and purée until smooth. Strain through a sieve if desired.

To make the slaw, combine the cabbage, radishes, cilantro, mint, chile, and onion in a bowl. For the vinaigrette, in a separate bowl, whisk together the vinegar, lime juice, mustard, shallot, salt, and pepper until the salt is dissolved. Gradually whisk in the olive oil and continue to whisk until emulsified. Cover and refrigerate the slaw and vinaigrette separately until you're ready to assemble the tostadas.

When you're ready to serve, toss the slaw with just enough vinaigrette to coat lightly. Pour oil to a depth of $1/8$ inch into a sauté pan and heat over medium-high heat. Add the tortillas one at a time and fry for 1 to 2 minutes until crispy. Drain on a rack, and sprinkle lightly with salt.

Heat a small amount of oil in a large skillet or nonstick pan over medium-high heat. Add the duck and reheat, tossing occasionally, to crisp it on the outside and heat it through.

To serve, place a mound of duck on each tortilla and drizzle it with the ancho salsa. Add a layer of slaw, and a drizzle of tomatillo salsa. Top it all off with a dollop of sour cream and garnish with cilantro sprigs. These tostadas do tend to get a bit high, so a knife and fork might help, although they taste best to me as finger food.

Because I am a primitive potter and bowls are about the only thing I can throw, I seem to be making a lot of soup at home these days.

Soups are versatile. They can be hearty and filling, or they can be the perfect diet dish (if you refrain from buttered crackers, cheese toast, and the ten thousand other great accompaniments on the planet). Here, I've tried to include several options for the dif-ferent seasons: asparagus and arugula in spring, curried lentil for fall, white vegetable with cilantro pesto for stick-to-your-ribs warmth in the winter. For summer, I could write a whole book on soups made with ripe tomatoes fresh from the garden—tomatoes with chiles, tomatoes with pimientos, tomatoes with basil and garlic, tomatoes with corn and tortillas. The possibilities are endless.

Asparagus Soup with Arugula and Crème Fraîche

Serves 6

This is an elegant start to a spring meal. The trick of blending the arugula or spinach in at the end helps keep the soup bright green. You can make the soup ahead. Just chill it over ice as soon as it's blended, then reheat it right before serving, and it will keep its bright green color.

2 tablespoons butter
2 leeks, white and light green parts only, quartered
$^1/_2$ onion, diced
3 cups chopped asparagus, tips reserved for garnish
1 cup peeled, diced Yukon Gold potatoes
1 teaspoon ground mace or freshly grated nutmeg
$1^1/_2$ teaspoons sea salt
$^1/_2$ teaspoon freshly ground black pepper, plus extra for garnish
5 cups water, chicken stock (page 218), or vegetable stock (page 215), or as needed
2 cups lightly packed arugula or spinach leaves
$^1/_2$ cup heavy whipping cream
6 tablespoons crème fraîche

Melt the butter in a large saucepan over medium heat, and cook the leeks and onion, stirring occasionally, for 5 to 6 minutes, until soft. Add the chopped asparagus, potatoes, mace, sea salt, and $^1/_2$ teaspoon pepper and cook gently, again stirring occasionally, for 8 to 10 minutes, until the vegetables are tender. Add the 5 cups water, and cook over medium-low heat for about 10 to 12 minutes, until the potatoes are soft enough to mash.

Meanwhile, blanch the asparagus tips in boiling water until just tender, refresh under cold water until cooled, and set aside.

When the potatoes are ready, transfer the soup, in batches, to a blender and blend with the arugula and cream until smooth. Strain through a fine-mesh sieve and reheat gently. Taste and adjust the seasonings as necessary. Thin with additional water or stock if the soup is too thick.

Ladle into bowls and top with a dollop of crème fraîche, the asparagus tips, and pepper.

Hot-and-Sour Mushroom Soup

Serves 8

Fresh lemongrass is difficult to find in areas without a large Southeast Asian population, but you can use lemon zest instead. If you are fortunate enough to have lemongrass, use the inner portion of the bulb end only, peeling away the tough outer layers. Save the rest for stocks or to season iced or hot teas.

3 tablespoons peanut oil

1 or 2 bulbs spring garlic, including most of the green, or 10 cloves garlic, sliced

2 leeks, white and light green parts only, julienned

2 jalapeño chiles or 1 pasilla chile, seeded and julienned

2 tablespoons minced lemongrass, bulb end only, or grated zest of 2 lemons

$1^{1}/_{2}$ tablespoons peeled and grated fresh ginger

1 teaspoon peeled and grated fresh turmeric root, or $^{1}/_{4}$ teaspoon ground turmeric

$2^{1}/_{2}$ pounds oyster, portobello, and shiitake mushrooms, trimmed and sliced (reserve trimmings for stock)

$1^{1}/_{2}$ teaspoons tamarind paste

2 tablespoons rice or Chinese black vinegar

2 tablespoons sugar

2 carrots, julienned

6 cups chicken stock (page 218)

1 teaspoon salt

$^{1}/_{2}$ teaspoon freshly ground black pepper

$^{1}/_{2}$ cup pineapple juice or minced fresh pineapple

Finely shredded fresh mint leaves, for garnish

Fresh chives, cut on the diagonal, for garnish

Heat the oil in a soup pot over medium-high heat. Add the garlic, leeks, and chiles and sweat for 6 to 8 minutes, until the leeks are soft. Add the lemongrass, ginger, and turmeric, and cook for 1 minute. Add the mushrooms and cook for 5 to 6 minutes, until tender and caramelized.

Combine the tamarind paste, vinegar, and sugar together in a small bowl, stirring until smooth. Add the mixture to the pot and cook for 2 minutes. Add the carrots and cook for 1 minute more, stirring. Add the chicken stock, salt, and pepper and bring just to a boil, skimming as necessary. Don't overcook the soup, as you want the flavors to be fresh and bright.

Stir in the pineapple juice just before serving. Ladle into bowls and sprinkle some mint and chives over each serving.

Red Tomato Gazpacho

Serves 6 to 8

This is a variation on the very first gazpacho I ever made, probably twenty years ago. I've learned a lot more about true Spanish gazpachos since then, but I often return to this simple version. It's what I eat when I am trying to diet, which is constantly in the summer. For photo, see page 53.

CROUTONS
1/2 baguette, cubed
1 1/2 tablespoons extra virgin olive oil

SOUP
1/2 red onion or 3 scallions, minced
5 large vine-ripened red tomatoes, peeled and diced
1 red bell pepper, seeded and minced
1 cucumber, peeled and diced
2 tablespoons rice vinegar
1 1/3 cups tomato juice
1 teaspoon salt
1/4 teaspoon freshly ground black pepper
1 pasilla chile, seeded and chopped
1/2 jalapeño chile, minced (with seeds if you like it hot, seeded if not)
3 tablespoons minced fresh cilantro

GARNISHES
2 to 3 tablespoons extra virgin olive oil
1/4 cucumber, peeled, seeded, and minced
1/4 red bell pepper, seeded and minced
3 tablespoons Lime Crème Fraîche (page 196) or Lime Sour Cream (page 196)

To make the croutons, preheat the oven to 350°. Spread the baguette cubes on a baking sheet and drizzle with the olive oil. Toast in the oven for 5 to 7 minutes, until golden brown and crisp. Set aside.

To make the soup, combine the red onion, tomatoes, bell pepper, cucumber, rice vinegar, and tomato juice in a blender and blend until smooth. Season with the salt and pepper to taste. You may strain the soup through a medium-mesh sieve at this point, if you like. Stir in the chiles, cilantro, and half of the croutons.

To serve, ladle or pour into well-chilled bowls. Drizzle each serving with olive oil and pass the remaining croutons and the cucumber, bell pepper, and crème fraîche for diners to garnish their soup as they wish.

Grape and Almond Gazpacho

Serves 6

I once made this gazpacho for a summer wine-tasting benefit attended by five hundred people. It was about 100° that day, and this refreshing, ice-cold soup was the hit of the party. It couldn't be quicker to make and is perfect for that hot day when no one wants to "cook." If you have them, chive blossoms make a beautiful addition to the garnishes.

SOUP

2 pounds seedless green grapes

1 small cucumber, peeled, seeded, and coarsely chopped

¼ cup almonds, toasted

2 scallions, white and light green parts only, coarsely chopped

¼ cup rice vinegar

½ cup plain yogurt

3 ounces cream cheese

2 tablespoons extra virgin olive oil

¼ cup buttermilk

½ to ¾ teaspoon salt

¼ teaspoon freshly ground white pepper

2 large dill sprigs, minced

⅛ to ¼ teaspoon ground cayenne pepper

GARNISHES

Minced fresh chives

Thin cucumber slices

To make the soup, combine the grapes, cucumber, almonds, scallions, vinegar, yogurt, cream cheese, olive oil, and buttermilk in a blender or food processor. Process until almost smooth, with just a bit of texture remaining. Stir in the salt, white pepper, dill, and cayenne until incorporated. Cover and refrigerate until cold.

To serve, ladle the cold soup into well-chilled bowls and garnish with the chives and cucumber slices.

Pear and Rutabaga Soup

Serves 6

I know the ingredients in this soup sound like a strange combination, but every time I serve it, people rave. Make sure the pears are ripe and the rutabagas are fresh. I haven't tried this recipe with turnips, but they should work fine, too, if you can't find rutabagas. If you prefer a chunky, chowder-style soup, dice the vegetables neatly and leave out the blending step.

2 tablespoons extra virgin olive oil
1 small onion, diced
1 tablespoon minced garlic
2 celery stalks, diced
1 large carrot, diced
1 pound rutabagas, diced
$^1/_2$ pound pears, peeled, cored, and chopped
1 tablespoon minced fresh thyme
1 bay leaf
1 whole clove
$^1/_8$ teaspoon ground cinnamon
1 cup white wine
6 cups vegetable stock (page 215) or chicken stock (page 218)
$^1/_2$ to 1 teaspoon salt, depending on saltiness of the stock
$^1/_4$ to $^1/_2$ teaspoon freshly ground black pepper
$^1/_2$ cup heavy whipping cream (optional)
Toasted almonds, for garnish (optional)
Minced fresh chives, for garnish (optional)
Chervil sprigs, for garnish (optional)

Heat the oil in a large saucepan over medium-high heat. Add the onion and garlic and cook, stirring occasionally, for about 6 to 8 minutes, until soft. Add the celery, carrot, rutabagas, pears, thyme, bay leaf, clove, and cinnamon, and cook, stirring occasionally, for about 8 to 10 minutes, until the vegetables are tender and fragrant. Add the wine, bring to a boil, and boil until almost all the liquid has cooked away. Add the stock and return the soup to a boil. Season with the salt and pepper (remember to taste first if you're using canned stock since it can be quite salty). Lower the heat to a simmer, and skim off any froth that comes to the surface. Cook for about 12 to 15 minutes, or until the vegetables are tender.

Remove the bay leaf and discard. Purée the soup in a blender (a food processor won't get it smooth enough), then strain through a fine-mesh sieve. At this point, the soup can be refrigerated until needed.

To finish, return the soup to the pot, add the cream, and heat until hot. Garnish with almonds, chives, and chervil and serve.

Tomato, Basil, and Tortilla Soup

Serves 6

This is incredibly quick to toss together, and there are about a million ways to dress it up or down, depending on your mood and what's in the cupboard. We serve it with Lime Crême Fraîche, but it's also excellent with a garnish of cheese, pesto, crisp tortilla strips, or croutons—whatever you happen to have around.

TORTILLA STRIPS
3 stale corn tortillas, julienned and sliced into 1-inch-long strips
Vegetable oil for frying

2 teaspoons salt plus additional salt for sprinkling on tortillas
1 tablespoon extra virgin olive oil
$^1/_2$ large red onion, coarsely chopped
$^1/_4$ head garlic, peeled and coarsely chopped
6 large ripe tomatoes, peeled and chopped
1 tablespoon tomato paste, if not using vine-ripened tomatoes
1 tablespoon minced fresh basil
1 tablespoon minced fresh parsley
1 tablespoon minced fresh chives
3 cups water, vegetable stock (page 215), or chicken stock (page 218)
$^3/_4$ teaspoon freshly ground black pepper
Lime Crème Fraîche (page 196) or Lime Sour Cream (page 196)
6 thick slices rustic country bread, grilled or toasted

Heat a heavy skillet filled $^1/_2$-inch-deep with vegetable oil over medium-high heat. When the oil is 365°, add the tortilla strips and fry until golden brown and crisp. Transfer the tortilla strips to paper towels and lightly salt.

Heat the olive oil in a large saucepan over medium heat. Add the onion and garlic, and sweat for about 10 to 15 minutes, until tender. Add the tortillas and cook, stirring, for 3 to 5 minutes, or until golden brown. Add the tomatoes, tomato paste (if necessary), and half each of the basil, parsley, and chives. Add the water and simmer for 20 to 30 minutes, or until thickened and flavorful. Season with the 2 teaspoons salt and pepper. At this point you can either leave the soup chunky or purée it, in batches, in a blender or food processor and reheat gently.

Just before serving, stir in the remaining herbs. Ladle into bowls and garnish with the crème fraîche and stick one slice of the bread in each soup (or float slices on top).

French Country-Style Vegetable Soup with Pistou

Serves 6

I have always thought of Mustards as a cross between a roadside rib joint and a French country restaurant. This soup is from Mustards' French country inn side. You need diced carrots and onions for both the stock and the soup, so you might want to prep enough for both all at once. The soup is served with pistou, the French version of pesto.

HAM HOCK STOCK
1 large, meaty ham hock
2 carrots, diced
1 onion, diced
¹/₂ bunch thyme
8 cups chicken stock (page 218)

PISTOU
1¹/₂ cups packed fresh basil leaves
¹/₄ cup grated Parmesan cheese
2 cloves garlic
¹/₂ cup extra virgin olive oil
¹/₄ teaspoon salt
¹/₈ teaspoon freshly ground black pepper

SOUP
3 tablespoons extra virgin olive oil
2 large carrots, diced
1 large onion, diced
1 large leek, white part and 1 inch of light green, diced
2 tablespoons minced garlic
¹/₂ head green cabbage, thinly sliced
2 cups cooked cannellini beans, with some of their cooking liquid (canned is okay)
¹/₄ teaspoon salt
¹/₈ teaspoon freshly ground black pepper

To make the stock, put the ham hock, carrots, onion, thyme, and stock in a saucepan and bring to a boil. Skim off any froth that rises to the surface, lower the heat, and simmer for 2 to 3 hours, until the meat is tender enough to fall off the bone. Strain the broth through a sieve. Pick out the meat from the sieve, removing any gristle or fat, and dice neatly. (You may do this ahead and refrigerate the stock and meat until needed.) Cool the broth in the refrigerator, then skim off any fat that has collected on the surface. Cover and return to the refrigerator until you are ready to make the soup.

To make the pistou, put the basil, Parmesan, and garlic in a blender or food processor and process briefly, until roughly chopped. With the motor running, slowly add the oil and continue processing until it is fully incorporated and the sauce is quite thick. Season with the salt and pepper and reserve until needed.

To make the soup, in a large stockpot, heat the olive oil over medium heat. Add the carrots, onion, leek, and garlic and sweat for about 10 minutes until slightly tender. Add the cabbage and cook until wilted, then add the reserved stock and ham hock meat and simmer for 30 minutes. Taste to see if flavors have melded.

If you are using canned cannellini beans, drain and rinse them. Add the cooked or canned beans to the pot, and simmer for 15 to 20 minutes, until the soup is thick and aromatic. Season with the salt and pepper.

Ladle into bowls and top each serving with a healthy dollop of pistou.

Roasted Squash Soup

Serves 6

Any of the winter squash varieties, such as Red Kuri, butternut, banana, acorn, or even pumpkin, will work for this soup. Although they are commonly thought of as fall and winter vegetables, you often start seeing them before the end of summer. When I'm baking potatoes, I often bake squash at the same time, some to serve as a vegetable and the extra to use for this soup. This is great with toasted walnut bread spread with a triple-cream cheese, for a nice supper in front of the fire.

2¹/₂ pounds winter squash
1 tablespoon extra virgin olive oil
1 red onion, diced
2 cloves garlic, smashed
¹/₂ large leek, white and light green parts only, thinly sliced into half-moons
1 carrot, peeled and diced
1 small russet potato, diced
¹/₄ teaspoon coarsely cracked cardamom
Finely grated zest and juice of ¹/₂ orange
2 tablespoons dry white wine
4 to 5 cups vegetable stock (page 215), chicken stock (page 218), or water
1 teaspoon salt
¹/₄ teaspoon freshly ground white pepper
¹/₄ cup heavy whipping cream (optional)

Preheat the oven to 400°. Halve or quarter the squash (or squashes), depending on size, and remove the seeds and fibrous membranes. Place the pieces on a baking sheet and roast for about 40 minutes, or until nicely caramelized and soft. When cool enough to handle, scoop out the flesh and set it aside.

Heat the olive oil in a large pot over medium-high heat. Add the onion and garlic and cook, stirring frequently, for about 10 minutes, until soft and golden. Add the leek and carrot and cook and stir for about 5 minutes, until tender. Add the potato, reserved squash, cardamom, and orange juice and zest and cook for 2 minutes. Add the wine and simmer until the wine is almost completely evaporated. Add 4 cups of the stock, adding more if necessary to achieve the right consistency, the add the salt and pepper. Bring to a simmer, and cook for 15 to 20 minutes, until the vegetables are soft.

Purée the soup, in batches, in a blender until smooth. Strain through a fine-mesh sieve placed over the pot and stir in the cream. Taste and adjust the seasoning. Ladle into bowls and serve.

Golden Gazpacho

Serves 6 to 8

After six or seven attempts, we finally got lemongrass to grow in our garden. It's like catnip—our dogs always eat it down to the ground before we can get to it! This recipe—a kind of Spanish-Vietnamese summer soup— is one of those crosscultural combos that California's great growing conditions allow us local chefs to make. It gets very hot in Napa Valley in the summer. That's when all I want to eat are cold soups, potato salads, and chilled melons, and this fits that profile. Yes, of course, you could use red tomatoes instead of yellow. The soup will be equally tasty, although it may not be as impressive looking.

SOUP

2$^1/_2$ pounds (5 large) golden tomatoes, peeled and cut up
1 cucumber, peeled, seeded, and diced
1 red bell pepper, seeded and diced
3 or 4 scallions, sliced
1 lemongrass stalk, bottom 2 inches of bulb end only, tough outer layers removed and very finely minced
2 tablespoons rice vinegar
$^1/_4$ cup olive oil
1 jalapeño chile, seeded and minced
$^1/_4$ to $^1/_2$ teaspoon salt
$^1/_8$ teaspoon freshly ground black pepper
Tabasco sauce

GARNISHES

3 to 4 tablespoons Lime Sour Cream or Lime Crème Fraîche (page 196)
1 handful croutons (page 212)
$^1/_4$ cup minced fresh cilantro, mint, basil, tarragon, or chives

To make the soup, purée the tomatoes in a blender, then strain through a medium-fine sieve placed over a large bowl. Stir in all the remaining soup ingredients, including Tabasco sauce to taste. Cover and refrigerate until cold.

To serve, ladle the cold soup into well-chilled bowls. Garnish each serving with an equal amount of the sour cream, croutons, and cilantro.

Yucatán-Style Chicken and Vegetable Soup

Serves 6 to 8

This rich, spicy broth gets its stunning color from achiote paste, a Yucatán spice paste made from achiote seeds, garlic, oregano, and cumin. (The seeds, which come from the annatto tree, are commonly used as a natural food coloring. They color, among other things, Cheddar cheese orange and butter a darker yellow.)

If you don't have time to smoke the tomatoes, use tomatoes fresh from the garden. Or you could get a nice smoky character by substituting 2 to 4 chipotle chiles in adobo or 2 to 3 tablespoons of pimentón, a Spanish paprika, for the serrano chiles. (Chipotles can be quite fiery, and much of the heat is in their seeds, so discard the seeds, start with a small amount of chile, and add more to your taste. I love putting all the garnishes for this soup on the side and letting everyone dress their own bowls as they want.

1 onion, thickly sliced
3 to 4 cloves garlic, unpeeled
2 to 4 serrano or árbol chiles
2 tablespoons peanut oil or extra virgin olive oil
1/4 teaspoon salt
1/8 teaspoon freshly ground black pepper
2 small zucchinis, diced
2 carrots, diced
1 teaspoon achiote paste (optional)
1 cup drained cooked garbanzo beans (canned is okay)
6 cups chicken stock (page 218)
1 bay leaf
2 cups Smoked Tomatoes (page 205)
3 boneless, skinless chicken breast halves
2 limes, halved

GARNISHES
2 jalapeño chiles, roasted, peeled, seeded, and minced
4 to 5 tablespoons minced fresh cilantro
1 avocado, pitted, peeled, and diced
Lime wedges
Crumbled feta cheese or queso añejo

Heat a sauté pan or griddle over medium-high heat. When it is hot, toss on the onion slices and the garlic and cook them in the dry heat, stirring now and then, for 3 to 5 minutes, until they are dark brown or almost black. Remove from the pan, dice the onions, and peel and slice the garlic. If you are using serrano chiles, mince them. If you are using árbol chiles, toast them briefly over a direct flame (a second will do), or toss them in a hot dry pan for 30 seconds or so, or until they are aromatic. Remove the seeds from the serranos or árbols if you want the soup less spicy.

Heat the oil in a large saucepan over medium-high heat. Add the charred onion, garlic, and chiles and sauté for several minutes. Season with the salt and pepper. Add the zucchinis, carrots, and achiote paste. Cook for several minutes more, stirring occasionally. Add the garbanzo beans, stock, bay leaf, and tomatoes. Bring to a boil, skim off any foam, and lower the heat to a simmer. When the vegetables are almost tender, add the chicken breasts and cook for 8 to 10 minutes, until just done. Remove the bay leaf before serving.

Remove the chicken breasts from the broth and shred the meat into soup bowls. Add some hot broth and vegetables to each bowl, then squeeze the juice from the lime halves into the bowls. Pass the garnishes at the table.

White Vegetable Soup

Serves 6

This winter soup has two variations: The one I think of as Latino-style is made with hominy, and I'd garnish it with Cilantro Pesto or fresh cilantro leaves. The other, more French version is made without the hominy, and I would garnish it with a crouton topped with blue cheese. The hominy version, which can be made with canned hominy, is substantial. You can serve it with some bread and a salad and you've got a meal. The French version is lighter and would make a nice appetizer for serving before grilled meats, such as lamb chops or steaks. Because the soup will be puréed, you don't need to be neat about chopping the vegetables.

2 tablespoons extra virgin olive oil

1 white onion, cut into wedges

2 small or 1 large leek, white parts only, sliced

2 parsnips, peeled, cored if the heart is hard and woody (reserve for stock), and cut up

1 turnip, peeled and cut up

1 large russet, yellow Finn, or Yukon Gold potato, peeled and cut up

2 cups sliced cauliflower

1 cup cooked white hominy (optional)

$\frac{1}{4}$ teaspoon salt

$\frac{1}{8}$ teaspoon freshly ground black pepper

1 cup white wine

6 cups chicken stock (page 218) or vegetable stock (page 215)

2 cups water

$\frac{1}{2}$ cup heavy whipping cream

Cilantro Pesto (page 194) or Blue Cheese Croutons (page 212), for garnish

Heat the olive oil in a large soup pot over medium-high heat. Add the onion and leeks and sweat for about 6 to 10 minutes, or until tender. Add the parsnips, turnip, potato, cauliflower, and the hominy, if making the Latino version. Cook uncovered, stirring occasionally, for several minutes. Add the salt and pepper and mix well. Then increase the heat to high, add the wine, and cook until almost all the liquid has cooked away. Lower the heat to medium-high, add the stock and water and bring just to a boil. Skim off any foam and lower the heat to medium. Cook, skimming as necessary, for 10 to 15 minutes, until vegetables are tender.

Purée the soup, in batches, in a blender. Return to the pot, add the cream, and reheat gently. Ladle into bowls.

If you've included the hominy, garnish with the pesto. If you have not included the hominy, serve topped with the croutons.

Cauliflower Soup with Truffles

Serves 6

The most important thing to remember with this soup is to keep it white, so cook it over low heat, "melting" the vegetables instead of browning or caramelizing them. Covering the soup as it cooks also seems to help keep it white. Purée the soup in a blender; a food processor just can't give you the velvety effect you want.

You have your choice of garnishes: a heady combination of mushrooms, Cognac, and truffle oil, or a simple sprinkling of chopped, blanched cauliflower. If you go for the truffle garnish, be careful, as sometimes wild mushrooms are foraged after a rain and they can be quite gritty. Clean them well, and be cautious with the soaking liquid, too.

Some folks are nervous about setting the alcohol on fire in sauces and other recipes like the one here for Mushroom-Truffle Garnish, but I have found that it is necessary if you want what you make to taste more like its ingredients than like alcohol. The step is a bit dangerous, however, so be careful. (Whoever said cooking was safe, anyway?)

2 tablespoons extra virgin olive oil or butter

1 onion, diced

2 celery stalks, diced

4 cloves garlic, diced

4 cups coarsely chopped cauliflower, plus 1 cup florets for garnish (optional)

1 to 2 teaspoons salt, depending on saltiness of stock

$^1/_2$ teaspoon freshly ground black pepper

$^1/_2$ cup dry white wine

5 to 6 cups chicken stock (page 218), vegetable stock (page 215), or water

2 russet, yellow Finn, or Yukon Gold potatoes, peeled and diced

MUSHROOM-TRUFFLE GARNISH

10 slices dried porcini mushrooms

$^1/_4$ cup Armagnac, Cognac, or brandy

2 tablespoons butter

1 shallot, minced

8 to 10 gratings of nutmeg

Pinch of salt

Pinch of freshly ground black pepper

1 to 2 tablespoons truffle oil

1 cup grated Parmesan or Asiago cheese

$^1/_3$ to $^1/_2$ cup heavy whipping cream (optional)

1 truffle, as big as you can afford, shaved (optional)

To make the soup, heat the oil in a large soup pot over medium heat. Add the onion, celery, and garlic and cook for about 8 minutes, or until hot. Add the 4 cups cauliflower and cook for another minute or two, stirring to coat with oil. Add the salt and pepper and cook for a minute more. Add the wine and cook until almost evaporated. Add the stock and potatoes and cook for 15 or 20 minutes, or until the cauliflower and potatoes are very tender. Don't rush, as you want the soup to be smooth when it is puréed.

Meanwhile, prepare the garnish. For the 1-cup cauliflower garnish, blanch the cauliflower florets in boiling salted water until crisp-tender. If they are small, this should only take 1 to $1^1/_2$ minutes. Drain and set aside.

to make the garnish, combine the mushrooms and Armagnac in a bowl and soak for about 10 minutes until rehydrated. Gently remove and finely chop the mushrooms, reserving the Armagnac.

Heat the butter in a small sauté pan over medium heat. Add the mushrooms, shallot, nutmeg, salt, and pepper and sauté for about 7 minutes, until tender. Pour in the reserved Armagnac, making sure that none of the grit from the mushrooms finds its way into the pan and gently splashing some over the edge of the pan so the liquor catches the flame from the burner and lights on fire in the pan. If you are cooking on an electric stovetop, use a match to light the Armagnac. The liquor may burst into flames, but this will only last for a moment or two and will burn off all of the alcohol flavor, making for a richer taste. Cook until almost dry, then stir in the truffle oil to taste.

To finish the soup, put the cheese and cream in a large bowl. Blend the soup, in small batches, in a blender. While it is still hot, pour it over the cheese and cream, stirring well with each addition. Serve it right away with a spoonful or two of the crisp-tender cauliflower or the mushroom-truffle garnish and several shavings of truffle over each serving. You may chill the soup and reheat it later, but make sure to do so slowly, so as not to scorch the cheese and cream.

Curried Cauliflower Noodle Soup

Serves 6

One day when I was craving chicken noodle soup, but cooking for vegetarian friends, I made this soup. It proved a good substitute for my craving; the turmeric in the curry gives the broth a warming, golden glow that makes one think of rich chicken soup. Depending on the heat of your curry powder, this soup could warm you up nicely on a cold winter day. It contains enough garlic and ginger to give the common cold a run for its money. Adding the coconut milk will make the soup richer and more chowderlike.

SOUP

2 tablespoons peanut oil or extra virgin olive oil

1 onion, sliced

8 cloves garlic, sliced

3 serrano or jalapeño chiles, seeded, if you don't want the heat, and minced

1 large carrot, halved lengthwise and cut into half-moons

8 pieces crystallized ginger, or $^{1}/_{3}$ cup peeled and grated fresh ginger

3 to 4 tablespoons curry paste, homemade (page 213) or purchased, or curry powder

1 cup dry white wine

2 sweet potatoes or white potatoes, peeled and julienned

1 small head cauliflower, sliced

8 cups vegetable stock (page 215) or chicken stock (page 218)

1 cup egg noodles

1 cup coconut milk (optional)

1 teaspoon salt

$^{1}/_{2}$ teaspoon freshly ground black pepper

GARNISHES

Cilantro Pesto (page 194) (optional)

Chopped fresh cilantro (optional)

Toasted sliced almonds (optional)

Minced fresh chives (optional)

To make the soup, heat the oil in a large pot over medium-high heat. Add the onion and garlic and sauté for several minutes, until translucent. Add the chiles, carrot, ginger, and curry, and cook, stirring, for several minutes more, or until the flavors are aromatic. Add the wine and cook until the wine is reduced by half. Add the potatoes, cauliflower, and stock and bring to a boil, skimming off any froth. Lower the heat to a simmer and cook for about 20 minutes, or until the vegetables are tender but not falling apart.

If you will be serving the soup as soon as it is done, add the noodles about 10 minutes before the vegetables are done. If you are not serving the soup right away, cook the noodles separately in boiling salted water and add them when you reheat the soup. When the vegetables are done, stir in the coconut milk and season with salt and pepper. Ladle into bowls and garnish with the pesto or sprinkle with the cilantro, almonds, and chives.

Spiced Lentil-Vegetable Soup

Serves 6 to 8

If you have any spice mix left over from this recipe, store it in an airtight container in a dark cupboard. A little bit of it combined with some olive oil makes a nice marinade for lamb chops, pork chops, or burgers. If you can find mini pappadams, crisp Indian lentil flatbreads, they make a great garnish for this soup.

SPICE MIX

1 tablespoon black peppercorns

1 tablespoon black mustard seeds

2 tablespoons coriander seeds

2 tablespoons ground turmeric

SOUP

1 or 2 dried chipotle or guajillo chiles, stemmed and seeded

3 tablespoons extra virgin olive oil

4 to 6 cloves garlic, minced

1 cup finely diced onions

1 cup finely diced carrots

$1/2$ pound beets, turnips, or rutabagas, cooked, peeled, and diced (page 71)

1 cup dry white wine

10 to 12 cups water or vegetable stock (page 215)

$1/2$ pound black or orange lentils, picked over and well washed

2 small or 1 large russet, yellow Finn, or Yukon Gold potato, peeled and diced

3 to 4 tablespoons peeled and grated fresh ginger

2 to 3 teaspoons salt

1 to 2 tablespoons champagne vinegar

GARNISHES

6 tablespoons plain yogurt

2 tablespoons finely minced fresh mint

Toasted mini pappadams (optional)

To make the spice mix, combine the peppercorns, mustard, and coriander in a dry skillet. Toast over medium-high heat for about 3 minutes (or less time, if toasting in a thin pan), until the seeds begin to pop. Let cool, then blend in a spice grinder or coffee grinder, or finely smash in a mortar with a pestle. Mix with the turmeric. Measure out 1 tablespoon for the soup, and store the remainder for other uses.

To make the soup, preheat the oven to 350°. Place the chiles in a shallow pan and toast for 2 to 3 minutes, until fragrant. Transfer the chiles to a bowl of warm water to cover for 10 to 15 minutes, until soft. Heat the oil in a large pot over medium-high heat. Add the garlic, onions, and chiles and cook, stirring occasionally, for 3 to 5 minutes, until their aroma fills the room. Add the 1 tablespoon spice mix, carrots, and beets and cook for 10 minutes more to develop the flavors. Add the wine and water and bring to a rolling boil. Add the lentils, potatoes, and ginger. Lower the heat to a simmer, cover, and cook for 15 to 20 minutes, until the lentils and potatoes are very tender, adding more water if needed. Season to taste with the salt and vinegar.

This soup may be blended and strained through a sieve, if desired, or left chunky. Ladle into bowls and serve with a dollop of yogurt, some mint, and mini pappadams.

Salads

The most wonderful part of being a chef in Northern California is that you can grow your own salad greens and herbs, and lots of vegetables, too, for ten to twelve months of the year. The garden teaches you volumes about the seasonality of produce and what tastes good with what: spring lamb with the mint that has begun to go wild and the rosemary that is in bloom; asparagus and marble-sized potatoes with that new explosion of tarragon that appeared out of nowhere. My rule is simple—eat from the garden whenever you can. It's nice to let Mother Nature write your menu.

Mixed Greens with Those Nuts and Blue Cheese

Serves 6

About 70 percent of the greens we use come from the Mustards garden six months out of the year. We grow mustard greens, red and green oak leaf lettuce, frisée, mizuna, tatsoi, curly cress, chervil, arugula and other tender lettuces and herbs.

Our basic, everyday mixed green salad is always open for interpretation, from the salad greens to the dressing to whether or not you want blue cheese on it. We use mesclun from Mustards' garden, often adding arugula, frisée, baby beet or chard leaves, or whatever else is tender and plentiful. According to Alice Waters, one of my heroes, mesclun is a Provençal word that simply means "mixed." In Chez Panisse Vegetables, *she describes how American grocery stores began offering mesclun during the late sixties and early seventies. This exotic treat was a far cry from the big three—iceberg lettuce, butter lettuce, and romaine.*

BALSAMIC AND SHERRY VINAIGRETTE
1 tablespoon sherry vinegar
1 tablespoon balsamic vinegar
1 shallot, minced
Pinch of fine sea salt
Pinch of freshly ground white pepper
3 tablespoons extra virgin olive oil
3 tablespoons pure olive oil

SHERRY VINAIGRETTE
1 tablespoon sherry vinegar
1 1/4 teaspoons Dijon mustard
1 shallot, diced
Pinch of salt
Pinch of freshly ground white pepper
3 tablespoons extra virgin olive oil
1 tablespoon pure olive oil

6 to 8 cups mixed greens
1/2 cup **Those Nuts** (page 212)
1/2 cup crumbled Maytag or Shraft blue cheese (optional)

To make the balsamic vinaigrette, whisk together the sherry vinegar, balsamic vinegar, shallot, salt, and pepper in a small bowl until the salt is dissolved. This should take about 30 seconds. Gradually whisk in the olive oils, and continue to whisk until fully emulsified. Taste and adjust the seasoning.

To make the sherry vinaigrette, whisk together the vinegar, mustard, shallot, salt, and pepper in a small bowl until the salt is dissolved. Gradually whisk in the extra virgin olive oil, then the pure olive oil, and continue to whisk until fully emulsified. Taste and adjust the seasoning.

Wash the greens, tear into bite-sized pieces, and spin dry. To serve, place the greens in a large bowl and dress with just enough vinaigrette to coat them. Portion them out onto chilled plates, and sprinkle the nuts and cheese over the top.

Arugula and Maytag Blue Cheese Salad with Maple-Sherry Vinaigrette

Serves 6

Arugula is definitely not a wimpy green. In fact, winter-grown arugula can be quite spicy and firm. I guess months of cold weather build character. A touch of maple syrup in the vinaigrette gives you a perfect sweet-hot combination. Maytag blue is a great domestic blue cheese that's made in Iowa. I use a lot of it because of its superior flavor and color, or maybe I use it out of loyalty to my Midwestern roots. Who knows? Grilled pears, apples, or peaches in season make nice additions, or you could turn this salad into an entrée with the addition of smoked chicken.

MAPLE-SHERRY VINAIGRETTE
3 tablespoons sherry vinegar
1 tablespoon real maple syrup
1 shallot, minced
$^1/_8$ teaspoon salt
Freshly ground black pepper
3 tablespoons extra virgin olive oil
6 tablespoons pure olive oil

$^3/_4$ to 1 cup walnuts
2 cups packed (not crushed!) arugula
1 cup watercress
2 cups mixed lettuces
4 ounces crumbled Maytag blue cheese
Freshly ground black pepper

To make the vinaigrette, whisk together the vinegar, maple syrup, shallot, salt, and pepper to taste in a small bowl until the salt is dissolved. Gradually whisk in the extra virgin olive oil and then the pure oil, and continue to whisk until fully incorporated. Taste and adjust the seasoning.

Preheat the oven to 350°. Spread the walnuts in a shallow pan and toast in the oven for 7 minutes, until fragrant. Set aside to cool. Wash the arugula, watercress, and lettuces, removing tough stems and tearing large leaves into bite-sized pieces. Spin dry and place in a bowl. Toss the greens with 3 to 4 tablespoons of the Maple-Sherry Vinaigrette, to coat lightly. Place the greens on salad plates and sprinkle liberally with the cheese, walnuts, and pepper.

Sean's Butter Lettuce Salad with Maytag Blue Cheese Dressing

Serves 8 to 10

This salad carries a double dose of blue cheese, so if you're a blue cheese lover, this one's for you. The dressing made me think how much alike my mom and our chef, Sean Mindrum, are: They are both German, and they both put sour cream and mayonnaise in their dressing. Brigid says this dressing reminds her of her mom's dressings as well, but her mom was Italian. So it must also be a seventies thing. There will be a bit of dressing left over: Try it with potato chips or any steamed green vegetable. Be creative!

DRESSING
¹/₄ cup sour cream
³/₄ cup mayonnaise
¹/₄ cup Maytag blue cheese
¹/₄ cup buttermilk
2 or 3 scallions, white and 3 inches of green, chopped
1 tablespoon freshly squeezed lemon juice
¹/₄ teaspoon salt
Pinch of freshly ground black pepper

2 heads Belgian endive, thinly sliced lengthwise
2 heads butter lettuce
1 head frisée, white and light green parts only
¹/₃ cup crumbled Maytag blue cheese
¹/₃ cup Those Nuts (page 212)

To make the dressing, combine the sour cream, mayonnaise, blue cheese, buttermilk, scallions, lemon juice, salt, and pepper in a blender and blend until smooth. Keep refrigerated until needed.

Wash the greens, tear into bite-sized pieces, and spin dry.

To serve, toss the greens together in a large bowl, then add enough dressing to coat the leaves lightly and toss again. Place the greens on salad plates. Garnish the salads with the remaining blue cheese and the nuts.

Warm Spinach and Frisée Salad

Serves 6

Buttery rich, caramelized roasted shallots play well against the some-what iron-y taste of the spinach, while the currants impart an unex-pected sweetness that contrasts well with the saltiness of the bacon in this interesting composition. You can roast the shallots in advance when you are roasting other food. Get everything you need prepared ahead of time, but don't combine it all until just before you are going to serve it.

6 shallots, peeled and sliced $1/2$ inch thick
1 tablespoon plus $1/4$ cup balsamic vinegar
4 tablespoons extra virgin olive oil
Salt and freshly ground black pepper
4 cups spinach leaves
3 to 4 cups frisée leaves
6 slices bacon, thinly sliced crosswise
6 tablespoons currants or raisins

Preheat the oven to 350°. Combine the shallots, the 1 tablespoon balsamic vinegar, 2 tablespoons of the olive oil, and a pinch each of salt and pepper in a small baking dish. Roast the shallots for 20 to 25 minutes, until golden brown and tender. Set aside to cool.

Remove the stems from the spinach and frisée, then wash, tear into bite-sized pieces if necessary, and spin dry. Place the spinach and frisée in a large heatproof bowl.

To make the dressing, cook the bacon in a large sauté pan over medium-high heat, stirring occa-sionally, until crisp. Using a slotted spoon, transfer the bacon pieces to the greens. Drain off and discard the bacon fat. Add the remaining $1/4$ cup balsamic vinegar to the same pan and cook over medium heat until reduced by half. Whisk in the remaining 2 tablespoons olive oil and season to taste with salt and pepper. Stir in the currants and roasted shallots.

Pour the hot dressing over the greens, toss quickly to combine, and serve immediately.

Thai Lamb and Ginger Salad with Curry Vinaigrette

Serves 6

Terry Lynch, a chef and partner at Mustards for many years, created this salad a long time ago. It's unusual to have lamb in a salad, but it is very tasty and satisfying and a nice way to surprise people. This salad works as an appetizer, or you can double the recipe and serve it as a cool and refreshing summer entrée. You need to plan ahead when you prepare this salad, however, as the lamb needs to marinate for at least 6 hours. The vegetables and greens can be prepared whenever it suits you.

The marinade calls for fish sauce, a staple cooking ingredient in Southeast Asia, much in the same way as soy sauce is in China. It is a clear, amber liquid with a strong aroma and a mildly fishy flavor. It's called nuoc mam in Vietnam and nam pla in Thailand. My favorite brand has three crabs on the label. The Bloomsdale spinach I call for is a "savoyed" or bubbly crunch leaf, and is often sold as "baby" spinach. It really holds up nicely in this type of salad.

CURRY VINAIGRETTE

1 tablespoon Patak's mild curry paste or homemade curry paste (page 213)

2 teaspoons Dijon mustard

2 tablespoons freshly squeezed lemon juice

2 tablespoons rice vinegar

1/2 teaspoon salt

3/4 teaspoon freshly ground black pepper

1/2 cup extra virgin olive oil

1/4 cup pure olive oil

MARINADE

3/4 teaspoon coriander seeds

3/4 teaspoon black peppercorns

Pinch of ground cayenne pepper

1 tablespoon peeled and grated fresh ginger

1/4 cup fish sauce

1/4 cup freshly squeezed lemon juice

1 tablespoon sugar

1/2 rack of lamb, boned and trimmed of fat and silverskin

1/2 cup shelled fava beans (about 1/2 pound unshelled), or 8 ounces haricots verts or green or yellow wax beans, tops and tails snapped off

1/2 cup cooked asparagus (about 1 bunch), broccoli (1 bunch), or pea pods (about 2 cups pods), chilled

2 cups Bloomsdale spinach or any other small variety

2 cups arugula

1 cup pea shoots or mixed Asian greens (such as tatsoi, baby bok choy, or mizuna)

1/2 bunch watercress

1 red Fresno chile, or 1/4 red bell pepper and 1 jalapeño chile, stemmed, seeded, and julienned

2 tablespoons peeled and finely julienned fresh ginger

3 scallions, white and light green parts only, cut on the diagonal

Basil, mint, and cilantro leaves

Freshly ground black peppercorns, for garnish

To make the vinaigrette, whisk together the curry paste, mustard, lemon juice, vinegar, salt, and pepper in a small bowl, until the salt is dissolved. Gradually whisk in the oils, and continue to whisk until fully emulsified. If you have any leftovers, this vinaigrette is great on all sorts of grilled vegetables, from asparagus and broccoli rabe to sweet or regular potatoes. It is also good on firm fish, poultry, and game.

continued from page 69

To make the marinade, crush the coriander seeds, peppercorns, and cayenne together in a mortar with pestle or grind in a spice or coffee grinder. Put the spices in a resealable plastic bag large enough to hold the rack of lamb. Add the ginger, fish sauce, lemon juice, and sugar, and mix well. Add the lamb, seal the bag closed, and refrigerate for 6 to 12 hours.

When ready to finish the dish, fill a stockpot halfway with water and bring to a rapid boil. Add the fava beans and cook until tender to the bite, removing them with a large skimmer. Add the asparagus, broccoli, or pea pods and repeat.

Remove the coarse stems from the spinach, arugula, pea shoots, and watercress, then wash and spin dry. All this can be done earlier in the day, if desired.

Shortly before serving, grill the lamb rack over high heat, turning the meat as the grill marks become strong and clear. The meat should be seared on the outside but rare inside, this should take 15 to 20 minutes. (If you want the meat more well done than that, I can't vouch for it.) Remove from the grill and allow to rest for 5 minutes.

Meanwhile, in a large bowl, toss together the salad greens, vegetables, chile, ginger, scallions, herbs, and just enough of the vinaigrette to coat lightly (be sure to whisk the vinaigrette thoroughly before adding it). Pile the greens and vegetables in the center of a large serving plate. Thinly slice the lamb crosswise into eighteen slices, and arrange the lamb slices around the salad. Drizzle with a little more vinaigrette, and finish with a generous amount of ground black pepper.

Blood Orange and Chioggia Beet Salad

Serves 6

Blood oranges begin showing up in our markets in December and are usually available until Easter. When we first started seeing them here, they were shipped in from Italy and were incredibly expensive. Now they are grown in California and are reasonably priced. If they are not available in your area, use any tasty eating oranges, or use mandarins or tangerines.

Chioggia beets are quite beautiful. They have circular stripes, so that if you cut them crosswise, each slice will look like a tiny target. If you can't get them, any small young beets will do. About 1 1/2 inches in diameter is a good size, and if you buy the beets with the green tops on, save all the tender, young leaves. Steam them as you would spinach, and season them with salt, pepper, lots of fresh lemon juice, and butter. They make a great vegetable accompaniment to grilled meats or fish.

3/4 cup walnut pieces
6 to 8 Chioggia or other beets
Olive oil, for coating, plus 1/4 cup pure olive oil
3 or 4 blood oranges
5 to 6 cups mixed peppery greens such as arugula and mesclun or watercress and mesclun
3 tablespoons balsamic vinegar
1 shallot, minced
1/2 teaspoon salt
1/4 teaspoon freshly ground black pepper
2 tablespoons extra virgin olive oil or walnut oil
Freshly cracked black pepper

Preheat the oven to 350°. Spread the nuts in a shallow pan and toast in the oven for 7 minutes, until fragrant. Set aside to cool. Leave the oven set at 350°.

To bake the beets, cut off the stems, leaving about 1 inch intact. Do not trim the root ends. Rub the beets with a little olive oil. Place in a baking dish, and bake for 20 to 30 minutes, until tender. The timing will depend on the age of the beets. When the beets are done, allow them to cool enough to handle, then peel and slice crosswise. (You can bake the beets a day ahead, although it is best to dress them while they are still a little warm.)

Using a zester or grater, remove enough zest from the blood oranges to measure 1 tablespoon and set it aside for the vinaigrette. Cut away all the pith from the orange, then section each orange by cutting between the flesh and membranes separating each segment. Put the orange sections in a large bowl along with the beets. Wash the greens, tear into bite-sized pieces, and spin dry. Add to the beets and oranges.

To make the vinaigrette, whisk together the vinegar, the reserved 1 tablespoon zest, shallot, salt, and pepper, until the salt is dissolved. Gradually whisk in the 1/4 cup pure olive oil and the extra virgin olive oil until the dressing is fully emulsified.

Add the vinaigrette to the salad and toss to coat evenly. Garnish with the walnuts and cracked pepper to taste. For a fancier presentation, dress the beets and oranges separately from the greens, put a pile of greens in the middle of each plate, and arrange the beets and oranges in an alternating pattern around the greens. Sprinkle the nuts over the salads and then the pepper.

Haricots Verts, New Potato, and Torpedo Onion Salad

Serves 4 to 6

I serve this salad when I'm not in the mood for greens. It's simple and it goes especially well with anything coming off the grill. We developed this salad when I had way too many onions in my home garden and brought them to work to use while they were fresh and sweet. Red torpedoes look nice in this salad—just the right size and color—but you can use any sweet onion, or even white or yellow torpedo onions if there are such things. I've never seen any, but that doesn't mean they don't exist.

1 pound small new potatoes
Juice of $^1/_2$ lemon
1 tablespoon Dijon mustard
$^1/_4$ teaspoon salt
$^1/_8$ teaspoon freshly ground black pepper
2 tablespoons crème fraîche or sour cream
1 tablespoon chopped fennel tops or fresh dill
$^1/_2$ pound haricots verts, baby Blue Lake beans, or other sweet, young green beans, ends trimmed
1 torpedo onion, thinly sliced crosswise

Boil the potatoes in heavily salted water for 12 to 15 minutes, until just fork tender.

While the potatoes are cooking, make the dressing: Whisk together the lemon juice, mustard, salt, and pepper in a small bowl until the salt is dissolved. Stir in the crème fraîche, then toss in the fennel.

When the potatoes are nearly done, toss the haricots verts into the same pot and boil until tender-crisp. The beans will take anywhere from 2 to 7 minutes, depending on how fresh and tender they are, so taste them as you go. For more control, you might want to cook the beans separately. Drain the potatoes and beans and put them into an ice bath. Drain them again when cool. (If you dress the potatoes when still warm, they absorb the dressing.)

Cut the potatoes in half and combine them in a serving bowl with the haricots verts and onion. Mix with the dressing, taste for salt and pepper, and serve. You may make this salad ahead and refrigerate it, although I do feel it tastes best freshly made.

Heirloom Tomato Salad

Serves 6

So many varieties of tomatoes are available here in California that it's impossible to decide which ones to grow. At Mustards, we grow mostly heirloom varieties, such as Brandywine, Golden Jubilee, and Sweet 100s. I'm fortunate to have an organic vegetable garden just outside my kitchen door, both at Mustards and at home. At the height of the season, I can actually serve tomatoes still warm from the garden. (Tomatoes taste best at room temperature, so never refrigerate fresh tomatoes.)

This salad looks nicest if you have tomatoes of different sizes and colors—we've used orange, red, yellow, and green zebra tomatoes in various combinations. Louise Branch, one of our former chefs, used to serve this salad out of huge pasta bowls, and it looked great. One more suggestion: Get the very best salt you can for this dish. I recommend gray sea salt from France. It has a nice mineral flavor and just a pinch will light a spark.

6 perfectly ripe tomatoes of varying sizes and varieties
8 to 10 perfectly ripe cherry and/or yellow pear tomatoes

VINAIGRETTE
1 tablespoon champagne vinegar
1 shallot, minced
$1/8$ teaspoon salt
1 teaspoon freshly ground coarse black pepper
3 tablespoons extra virgin olive oil

3 tablespoons fresh thyme leaves
6 tablespoons fresh tarragon leaves
$1/2$ to 1 tablespoon coarse sea salt, French gray sea salt, or Maldon flake salt
6 slices rustic country bread, each $1/2$ inch thick
Extra virgin olive oil
$1/4$ pound fresh goat cheese or other soft, spreadable cheese (optional)
Freshly ground black pepper

Cut the larger tomatoes into different shapes, such as wedges and thick slices. Leave the cherry and yellow pears whole or cut them in half. Arrange the tomatoes attractively on a large serving platter or in a pasta bowl.

To make the vinaigrette, whisk together the vinegar, shallot, salt, and pepper in a small bowl, until the salt is dissolved. Gradually whisk in the olive oil, and continue to whisk until fully emulsified.

When you're ready to serve, drizzle some vinaigrette over the tomatoes and sprinkle on the thyme and tarragon leaves. Sprinkle with the salt. Grill or toast the bread at the last minute, brush it with the olive oil, smear it with the cheese, if desired, and tuck it in around the tomatoes. Drizzle any remaining vinaigrette or oil over the bread and grind black pepper over all.

Grilled Potato Salad with Goat Cheese, Fried Garlic, and White Truffle Vinaigrette

Serves 6

The truffle oil, the garlic, and the grilled potato aromas give this salad an earthly character. It's definitely not a traditional salad, but it would make an elegant first course to a simple grilled fish or steak dinner. You could use any type of ripened goat cheese. We use local goat cheese producers Bermuda Triangle from Cyprus Grove or Taupinière from Laura Chenel. Morbier, a French cheese made from cow's milk is another possibility. Make sure whichever cheese you use is at room temperature before you serve it. Get the tiniest red creamer potatoes you can find, no more than 1 1/2 to 2 inches in diameter. For the vinaigrette, you will probably need to go to a specialty food store to find white truffle oil. Buy the smallest container you can find, and store the unused portion in the refrigerator. A little truffle oil is good on polenta, in any mushroom sauce or soup, or drizzled over grilled portobellos.

WHITE TRUFFLE VINAIGRETTE
2 tablespoons balsamic vinegar
Tiny pinch of salt
A few grinds of black pepper
3 tablespoons extra virgin olive oil
3 tablespoons white truffle oil
1 tablespoon sliced shallot

12 small red creamer potatoes
6 or 7 large cloves garlic
1/4 cup plus 1 tablespoon extra virgin olive oil
1 1/2 cups arugula leaves
1 1/2 cups frisée leaves
Salt and freshly ground black pepper
3 tablespoons minced fresh tarragon
3/4 pound aged goat cheese, cut into 12 equal pieces
Fresh chive blossoms (optional)

To make the vinaigrette, whisk together the vinegar, salt, and pepper in a small bowl, until the salt is dissolved. Gradually whisk in the oils, and continue to whisk until fully emulsified. Stir in the shallot.

Boil the potatoes in heavily salted water for 12 to 15 minutes, until just fork tender. Drain them and allow them to cool. When cool, slice them in half if small, or into thirds if large.

To prepare the garlic, peel the cloves and slice them paper-thin, removing the green sprout if it has started to form. Put the 1/4 cup olive oil in a sauté pan along with the garlic and heat to medium-high. Cook, stirring almost constantly, until the garlic turns a light golden brown. (Be careful: If the garlic gets even slightly overcooked, it will be bitter.) Using a slotted spoon, transfer the garlic to paper towels to drain.

Have all the salad ingredients ready for final assembly of the salad. Wash the arugula and spinach, tear the leaves into bite-sized pieces, and spin dry. Lightly coat the potatoes with the remaining 1 tablespoon olive oil, season with salt and pepper, and grill over a medium fire for about 2 minutes on each side, until golden brown. Place the potatoes in a large bowl, add the arugula, frisée, and just enough vinaigrette to coat lightly. Gently mix in the tarragon.

To serve, divide the salad among serving plates, mounding it in the center. Arrange two thin slices of goat cheese across from each other on the salad. Sprinkle with some of the garlic and the chive blossoms. Drizzle about 1/2 teaspoon additional dressing on each salad.

Grilled Salmon Salad

Serves 6

If at all possible, make this with the wild king salmon that comes out of the Pacific Northwest. This is definitely a main-course salad.

8 to 10 cups mesclun or other mixed greens

BALSAMIC-HONEY-MUSTARD VINAIGRETTE

$^1/_4$ cup balsamic vinegar

1 tablespoon honey

$1^1/_2$ teaspoons Dijon mustard

1 shallot, minced

Sea salt and freshly ground black pepper

$^1/_2$ to $^3/_4$ cup extra virgin olive oil

6 king salmon fillets, about $^1/_4$ pound each, skinned

Extra virgin olive oil

Salt and freshly ground black pepper

2 cups haricots verts or small green or baby Romano beans (about $^3/_4$ pound)

2 cups yellow wax beans (about $^3/_4$ pound)

2 cups small gold or red beets (about 2 bunches), cooked (page 71)

4 cups yellow Finn, Yukon Gold, or small red potatoes (about $^3/_4$ pound to 1 pound, about 18 small potatoes), halved and roasted

Lemon Aioli (page 201)

Lemon wedges, for garnish

Dill sprigs, fennel leaves, or minced fresh chives, for garnish

Wash the greens, tear into bite-sized pieces, and spin dry.

To make the vinaigrette, combine the vinegar and honey in a small saucepan and bring to the boil. Cook until reduced by half, then set aside to cool. Add the mustard, shallot, and salt and pepper to taste and whisk until the salt is dissolved. Gradually whisk in the olive oil, and continue to whisk until fully emulsified. All this can all be done early in the day, if you wish.

Fill a stockpot halfway with water and bring to a rapid boil. Add the beans and cook for 2 to 3 minutes, or until tender to the bite, then shock in ice-cold water and set aside while you cook the salmon.

Lightly brush the salmon with olive oil, and season with salt and pepper. Grill over a medium fire, turning as needed, for 2 to 3 minutes on each side. The timing will depend on how thick the pieces are and how rare you like your salmon.

While the salmon is cooking, dress the beans, beets, and potatoes with just enough of the vinaigrette to coat lightly and season with salt and pepper. Dress the greens separately, again using the vinaigrette, and place them in the center of salad plates. Arrange the vegetables around the greens, and top the greens with the salmon. Put a generous dollop or two of aioli on each fish fillet. Garnish with the lemon wedges and herbs and grind pepper over all to finish.

Chinese Chicken Salad with Sesame Noodles and Rice Vinegar Cucumbers

Serves 6

I can't imagine how many of these we've served at Mustards over the years—thousands, for sure. This is a fairly complicated recipe, but keep in mind that a lot of the work can be done ahead of time. You can poach the chicken and shred it up, and pre-pare the salad greens and make the dressings early in the day, then you'll be way ahead of the game. The cucumbers can be prepared up to 2 hours in advance. All you'll need to do at the end is prepare the pasta and arrange the salad. It seems like a lot of work, but this is a great entrée or party dish, and you'll get tons of com-pliments, so don't be afraid.

You may need to make a trip to an Asian market to pick up some of the more unusual ingredients—star anise, chile paste with fermented black beans, black vinegar, black soy sauce, Szechuan peppercorns, and tahini, for instance. (If you can't find tahini or just don't want to add another condiment to your collection, peanut butter works fine.)

RICE VINEGAR CUCUMBERS

2 cucumbers, peeled, seeded, and cut into $^{1}/_{4}$-inch-thick rounds
$^{1}/_{4}$ teaspoon salt
1 large carrot, julienned
1 clove garlic, minced
1 tablespoon peeled and grated fresh ginger
1 tablespoon minced fresh mint
2 scallions, white parts only, minced
$^{1}/_{4}$ cup rice vinegar
2 teaspoons sugar

CHICKEN

$^{1}/_{4}$ cup Chinese rosé wine or 2 tablespoons dry white wine plus a shot of Scotch
$^{1}/_{4}$ cup rice vinegar
$^{1}/_{2}$ cup soy sauce
2 tablespoons sugar
1 cinnamon stick
1 teaspoon grated orange zest
$^{1}/_{4}$ cup peeled and grated fresh ginger
3 pods star anise
2 teaspoons Szechuan peppercorns
2 teaspoons kosher salt
4 cups water
3 large bone-in, skin-on whole chicken breasts

TAHINI DRESSING

2 tablespoons soy sauce
1 or 2 cloves garlic
1 tablespoon peeled and grated fresh ginger
2 tablespoons sesame tahini or natural peanut butter
$^{1}/_{4}$ cup peanut oil
1 tablespoon sesame oil
1 tablespoon rice wine vinegar
2 teaspoons sugar
$^{1}/_{8}$ to $^{1}/_{4}$ teaspoon Lee Kum Kee black bean chile sauce
$^{1}/_{4}$ teaspoon red chile flakes

CABBAGE SALAD

3 cups arugula leaves or mixed salad greens
3 to 4 cups shredded green cabbage
1 cup fresh cilantro leaves

VINAIGRETTE

1 tablespoon rice vinegar
$1^{1}/_{2}$ teaspoons minced shallot
$1^{1}/_{2}$ teaspoons Dijon mustard
Pinch of salt
Pinch of freshly ground black pepper
1 tablespoon sesame oil
2 tablespoons peanut oil

SESAME NOODLES

1 pound spaghettini
2 tablespoons sesame oil
2 tablespoons black soy sauce
1 teaspoon Chinese black vinegar
1 tablespoon sugar
$1^{1}/_{2}$ teaspoons black bean paste with chile
$^{1}/_{4}$ cup minced scallions

$^{1}/_{4}$ cup Those Nuts (page 212), chopped
3 scallions, white and light green parts, thinly sliced on the diagonal
Cilantro sprigs for garnish (optional)

continued from page 79

To make the cucumbers, sprinkle the cucumber slices with salt, allow to sit for 20 minutes, then squeeze gently and drain.

Combine the cucumbers, carrot, garlic, ginger, mint, and scallions in a bowl. Combine the rice vinegar and sugar in a small saucepan, bring to a boil, stirring to dissolve the sugar, remove from the heat, and allow to cool.

Pour the cooled vinegar over the vegetables and allow them to marinate at room temperature, tossing occasionally, until you are ready to assemble the salad. This can be done up to 2 hours ahead of serving.

To prepare the chicken, combine the wine, vinegar, soy sauce, sugar, cinnamon, orange zest, ginger, star anise, Szechuan peppercorns, salt, and water in a large pot. Bring to a boil, lower the heat to a simmer, and add the chicken breasts. Simmer, uncovered, for 12 to 15 minutes. The breasts should be just firm to the touch, and when poked with a skewer, the juices should run clear or slightly pink, as the meat will continue cooking as it cools. Allow the chicken to cool in the poaching liquid, then skin and bone the breasts and shred the meat into bite-sized pieces. Drizzle the meat with a little of the poaching liquid, then cover and refrigerate until you're ready to assemble the salad. You can freeze the leftover poaching liquid for another use.

To make the tahini dressing, combine all the dressing ingredients in a blender or food processor and purée until smooth. Refrigerate it until you're ready to assemble the salad.

To make the cabbage salad, wash the arugula, tear the leaves into bite-sized pieces, and spin dry. Combine the cabbage, arugula, and cilantro and refrigerate until needed.

To make the vinaigrette, whisk together the rice vinegar, shallot, mustard, salt, and pepper in a small bowl, until the salt is dissolved. Gradually whisk in the oils, and continue to whisk until fully emulsified. Set the vinaigrette aside.

To prepare the noodles, cook the spaghettini in boiling salted water for about 11 minutes, until al dente. Drain and rinse under cold water until just warm. In a small bowl, combine the sesame oil, soy sauce, vinegar, sugar, black bean paste, and scallions; then toss this with the noodles. Set aside until ready to serve.

To assemble the salad, combine the cabbage salad with the rice vinegar cucumbers in a large bowl, and toss with just enough of the cabbage salad vinaigrette to coat the vegetables lightly. Place a mound of sesame noodles at either end of the serving platter, and put the cabbage salad in the middle. Top the salad with the shredded chicken, drizzle with the tahini dressing, and garnish with the almonds, scallions, and several sprigs of cilantro.

Beet and Goat Cheese Salad with Balsamic Vinaigrette

Serves 6

Beets are one of the three vegetables I can get my husband to eat. (The other two are potatoes and frozen English peas!) Since beets are also one of my favorites, we eat a lot of them. You can use any variety that you can find, keeping in mind that baby beets are extra good. A mixture of gold and red beets makes a great looking salad. Mizuna is a spiky Japanese green that most closely resembles dandelion greens in flavor. If you can't find mizuna, dandelion greens, arugula, frisée, or escarole would be tasty substitutions.

While the beets are roasting, you can get everything else ready: the vinaigrette, the garlic, the greens, the cheese. Final assembly will be a snap.

BALSAMIC VINAIGRETTE
1 tablespoon balsamic vinegar
$^1/_2$ shallot or 1 bulb spring garlic, minced
$1^1/_2$ teaspoons Dijon mustard
Pinch of salt
Pinch of freshly ground black pepper
3 to 4 tablespoons extra virgin olive oil

1 bunch large beets or 2 bunches baby beets
Olive oil for rubbing on beets
Salt
$^1/_2$ pound spring garlic, or 6 to 8 cloves garlic
1 head radicchio
1 bunch mizuna, dandelion greens, or arugula
$^1/_2$ cup crumbled mild fresh goat cheese (a *crottin* or *cabécou* would be good)

To make the vinaigrette, whisk together the vinegar, shallot, mustard, salt, and pepper in a small bowl until the salt is dissolved. Gradually whisk in the olive oil, and continue to whisk until fully emulsified. Taste and adjust the seasoning.

Preheat the oven to 375°. Cut off the stems from the beets, leaving about 1 inch intact. Do not trim the root ends. Rub the beets with a little olive oil and sprinkle with salt. Place in a baking pan and bake for 30 to 50 minutes, until tender. The timing will depend on the age and size of the beets. If they seem to be cooking too slowly, add $^1/_2$ inch of water to the pan and cover it. When the beets are done, allow them to cool enough to handle, then peel and quarter them lengthwise. Toss the warm beets with enough of the vinaigrette to coat them, and allow them to marinate for 20 minutes to 1 hour.

If you are using spring garlic, slice the bulbs and blanch them in boiling water for 30 seconds to 1 minute, depending on how tender they are. If you are using regular garlic, peel, slice, remove the green sprout, if any, and blanch for 1 minute. Wash the radicchio and mizuna, tear into bite-sized pieces, and spin dry.

To serve, combine the radicchio, mizuna, garlic, and beets in a large bowl and toss with enough of the vinaigrette to coat lightly. Arrange on salad plates with the beets on top, and sprinkle with the goat cheese. You can drizzle with additional vinaigrette, if desired.

I still remember that first winter, sitting cross-legged on the floor in front of the smoker with a whole cord of wet green wood. It was seventeen years ago, and I was wondering just how I was going to get the damned thing going, and  at the same time thinking about the pioneer women who had gone through the same thing. Well, I put the wet wood in the gas oven, along with a batch of chocolate pecan cakes, so that the logs would dry out. When they started burning, I tossed them into the smoker.

All my cooks were convinced I was nuts, but I got that smoker going.

Our smoker is a huge brick chamber, about as big as a good-sized bank safe. It was built for us by a German bricklayer, whose name I've since forgotten, and by Ernesto Vanucchi, an Italian ironworker. They got a lot of help from my then-partners, Bill Upson and Bill Higgins, who acted as hod carriers and beer suppliers, and from friends who would drop by to check the progress and give advice. I remember we bent the rebars by making a mark where we needed the bend, sticking the bars in the slots on a dumpster (the lifting brackets), and somehow bending them with a pickup truck I had borrowed from an old boyfriend. On the last day, with one piece of rebar to go, a friend of one of the Bills stopped by and asked why we hadn't rented a rebar bender.

Cindy Says

For home cooks, there's no need to engage in a do-it-yourself rebar-bending project in your backyard, unless you want to, of course. There are plenty of good portable smokers and grills to choose from these days, some of which can function as both. There are even alternatives for those of you who don't have access to a grill, or who don't feel up to getting it going. Several companies, including Le Creuset and Lodge, make ridged cast-iron pans for use on an ordinary cooktop. Just season them with cooking oil or use a cooking spray. These won't give the wonderful flavor of wood smoke, but they are a first-class substitute. You could also grab a mini hibachi, head for your local park, and have a cookout there.

CHOOSING A GRILL: When buying a grill, take a good look at the grate. Finer grates are better for fish and vegetables. If you already have a grill with widely spaced bars and have a problem keeping your vegetables or other items from falling through them, purchase some fine-mesh baskets at a specialty cookware shop. Load smaller items into these, place them on the grill, and your problem is solved. In a pinch, you can set a cake cooling rack crosswise on top of your grill's grate. It works well, too.

In a perfect world, all grates would easily move up and down as needed. If you can't raise and lower yours, you'll have to be patient and wait for the coals or wood to reach the perfect cooking temperature. Another option is a Tuscan fireplace grill, which fits inside your fireplace and can be raised and lowered as needed.

ABOUT THE FIRE: We use mostly oak— red oak—for both the grill and our wood-burning oven-smoker. We also use applewood whenever I can find it, and almond wood on occasion. Part of the fun of having a wood-burning oven and grill is hearing about people who are pulling out trees or pruning their orchards. Of course, since we're in the Napa Valley, we burn our share of grapevines, too. At home I use mesquite charcoal and branches from manzanita bushes and/or madrone trees. These two native shrubs grow all around our area.

Do not use lighter fluid to get your fire started. Roll up some newspaper and try to join the one-match club. A true grilling artist can get a grill going with a single match. Alternatively, use an electric starter and no matches at all. About 15 to 20 minutes before you start cooking, let the fire burn until the coals are lightly coated with white ash. If you're using wood, you'll want some flame. If you're cooking with charcoal, you don't want any at all.

SOME COOKING BASICS: Brush off the grate with a grill brush and oil it after each use, so as not to pass the flavor of one food on to the next. If you're grilling marinated meats or vegetables, and the marinade did not have any oil in it, dip a rolled-up rag in cooking oil (peanut, olive, or vegetable is best) and rub a *light* coating on the grill to keep the meat from sticking. If the food to be grilled has a heavy marinade, avoid flare-ups by letting it drain for several minutes before placing it on the grill. When grilling meat, set aside some of the marinade for basting *before* you marinate the meat; it is generally con-sidered unsafe to baste with a marinade that has been in contact with raw meat. Baste with the reserved marinade as the food cooks. Let the marinade glaze the grill items nicely before taking them off the grill, otherwise the marinade will have a "raw" taste. Don't move them around too much, and be sure to let them sear first. Turning foods too soon will cause them to stick and tear. With all grilled meats, fish, and poultry, it's nice to make crosshatch marks on the side that will be served face-up. To make restaurant-style crosshatch marks, rotate the meat or fish a quarter turn halfway through cooking on each side.

Japanese-Inspired Beef Filet "Rolls"

Serves 6

As a child growing up in Minnesota, I loved going to the one Japanese restaurant in our city where you sat on the floor and they cooked at your table. Now I am lucky enough to live in an area with many excellent Japanese restaurants, sushi bars, and markets. The marinade for this dish is a delicate version of a teriyaki sauce, inspired by my many trips to Japan.

This is a great party dish, as so many elements of it can be done ahead, and it's fun to eat. You grill and slice the steaks just before serving, then your guests build their own rolls by filling a mustard green leaf with slices of tender filet mignon and whatever condiments they like, rolling it up, and dipping it into a lemon-soy sauce or a ginger-flavored butter sauce. I like to use red Japanese mustard greens for the color, but you can easily switch to green mustard greens if you can't find the red variety. The greens are not cooked, so look for tender, young leaves. Butter lettuce, plus some arugula or watercress for the spiciness, would also work.

3 pounds beef tenderloin, center-cut section, fat and silverskin removed
1/3 cup sake
1/3 cup tamari soy sauce

1/2 cup Ginger Butter (page 206)
4 to 6 cups red Japanese mustard greens
1 cup finely grated daikon radish
1 or 2 red Fresno chiles, julienned
1/4 cup sesame seeds, toasted
2 tablespoons freshly cracked coarse black pepper
6 to 8 scallions, white and light green parts only, thinly sliced on the diagonal

LEMON-SOY DIPPING SAUCE
1/4 cup freshly squeezed lemon juice
1/4 cup soy sauce
3 tablespoons rice vinegar
3 tablespoons mirin
1 1/2 teaspoons tamari soy sauce

Cut the tenderloin into 6 equal-sized steaks. Combine the sake and tamari, pour it over the meat, and let it marinate overnight in the refrigerator, turning it several times.

Prepare the butter and put it into a small saucepan that you don't mind placing right on the grill. Trim the large stalks off the greens, leaving the leaves whole, then wash and spin dry. Divide the greens between two bowls, one for each end of the table. Put the radish, chiles, sesame seeds, black pepper, and scallions in small dishes, one set for each guest or for each couple to share from.

To make the dipping sauce, combine the lemon juice, soy sauce, rice vinegar, mirin, and tamari in a small bowl and mix well. Divide the dipping sauce among individual small dishes. Have everything out before you grill the steaks.

When you're ready to serve, grill the steaks to the desired degree of doneness, basting often with the marinade. Cook 3 minutes per side for medium, less for rarer meat, more for well done. Rotate the steaks a quarter turn halfway through cooking on each side to get nice grill marks. If you're grilling a whole piece of tenderloin, you'll be working with a round piece of meat. You might find it easier to use an instant-read thermometer, grilling the meat to 118° to 120° for very rare, 125° to 130° for rare, 130° to 140° for medium-rare, 135° to 145° for medium, 150° for medium-well, and 165° for well done. Just before the meat comes off the grill, melt, but don't brown, the butter. Thinly slice the steaks for your guests and drizzle each serving with a small amount of the butter. (Alternatively, you could serve the butter in small dishes for everyone to choose between it and the lemon-soy sauce.) Each person takes a mustard leaf, puts a slice or two of beef on it, adds some radish, sesame seeds, chiles, pepper, and scallions, rolls it up, and dips it in sauce.

Steak and Potatoes "Truck Stop Deluxe"

Serves 6

I don't remember when we started calling the restaurant a truck stop deluxe, but it had something to do with an eighteen-wheeler taking up most of the parking lot, causing quite a few Mercedes Benzes and Cadillacs to park on the highway. You won't find steaks like these at any other truck stop I know. For one thing, they weigh in at 14 to 16 ounces. For another, they're flavored with a smoky chipotle marinade that will warm your soul. And then there's the red wine sauce.... All you need is a great Cabernet to enjoy with it. Incidentally, the chipotle marinade is also good on quail, duck, and chicken.

6 (14- to 16-ounce) dry-aged prime Angus New York strip steaks
1 tablespoon Maldon flake salt or other sea salt

CHIPOTLE MARINADE
2 chipotle chiles in adobo sauce, drained
2 cloves garlic
3 tablespoons tomato juice
$^1/_2$ cup extra virgin olive oil
$^1/_4$ cup tamari soy sauce
2 tablespoons sherry vinegar
$^1/_2$ bunch basil, chopped
$^1/_2$ bunch oregano, chopped
$1^1/_2$ teaspoons freshly ground white pepper
$^3/_4$ teaspoon salt

RED WINE BUTTER SAUCE
1 cup Merlot or Cabernet Sauvignon
2 bay leaves
$^1/_2$ teaspoon freshly ground black pepper
$^1/_2$ teaspoon salt
$^1/_2$ cup butter, cut into small pieces
2 tablespoons minced chives
1 tablespoon minced tarragon

Mustards' Mashed Potatoes (page 178) or Roasted Potatoes (page 189)

Liberally sprinkle both sides of the steaks with the sea salt, cover, and refrigerate for at least 3 hours and up to 24 hours.

To make the marinade, put the chiles and garlic in a blender or processor and purée until well mixed and smooth. Add the tomato juice, olive oil, tamari, vinegar, basil, oregano, pepper, and salt and purée until well mixed and smooth. Dip the steaks in the marinade to coat them (don't soak them in it), place in a nonreactive dish, cover, and refrigerate for 3 to 4 hours. (Alternatively, you can omit the marinating and instead baste the steaks with the marinade as you grill them.)

To make the sauce, combine the wine, bay leaves, salt, and pepper in a nonreactive saucepan and bring to a boil over high heat. When the pan is almost dry, remove from heat, discard the bay leaves, and beat in the butter, whisking constantly so it doesn't "break." If the butter does separate, add a few drops of cold water to bring the sauce back together, and don't let it get too hot. Strain the sauce through a fine-mesh sieve placed over a bowl, then fold in the chives and tarragon. Taste to see if it needs more salt. Keep warm until needed.

continued from page 87

Prepare the potatoes before you put the steaks on the grill.

Place the steaks over the hottest part of the grill and grill, giving them a quarter turn to get nice crosshatch marks on both sides and basting with marinade as needed. Plan on 6 to 8 minutes on each side for medium-rare, although timing will depend on the thickness of the steaks and on how hot your coals are. For more well-done meat, rake out the coals for longer, slower cooking, in which case it could take up to 20 minutes in all.

To serve, transfer the steaks to dinner plates and pour some of the sauce over each steak. Pass the remaining sauce at the table. Serve the potatoes on the side.

Veal Chops with Roasted Red Bell Pepper and Black Olive Relish

Serves 6

I love the flavor of wood-grilled veal. We use western veal at Mustards, which is not the fancy milk-fed formula veal. These animals actually get out and about, so they have fed on grasses and their meat is not as white. To my mind, this meat is tastier and is not as delicate as the formula veal, which doesn't hold up as well on the grill. We serve the chop with sautéed greens, such as spinach, red chard, mustard or beet greens, and grilled polenta on the side. The relish should be prepared ahead.

The relish is similar to Tapenade (page 96), which you could substitute, but I like the juicy richness of the red pepper with the veal, and the contrasting colors are spectacular.

ROASTED RED BELL PEPPER AND
BLACK OLIVE RELISH
2 red bell peppers, roasted, peeled, seeded, and diced
1/4 cup oil-cured black olives, pitted and finely chopped
2 tablespoons finely shredded fresh basil
2 cloves garlic, minced
1/2 red onion, minced
1 tablespoon extra virgin olive oil
Pinch of freshly ground black pepper
Salt

6 (10-ounce) bone-in veal loin chops

MARINADE
3 tablespoons minced fresh cilantro
1 jalapeño chile, seeded and minced
2 tablespoons sherry vinegar
1 tablespoon dark soy sauce
Juice and zest of 1 orange
2 tablespoons extra virgin olive oil
1/4 red onion, very thinly sliced
2 cloves garlic, minced
3 tablespoons honey
1/2 teaspoon salt
1/4 teaspoon white pepper

Sautéed Greens (page 170)
Polenta (page 185), chilled

To make the relish, combine all the ingredients, except the salt, in a small bowl and mix well. Taste for salt. If the olives are on the salty side, you may not need any at all. This can be made up to 3 hours ahead and kept refrigerated until needed. Remember to bring it to room temperature before serving.

Put the chops in a clean plastic bag and lightly sprinkle with water to prevent the meat from tearing when pounded. Pound the chops with the smooth side of a meat mallet to flatten them slightly. To make the marinade, combine all the ingredients in a bowl and mix well. Rub the marinade into the chops and marinate for at least 6 hours and up to overnight in the refrigerator.

Shortly before you're ready to start grilling, sauté the greens and set them aside (it's okay to serve them warm). Bring the relish to room temperature, and have the polenta ready to go on the grill.

Grill the chops over a medium fire, rotating them a quarter turn on each side to create nice cross-hatch marks. One-inch-thick chops should take 4 to 5 minutes on each side to cook to medium. Reduce or increase the time for your desired doneness. Put the polenta on the grill as the chops are finishing: Move the chops to the outside of the grate, and grill the polenta in the center where more of the heat is concentrated.

To serve, place the polenta off to one side of the plate. Position the veal chop with the bone toward the inside, along but not over the polenta. Place a pile of the greens at the point where the bone and main part of the loin connect, and top the meat with a spoonful of relish. Pass additional relish at the table.

Spicy Mustard and Garlic Poussin with Black Beans and Tomatillo-Avocado Salsa

Serves 6

In the summer, I love to use this marinade and grill any kind of bird I can get my hands on. Poussin is a variety of chicken that is fully matured at a smaller size and younger age. The meat is sweet and has a nice firm texture, and the skin is not too fatty or tough. It runs about 15 ounces, bone in. Figure on one per person, if you don't have many before-dinner snacks or accompaniments; otherwise, half a bird per person will do fine. Most butchers will have to special-order poussins for you, or you can substitute squabs, Cornish game hens, or regular chicken. You can also use quail, but then you should plan on two birds per person. This is a simple entrée; just remember to give the beans a 2-hour head start. To finish off the meal, make one of Brigid's great sorbets or set out a bowl of fresh fruit.

TOMATILLO-AVOCADO SALSA
12 to 14 tomatillos, papery husks removed
2 small avocados, pitted and peeled
3/4 cup extra virgin olive oil
1/4 cup rice vinegar
3 cloves garlic
1 teaspoon cumin seeds, toasted and ground
1/2 bunch cilantro, leaves only
2 teaspoons dried Mexican oregano (optional)
1/2 teaspoon salt
1/4 teaspoon freshly ground black pepper

6 poussins or squabs

MARINADE
4 serrano chiles, minced
Juice of 2 to 3 limes
1/2 cup extra virgin olive oil
1/4 cup red wine vinegar
1/4 cup Dijon mustard
1/4 cup honey
5 to 6 cloves garlic, minced
1/2 bunch cilantro, minced
3/4 teaspoon salt
1/2 teaspoon freshly ground black pepper

Erasto's Chile and Orange Black Beans (page 183)
3 limes
1/4 pound fresh goat cheese or *queso fresco*, crumbled
Cilantro sprigs for garnish

To make the salsa, combine all the ingredients in a blender or food processor and purée until smooth and liquid, but not thin. Refrigerate until needed.

Prepare the birds one of two ways: Cut out the backbone with a pair of poultry shears and flatten them with a sharp whack to the breastbone, or quarter them, yielding two pieces of breast and two leg-and-thigh portions for each bird. Combine all the marinade ingredients in a large bowl or platter that will hold all the birds and mix well. (Use the juice of all 3 limes if you like a stronger citrus taste.) Toss the birds in the marinade to be sure they're well coated, and allow them to marinate overnight if you can, but at least a couple of hours if not.

Have the black beans and the salsa ready to serve before cooking the poussins. Tuck the wing tips of the poussins behind the shoulders to hold the wings off the breast so the skin will caramelize nicely. Grill the poussins over a medium-hot fire on each side, until cooked through, 8 to 10 minutes per side. (Squabs are better cooked to medium-rare, 6 to 8 minutes per side. Quail are quick to cook, so 2 1/2 to 3 minutes per side will do.) To grill the limes for garnish, cut them in half crosswise and place them on the grill cut side down. They should turn a nice golden brown in 2 to 3 minutes.

To serve, arrange the birds alongside the beans on dinner plates, and top each bird with a tablespoon of the salsa, chilled at room temperature. Sprinkle with the crumbled cheese and garnish with the cilantro sprigs and grilled limes. Put the remaining salsa in a bowl and pass at the table.

Grilled Halibut with Tomato Vinaigrette

Serves 6

When we can get the local halibut, it's all we serve. Its season is so short, however, that we often use the Alaskan halibut, as it is more plentiful and nearly as good. If you end up with leftover vinaigrette, it is also great as a dip for chunks of grilled crusty country bread. Remember to have everything ready before you put the fish on the grill. (Allow 50 minutes for the potatoes, for example.) Tuna or swordfish would be nice substitutions for the halibut.

TOMATO VINAIGRETTE
$^1/_2$ bulb spring garlic, sliced, or 4 or 5 cloves garlic, sliced
$1^1/_2$ tablespoons balsamic vinegar
Pinch of salt
Pinch of freshly ground black pepper
$4^1/_2$ tablespoons extra virgin olive oil
2 large tomatoes, peeled, seeded, and diced
1 tablespoon finely shredded fresh basil, chives, or tarragon or whole small leaves

Roasted Potatoes (page 189)
Sautéed Greens (page 170)
6 (6-ounce) halibut fillets
Salt and freshly ground black pepper
Extra virgin olive oil

To make the vinaigrette, combine the garlic, vinegar, salt, and pepper in a bowl and whisk until the salt has dissolved. Gradually whisk in the olive oil and continute to whisk until the oil has fully emulsified. Add the tomatoes and toss to coat. Stir in the herbs just before serving.

Prepare the vinaigrette, the potatoes and the greens.

Season the halibut fillets with salt and pepper and lightly brush with olive oil. Grill over hot coals, rotating a quarter turn halfway through cooking on each side to get nice grill marks. For medium-rare, the fish should be on the grill no more than 3 to 5 minutes total; for medium, plan on 1 or 2 minutes longer if your fillets are thick. The rule of thumb is 8 to 10 minutes cooking time per inch of thickness.

To serve, put the greens alongside the fish and arrange the potatoes around them or in a separate bowl. Spoon some of the sauce of your choice over the fish and serve the remainder on the side.

Grilled Beef Tenderloin con Tres Salsas

Serves 6

Why make three salsas? Well, the avocado salsa is almost a salad accompaniment, and the other two are a good excuse for serving warm fresh tortillas. The three together give the tenderloin a boost, as it is the least flavorful of all the primal cuts. Besides, with three salsas, you are certain to impress your guests.

Use only juicy and flavorful, summer-garden tomatoes for the salsas. For the best flavor, serve the Tomato-Cumin Salsa and the Avocado and Pumpkin Seed Salsa at room temperature. You can make them earlier in the day, and then pull them out of the refrigerator a bit before you want to serve them. (If you're making all three salsas, here's a tip on crossover ingredients: altogether you need 7 or 8 large tomatoes, 3 tablespoons minced cilantro, and 5 tablespoons lime juice.)

One of the recipe testers bought pork tenderloin instead of the beef and said the dish was still wonderful. Lightly grilled corn tortillas for mopping up the juices and Erasto's Chile

Avocado and Pumpkin Seed Salsa (page 202)

TOMATO-CUMIN SALSA
1/2 teaspoon cumin seeds, toasted and ground
2 cups peeled, seeded, and diced
    tomatoes (about 5 small or 3 large tomatoes)
3 scallions, white and light green parts only,
    minced
1 tablespoon rice vinegar
1 tablespoon freshly squeezed lime juice
5 tablespoons extra virgin olive oil
1 jalapeño chile, seeded and minced
1 tablespoon minced fresh cilantro
1/4 teaspoon salt, plus more to taste as needed
1/4 teaspoon freshly ground black pepper

TOASTED CHILE-TOMATO SALSA
1 dried New Mexico or guajillo chile, stemmed and seeded
1 dried pasilla or ancho chile, stemmed and seeded
1/2 cup hot water
1/2 red onion, cut into large chunks
3 cloves garlic
4 or 5 tomatoes, cored
2 tablespoons extra virgin olive oil
Salt

6 (9-ounce) beef tenderloin steaks
Salt and freshly cracked black pepper
Extra virgin olive oil
2 tablespoons butter
Roasted Potatoes (page 189) or Grilled Potatoes
    with Rosemary and Garlic (page 180)
Corn tortillas, warmed

To make the tomato-cumin salsa, combine all the ingredients in a bowl and mix well. Taste and add more salt if needed. Cover and refrigerate, then bring to room temperature before serving.

To make the chile-tomato salsa, toast all the chiles in a small skillet over medium-high heat for 1 1/2 to 2 minutes, until fragrant. Remove from the heat, add the hot water, and set aside to soften.

Heat a medium skillet over high heat and add the onion, garlic, and tomatoes. (Yes, this is a dry skillet! You want to char the onion and garlic.) Cook for 8 to 10 minutes, until tender and a bit charred. Combine the softened chiles and the charred tomato, onion, garlic, and enough chile-soaking water to loosen the mixture in a food processor or blender and purée until thick and smooth, but not watery.

Heat the olive oil in a skillet over medium-high heat and add the puréed sauce. Cook, stirring frequently, for about 5 minutes, until slightly thickened. Add salt to taste and strain through a medium-mesh sieve. Reheat before serving as directed in the above recipe.

and Orange Black Beans (page 183)
or Roasted Potatoes (page 189)
would make great accompaniments.
Remember to roll up your sleeves
before you begin to eat.

If you've chilled the Avocado and Pumpkin Seed Salsa or the Tomato-Cumin Salsa, allow them to come to room temperature. Time your preparation of any other accompaniments (beans or potatoes) so that they'll be ready when the steaks come off the grill.

To prepare the steaks, sprinkle them with salt and pepper at least 1 hour prior to cooking. (This step may be done as far as 24 hours in advance; cover and refrigerate the steaks.) Brush the steaks on both sides with olive oil and grill over a medium-hot fire for 3 to 5 minutes, rotating them a quarter turn to get nice crosshatch marks when the meat moves freely and no longer sticks to the grill. Flip the steaks and cook for another 3 to 5 minutes, again rotating the steaks to make nice grill marks.

To finish the chile-tomato salsa, melt the butter in a medium-sized skillet over medium-high heat. Add the salsa and heat, stirring, until the butter is incorporated and the salsa is hot.

To serve, spread a little of the chile-tomato salsa on each serving plate and place a steak in center, topped with a healthy spoonful each of the Tomato-Cumin Salsa and Avocado and Pumpkin Seed Salsa. Serve with potatoes and corn tortillas.

Hanger Steak with Watercress Sauce

Serves 6

The hanger steak, or butcher's tenderloin, is a long, narrow, thick piece of meat with a sirloinlike texture. It needs to be "pinned" and marinated to make it tender enough to grill. The Jaccard Company makes a simple handheld tenderizing tool that you can get through some specialty cookware shops (or on the Internet). One quick jab along the length of the meat on each side is all you need. In the absence of the tool, you can poke the meat all over with a skewer. The rarer the better, when it comes to cooking less expensive cuts as they become tougher the longer they cook. You could also use top sirloin butt steaks, rib eyes, or skirt steak. Store unused marinade in the refrigerator, and use it for grilling other steaks, or for pork chops or lamb shoulder chops.

The sauce was created by Greg Gevurtz, one of our former chefs. It's great with this steak, and it also works well with grilled salmon or halibut. Sometimes when we indulge in kitchen "snacks," we use it as a dip for our french fries (of course, we douse the fries in Tabasco sauce first).

3¹/₂ pounds hanger steak

MARINADE
5 cloves garlic, minced
2 teaspoons peeled and minced fresh
   ginger
¹/₄ cup soy sauce
1 tablespoon yellow, black, or brown mustard
   seeds, lightly toasted
2 tablespoons coarse-grain mustard
1 tablespoon Dijon mustard
¹/₄ cup extra virgin olive oil
¹/₄ cup sherry vinegar
1 teaspoon freshly ground black pepper
¹/₂ teaspoon salt

WATERCRESS SAUCE
¹/₂ cup mayonnaise
¹/₄ cup sour cream
1 teaspoon chopped shallots
2 cloves garlic
¹/₂ bunch watercress, coarse stems removed
1¹/₂ teaspoons Dijon mustard
1 teaspoon freshly squeezed lemon juice
Pinch of salt
Pinch of freshly ground black pepper

Onion Jam (page 206)
Mashed Potato Pancakes with Jarlsberg Cheese
   (page 181)

Cut the meat into 6 steaks, about 9 ounces each. Trim off any surface fat, and pin the meat with a Jaccard tenderizing tool or with a skewer. To make the marinade, combine all the ingredients and mix well. Place the steaks in a nonreactive dish, pour the marinade over them, cover, and marinate in the refrigerator for at least 3 hours and up to 12 hours maximum. If you marinate the meat longer than 12 hours, the marinade macerates, or slightly "cooks," the meat enough that it will no longer cook up rare on the grill.

To make the sauce, combine all the ingredients in a food processor or blender and whirl until bright green and puréed to a desired consistency. I prefer it with a bit of texture, but you can make it as smooth as you like. Cover and refrigerate until you are ready to serve.

Grill the steaks over medium-hot fire for 3 to 5 minutes, rotating them a quarter turn to make nice crosshatch grill marks when the meat moves freely and no longer sticks to the grill. Flip the steaks and cook for another 3 to 5 minutes, again rotating the steaks to make nice grill marks. Transfer the steaks to dinner plates and serve with the sauce, jam, and potato pancakes.

Double Lamb Chops with Tapenade and Polenta

Serves 4 to 6

This is a quick supper with lots of flavor, the kind I like best. Have your butcher french the lamb chops for you, that is, cut off the fat just above the beginning of the loin and any meat between the bones, leaving the ends of the bones exposed. Lamb loin chops, which look like little T-bones, would also work. You can cook the polenta while the coals are getting ready.

The olive relish is best left rough and chunky. I typically use niçoise or kalamata olives, but I have made the tapenade with green picholine olives as well.

TAPENADE
1 cup oil-cured black olives
2 teaspoons freshly grated orange or lemon zest
1¹/₂ tablespoons chopped fresh parsley
3 tablespoons extra virgin olive oil
2 to 3 tablespoons coarsely chopped celery hearts and leaves
Freshly ground black pepper
Salt

8 double-bone rack lamb chops
2 to 3 tablespoons chopped fresh thyme
¹/₄ cup chopped fresh mint
2 cloves garlic, mashed
¹/₂ teaspoon salt
1 teaspoon freshly ground black pepper
Extra virgin olive oil
Polenta (page 185)

To make the tapenade, pit and coarsely chop the olives. Place in a bowl and add all the remaining ingredients, except the salt. Taste and add salt if necessary. It may not need any as the olives may provide all the salt you need. Serve at room temperature.

Cut each rack into four 2-bone chops. In a mortar, mash together the thyme, mint, garlic, salt, and pepper with a pestle, or just use a good knife on a cutting board. Smear the spice mix on the meaty sides of the chops, and let them marinate for 2 hours at room temperature, or for as long as overnight in the refrigerator.

Have both the polenta and the tapenade ready before you cook the lamb chops. Lightly brush the lamb chops on both sides with olive oil. Place on the grill and grill, rotating the chops a quarter turn on each side to create nice crosshatch marks, for about 5 minutes total for medium-rare.

To serve, put a mound of polenta in the center of each plate, arrange the lamb chops around it, and pass the tapenade separately.

Achiote-Marinated Chicken Breasts with Black Beans and Mango Salsa

Serves 6

Boneless, skinless chicken breasts may be healthy for us, but they do need strong and interesting seasonings to make for great eating. Achiote paste does the job in this recipe. It's an intensely flavored Yucatecan seasoning made from annatto seeds, oregano, cumin, coriander, cinnamon, and garlic. Some of our testers had a hard time finding the paste. If you'd like to make your own achiote paste, Diana Kennedy has a great recipe for it in her book, Mexican Regional Cooking. She calls it recado rojo. Another great recipe, also called recado rojo, can be found in Rick Bayless's Authentic Mexican Regional Cooking from the Heart of Mexico.

You can use bone-in, skin-on breasts, too. Just be sure to cook them over a slower fire, skin side down first, to render the fat, then slowly, bone side down, until cooked through. The beans can be done ahead and reheated when needed. If mangoes aren't available, substitute papaya or avocado in the salsa. You could also use the Avocado and Pumpkin Seed Salsa (page 202) or the Salsa Ranchera (page 197).

6 skinless, boneless whole chicken breasts

ACHIOTE MARINADE
4 ounces achiote paste
$^1/_2$ cup freshly squeezed orange juice
$^1/_2$ cup rice vinegar
$1^1/_4$ teaspoons minced fresh oregano or 2 teaspoons dried Mexican oregano
$1^1/_4$ teaspoons cumin seeds, toasted and ground
$^1/_4$ teaspoon sea salt
$^1/_4$ teaspoon black pepper
1 tablespoon minced garlic
$^1/_3$ cup extra virgin olive oil

Erasto's Chile and Orange Black Beans (page 183)
Lime Crème Fraîche (page 196)
Mango Salsa (page 203)

Split each chicken breast into 2 pieces and trim off the coarse membrane in the middle. Lay the breasts flat inside a plastic bag, and sprinkle with a bit of cold water to keep them from sticking when pounded. Lightly pound the breasts with a rolling pin or wine bottle to flatten them slightly. To make the marinade, combine all the ingredients in a bowl and mix well. Spread it over the chicken breasts, making sure they are well coated. Marinate for at least 1 hour, or as long as overnight in the refrigerator.

At some point between marinating and grilling, prepare the black beans, crème fraîche, and salsa. Before you put the chicken on the grill, start reheating the beans, and have the salsa and crème fraîche on hand.

Place the chicken on the grill and grill, rotating the meat a quarter turn halfway through the cooking on each side to make nice grill marks. Plan on $2^1/_2$ to $3^1/_2$ minutes on each side.

We serve this in wide, deep bowls with the chicken breasts on top of the black beans, the salsa spooned over the chicken, and the crème fraîche drizzled over all.

Mongolian Pork Chops

Serves 6

Jerry Schlink and Herb Schmidt, two of our original regulars, patiently stuck with me as I experimented with different pork chop marinades for about a week. When I hit on the perfect match, the guys wrote their compliments on a napkin and my then-partner, Bill Higgins, framed it to remind me that if it ain't broke, don't fix it. During March 2000, which was not a particularly busy month, we sold 1,581 Mongolian Pork Chops. Yikes! In the winter we serve them with Braised Red Cabbage, hot, sweet Chinese-style Mustard Sauce, and mashed potatoes. In the summer, we might switch to sugar snap peas or haricots verts. You'll have extra marinade, which keeps well, refrigerated, and can be used for baby back ribs or chicken (especially chicken wings, which when smoked then grilled are great). There are two special ingredients that really make the marinade: hoisin sauce, which is a slightly sweet Chinese bean paste, and a black bean paste with chiles that is pretty spicy. Look for them in Asian markets. Try to find brands that do not contain MSG.

6 (10-ounce) center-cut double pork chops

MONGOLIAN MARINADE

1 cup hoisin sauce
1 tablespoon sugar
1 1/2 tablespoons tamari soy sauce
1 1/2 tablespoons sherry vinegar
1 1/2 tablespoons rice vinegar
1 scallion, white and two-thirds of the green parts, minced
1 teaspoon Tabasco sauce
1 1/2 teaspoons Lee Kum Kee black bean chile sauce
1 1/2 teaspoons peeled and grated fresh ginger
1 1/2 tablespoons minced garlic
3/4 teaspoon freshly ground white pepper

1/4 cup fresh cilantro leaves and stems, minced
1 tablespoon sesame oil

Braised Red Cabbage (page 169)
Mustards' Mashed Potatoes (page 178)
Chinese-Style Mustard Sauce (page 196)

Trim the excess meat and fat away from the ends of the chop bones, leaving them exposed. Put the pork chops in a clean plastic bag and lightly sprinkle with water to prevent the meat from tearing when pounded. Using the smooth side of a meat mallet, pound the meat down to an even 1-inch thickness, being careful not to hit the bones. Alternatively, have your butcher cut thinner chops and serve 2 per serving. To make the marinade, combine all the ingredients in a bowl and mix well. Coat the pork chops liberally with the marinade and marinate for 3 hours and up to overnight in the refrigerator.

Prepare the cabbage, mashed potatoes, and mustard sauce, coordinating the timing so that the side dishes will all be ready when the chops come off the grill.

Place the chops on the grill and grill for 5 minutes on each side, rotating them a quarter turn after 2 to 3 minutes on each side to produce nice crosshatch marks. It's good to baste with some of the marinade as the meat cooks. As with all marinated meats, you want to go longer and slower on the grill versus shorter and hotter, because if the marinated meat is charred, it may turn bitter. The pork is ready when it registers 139° on an instant-read thermometer.

Serve the pork chops with the cabbage and mashed potatoes. Offer the mustard sauce on the side for dipping.

Grilled Salmon with Red Beet and Orange Relish and Coarse-Grain Mustard Beurre Blanc

Serves 6

The combination of orange salmon, white mashers, and bright red relish make this a striking plate. If salmon isn't to your liking, this trio would also be nice, although not quite as colorful, with sturgeon or halibut.

RED BEET AND ORANGE RELISH
3 beets
Finely grated zest and juice of 1 orange
1 tablespoon sherry vinegar
2 pinches of salt
Pinch of freshly ground black pepper
3 tablespoons extra virgin olive oil
1 tablespoon minced fresh mint or chives

Celery Root Mashers (page 179)
Coarse-Grain Mustard Beurre Blanc (page 208)
6 (6-ounce) salmon fillets
Extra virgin olive oil
Salt and freshly ground black pepper

Trim the beets, leaving 1 inch of the stem and the roots attached to help retain color and flavor. Bake the beets until tender when pierced with a fork (see page 71 for instructions on how to bake beets). Allow the beets to cool just enough to handle, then peel and dice them.

Combine the orange zest and juice, vinegar, salt, and pepper in a small bowl, and whisk until the salt has dissolved. Gradually add the olive oil, whisking continuously until the oil has emulsified completely. Stir in the beets and mint (best done while the beets are still warm). This tastes best when freshly made, but if necessary, you can make it ahead and refrigerate until needed, but bring to room temperature before serving.

The relish, mashed potatoes, and beurre blanc should be completely ready before the fish goes on the grill. Keep the mashers and beurre blanc warm in the tops of double boilers as you proceed with the fish.

Brush the salmon fillets with olive oil and season each with several sprinkles of salt and pepper. Grill over a medium fire for $2\frac{1}{2}$ to 3 minutes per side (less if the fillets are less than $\frac{1}{2}$ inch thick), rotating a quarter turn halfway through cooking on each side to get nice grill marks. For medium-rare, the fish should be on the grill no more than 3 to 5 minutes total; for medium, plan on 1 or 2 minutes longer if your fillets are thick. The rule of thumb is 8 to 10 minutes cooking time per inch of thickness.

To serve, place the mashers in the center of the plate with the fish alongside, and top with a spoon-ful of the beet relish. Drizzle the warm beurre blanc about, and pass the rest at the table.

Columbia River Sturgeon with Brussels Sprouts and Thyme and Parsley Beurre Blanc

Serves 6

As with all firm, oily fish, sturgeon grills perfectly. It seems to me that the Columbia River sturgeon are always running when we get our first brussels sprouts, and that's when this combination goes on the menu. We've converted many a non-brussels-sprouts-eater with it. When shredded, the sprouts take on a nutty roasted flavor, and combined with the bacon they can become addictive. Monkfish or trout would be nice with this combination as well. Get the mashed potatoes and beurre blanc started about 45 minutes before you plan to serve, and keep them warm. Allow about 15 minutes to cook the brussels sprouts.

Mustards' Mashed Potatoes (page 178)
Thyme and Parsley Beurre Blanc (page 208)
2 pounds brussels sprouts
3 or 4 slices bacon, thinly sliced crosswise
Extra virgin olive oil
2 shallots, minced
$^1/_4$ to $^1/_2$ cup chicken stock (page 218), vegetable stock (page 215), or water
Salt and freshly ground black pepper
6 (6-ounce) sturgeon fillets

Prepare the potatoes and beurre blanc and keep them warm. Trim off the ends of the brussels sprouts and pull off the outer leaves. Slice the sprouts lengthwise $^1/_4$ inch thick, and set them aside.

Cook the bacon in a large skillet over medium heat, stirring occasionally, for 3 to 5 minutes, until crisp. Using a slotted utensil, transfer to paper towels to drain from the pan.

In the same skillet, heat 2 tablespoons olive oil over medium heat and cook the shallots, stirring occasionally, for 5 minutes, until golden. Add the brussels sprouts, stir to coat with the oil, and cook for about 3 to 5 minutes, until they turn bright green and are just starting to wilt. Add the stock and bring to a boil over high heat. Cook the sprouts for 7 to 10 minutes, until wilted and tender but not mushy, adding more liquid if necessary. Add the reserved bacon and toss to combine, then season to taste with salt and pepper. These can hold for a moment while you finish the fish.

When grilling the fish, make sure the coals have a nice white coat of ash over them. Season the fish with salt and pepper, then brush with oil. Grill the fillets, rotating a quarter turn halfway through cooking on each side to get nice grill marks. For medium-rare, the fish should be on the grill no more than 3 to 5 minutes total; for medium, plan on 1 or 2 minutes longer if your fillets are thick. The rule of thumb is 8 to 10 minutes cooking time per inch of thickness.

To serve, arrange the brussels sprouts on the lower part of the dinner plates, with the fish and mashers almost touching in the center. Drizzle the sauce over the fish and pass any additional sauce at the table.

Grilled Tuna with Moroccan Pepper Salad and Grilled Potatoes

Serves 6

I love all kinds of tuna. Yellowfin, or ahi, as everyone here in California calls it, is the most popular. Near the San Francisco Bay, we get fresh albacore tuna in season, which is my favorite. It's very tasty, but it needs to be cooked very carefully, as it has a lower fat content than ahi tuna and can dry out easily.

If you want a milder salad, use orange or red bell peppers or 4 Anaheim chiles in place of the pasilla. Any leftover peppers are great tucked into a grilled cheese sandwich, placed on grilled bread with fresh basil, or added to grilled chicken or a firm, oily fish, such as swordfish, shark, or mahi mahi.

MOROCCAN PEPPER SALAD
1 to 2 teaspoons pure olive oil
¹/₂ large red onion, thickly sliced
1 tablespoon freshly squeezed lemon juice
¹/₂ teaspoon cumin seeds, toasted and ground
¹/₂ teaspoon salt
¹/₄ teaspoon freshly ground black pepper
3 to 4 tablespoons extra virgin olive oil
2 large pasilla chiles, roasted, peeled, seeded, and cut into wide strips
1 large red bell pepper, roasted, peeled, seeded, and cut into wide strips

Grilled Potatoes with Rosemary and Garlic (page 180)
6 (6-ounce) ahi or albacore tuna fillets
Salt and freshly ground black pepper
1 teaspoon pure olive oil

Heat the olive oil in a frying pan over medium heat and sauté the onion for about 3 to 5 minutes until nicely caramelized and tender (or brush with olive oil and grill).

To make the vinaigrette, whisk together the lemon juice, cumin, salt, and pepper in a bowl. Gradually whisk in the olive oil, and continue to whisk until fully emulsified. Add the onion, chiles, and bell pepper and toss to combine. Taste and adjust the salt, if necessary.

You will need to coordinate the grilling of the potatoes with the grilling of the tuna. To grill the tuna, season it with salt and pepper and lightly brush with the remaining 1 teaspoon olive oil. Grill over a medium-hot fire, rotating a quarter turn about halfway through cooking on each side to get nice crosshatch marks. It will take 1¹/₂ to 2 minutes per side at most for ¹/₂- inch-thick fillets.

To serve, arrange the potatoes on large plates, nestle the tuna in the center, and top with the marinated peppers.

Chilean Sea Bass with Sake-Braised Shiitakes and Grilled Asparagus

Serves 6

Chilean sea bass is a tender, sweet, white-fleshed fish with a high oil content. It is quite popular here in California, to the point where it has almost been fished out. If you have trouble finding it, halibut, sea bass, cod, or grouper will work well. You can make the mushrooms ahead and reheat them when needed. I have also used the mushrooms for grilled beef fillet steaks with good results. Basmati rice or wild rice will finish off this main course nicely. Just remember that wild rice needs extra time to soak. Stir-fried bok choy, with scallions and toasted sesame seeds, makes a good substitute when asparagus is out of season.

SHIITAKES
1¼ pounds fresh shiitake mushrooms
1 to 1½ tablespoons sesame oil
¼ cup mirin
¼ cup tamari soy sauce
¼ cup rice vinegar
1 cup chicken stock (page 218) or vegetable stock (page 215)

Steamed Basmati Rice (page 189) or Wild Rice (page 191)
6 (6-ounce) Chilean sea bass fillets
36 asparagus spears
Extra virgin olive oil
Salt (gray sea salt preferably)
Freshly ground black pepper

To prepare the shiitakes, cut the stems from the mushrooms and place the caps in a bowl (reserve the stems for broth). Toss the mushrooms with the sesame oil and let stand for 30 minutes. Heat a heavy sauté pan over medium-high heat and sear the mushrooms. Stir in the mirin, tamari, and rice vinegar, increase the heat to high, and reduce by one-fourth. Add the stock, reduce the heat to medium-low, and simmer, uncovered, for 15 to 25 minutes, until the mushrooms are tender.

Start the rice before you fire up the grill, so it will be done just when needed. The asparagus and fish will take less than 10 minutes to grill. If your timing is off and the rice finishes early, it will keep warm covered, with a towel thrown over the pot for extra insulation.

Lightly brush the fish and the asparagus with olive oil and season with salt and pepper. Pencil-thin asparagus spears will heat through as they caramelize on the grill; thicker spears need a bit more time. Put the asparagus on the grill and then the fish. (The asparagus will hold while you grill the fish if you don't have room on the grill for both at the same time.) You want the asparagus to caramelize slightly on all sides. Cook the bass for 2 to 3 minutes per side, rotating the fish a quarter turn on each side to create nice crosshatch marks. To serve, place the asparagus and rice at the top of the plate, place the fish in the center, and top the fish with the mushrooms and their juices.

Tea-Smoked Duck with 100-Almond Sauce and Ginger Pickled Mango

Serves 4 to 6

Chris Torla, one of our former sous chefs, developed this recipe based on research he did on the Chinese cooking technique of tea smoking. The ducks are soaked first in a star anise-flavored brining solution, then smoked with a combination of tea leaves, rice, and sugar added to the coals. The result is an indescribably delicious, juicy duck with a beautiful mahogany-colored, extra-crispy skin. It's not a quick dish to prepare, with all the steps of brining and smoking, but none of the steps is that difficult, and the end results are very tasty. It's also a nice way to do chickens.

The duck and its sauce has been on our menu for a long time. One year, Terry Lynch, another former chef, and I took it to London with the Napa Valley Vintners for a special lunch featuring California wines. The duck was well received, as were the Zinfandels and Merlots that were presented. At the restaurant, we serve half a duck per person, but, depending on your appetizer and dessert, you might want to serve only a quarter

100-ALMOND SAUCE

2 tablespoons peanut oil

1 large onion, very thinly sliced

1½ tablespoons peeled and grated fresh ginger (about a 1-inch piece)

2 cloves garlic, minced

Pinch of red chile flakes

¼ teaspoon ground turmeric

½ teaspoon salt

1½ cups chicken stock (page 218)

2 cups coconut milk

¾ cup almonds, toasted and finely chopped

GINGER PICKLED MANGO

1 firm ripe mango

2-inch piece fresh ginger, peeled and thinly sliced

¼ jalapeño chile, seeded and thinly sliced

½ cup sugar

½ cup rice vinegar

½ cup water

Pinch of red chile flakes

2 shallots, thinly sliced

2 (4½- to 5-pound) ducks

BRINE

4 quarts water

¾ pound kosher salt

2 pounds brown sugar

½ cup black peppercorns

½ cup whole star anise

TEA SMOKE MIXTURE

2 cups oolong tea leaves

1 cup sugar

1 cup rice

Steamed Basmati Rice (page 189)

Sautéed Greens (page 170)

To make the sauce, heat the oil in a large shallow pan over medium-high heat. Add the onion and sauté, stirring often, for 10 to 12 minutes, until translucent. Do not caramelize the onion. Add the ginger and garlic and cook for 2 minutes. Add the chile flakes and turmeric and cook, stirring, for 2 minutes more. Stir in the salt, stock, and coconut milk and bring to a boil. Reduce the heat to a gentle simmer and cook for about 5 minutes, until the onions are very tender and the sauce has reduced by one-fourth and is somewhat thickened. Add the almonds and cook for 5 minutes more to develop the flavors. Taste and adjust the seasoning.

Wrestling with a mango can be a little messy, but here's one way to attack it: Make two lengthwise cuts all the way across on either side of the pit, so you end up with one piece that's mostly pit and two that are flesh and skin. Peel the outer sections, then lay them on a cutting board, flat side down. Cut them into thin lengthwise slices and transfer the slices to a bowl. If you can slice any fruit off the pit, add that to the bowl.

Combine all the remaining ingredients in a saucepan and bring to a boil. Remove from the heat, allow to cool, and then pour it over the mango slices. Marinate for at least 2 or 3 hours, or better yet, cover and refrigerate overnight.

continued from page 107

*per person. The sauce reheats beauti-
fully, so you can make it as much as 4
days ahead. Refrigerate, then reheat it
just before serving.*

*When shopping for mango to
make the pickles, you may you may
find quite a few varieties available off
and on during the season, but one of
the best is the Manila mango, a
bright yellow, sweet, juicy fruit.
Mangoes are ripe when they are only
slightly soft to the touch.*

Remove the excess fat from the ducks and clean out the cavities. Prick the skins all over with a skewer or toothpick, being careful not to poke into the meat. Bring a large pot of water to a boil (the pot needs to be big enough to hold a whole duck and you need enough water to submerge it completely). Carefully lower the first duck into the boiling water and blanch it for 1 minute. Remove it to drain, and repeat with the remaining duck. This process helps to open the pores and let in the marinade. Later, as the skin tightens during the smoking process, the same holes allow the rendered fat to escape.

Combine all the ingredients for the brining solution in a large pot and bring to a boil. Simmer for 10 minutes, then cool for 10 minutes. Put the ducks in the brine, weight them down with several plates to keep them submerged, and leave them in the solution overnight in the refrigerator. Remove the ducks from the brine, drain them, and place them on a rack set on a tray in the refrigerator to dry. This should be done 24 hours ahead. This drying step is what makes the skin crispy in the end.

To prepare the tea smoke mixture, put the tea, sugar, and rice in a bowl and mix well. Smoke the ducks for 3 hours, following the manufacturer's instructions for smoking over water. Add about $^1/_2$ cup of the tea mixture to the coals every 20 minutes. (Any leftover tea mixture will keep well at room temperature in a resealable plastic bag.) When the ducks are dark brown and the fat has rendered out, they are ready.

Allow the ducks to cool down enough to handle. Cut the birds in half down through the breastbone, then cut off the leg where it joins the breast. You can cut the breast meat away from the ribcage and bone the thigh for easier eating, if desired. The ducks can be prepared a day ahead to this point. To finish, grill the pieces over medium-hot coals for 5 to 8 minutes, to crisp the skin and heat through just before serving. Turn them often so they don't char.

To serve, spoon some of the sauce on the bottom of each plate, then place a mound of steamed rice in the center, arrange the duck alongside the rice, and add the spinach around the outside in several small piles. Top with a few slices of the pickled mango.

Thai Garlic Crab

Serves 6

When fresh live crabs are not available, we do lobsters this way. We prefer to use live crabs or lobsters, as the precooked ones can be salty and/or dry. If you have to use precooked crab, taste a bit for salt and tenderness and adjust accordingly. Reduce the amount of tamari in the marinade, and marinate the crabs for less time. Make sure you have plenty of finger bowls and lots of napkins for this meal—and bibs are not out of the question.

4 live Dungeness crabs, 2^1/$_2$ to 3 pounds each, or 12 blue crabs

MARINADE
5 cloves garlic, smashed
^{1}/$_2$ stalk lemongrass, bulb end only, minced
1 bunch cilantro, minced
2 tablespoons minced fresh Thai or regular basil
^{1}/$_2$ cup coconut milk
3 tablespoons rice vinegar
3 tablespoons tamari soy sauce
^{1}/$_3$ cup extra virgin olive oil
1 teaspoon freshly cracked black pepper
1 jalapeño chile, seeded and minced
Salt

Steamed Basmati Rice (page 189) flavored with star anise
Chinese-Style Mustard Sauce (page 196) or Ginger Butter (page 206)

Fill the largest pot you have three-fourths full of water and bring to a boil. Add salt to the water until it tastes really salty, like the ocean, then drop the crabs into the boiling water. (If you don't have a pot large enough, do this in two batches, allowing the water to come to a boil between batches.) Cook Dungeness crabs for 7 minutes and blue crabs for 3 to 4 minutes. Remove them from the water and allow them to cool.

Meanwhile, make the marinade: Combine all the ingredients in a large bowl and mix well. When the crabs are cool enough to handle, clean them by removing and discarding the top shell, apron, gills, and internal organs. Remove or crack the legs, leaving the meat intact, and cut the bodies in half. This allows the marinade to permeate and also makes eating easier later on. Toss the crab with the marinade to coat all the pieces, and allow to marinate for 1 to 4 hours.

Start the rice about 30 minutes before serving. Grill the crab over a hot fire, cooking only long enough to warm the crab through and give it a smoky flavor. This should take 3 to 5 minutes on each side. Often we set an old tin or aluminum pie pan over the crab for 1 or 2 minutes to hold in the smoke a bit.

To serve, arrange the crab on a serving platter and spoon the rice into a bowl. The mustard sauce makes a nice dipping sauce, as does the butter.

Honey-Glazed Spiced Duck with Wild Rice and Tomatoes in Ginger Vinaigrette

Serves 4 to 6

I developed this dish after my first trip to Hong Kong in 1985—all those glistening, mahogany-colored roasted ducks hanging in the Chinese poultry markets inspired me. In my version, the ducks are cooked by an entirely different process—there's no roasting at all, because the ducks are steamed, then smoked, then finished on the grill. They look just as good, though, and taste wonderful.

In the restaurant, we serve half a duck per person, so each person can have breast and leg meat and not be disappointed. I can never eat that much at one sitting, but I see very few plates coming back with food on them. Still, depending on what the rest of the meal consists of, and depending on your guests' appetites, you might want to cut back on the serving size. If you can get parts, duck legs cooked this way come out the best, and they are less expensive, too. One leg-and-thigh portion per person should do it.

For steaming we use a Chinese-style bamboo steamer, but any type of

2 (4½- to 5-pound) whole ducks, or 4 to 6 duck legs

SALT CURE
5 whole cloves
1-inch piece cinnamon stick
2 whole star anise
1 tablespoon Szechuan peppercorns
1 tablespoon coriander seeds
¼ cup salt

HONEY GLAZE
½ cup honey
¼ cup soy sauce
1 tablespoon rice vinegar

STEAMING BROTH
1 cup water
1 cup rice vinegar
1 cup soy sauce
2-inch piece fresh ginger, peeled and smashed
½ stick cinnamon
5 cloves garlic

Tea smoke mixture (page 107)
Wild Rice (page 191)

TOMATOES IN GINGER VINAIGRETTE
6 ripe tomatoes
2 tablespoons rice vinegar
1½ tablespoons peeled and grated fresh ginger
3 scallions, white and light green parts only, minced
⅛ teaspoon table salt
Freshly ground black pepper
6 to 9 tablespoons extra virgin olive oil
French gray sea salt

Remove excess fat from the ducks and clean out the cavities. If you are using duck legs, trim away any excess fat. Prick the skins all over with a skewer or toothpick, being careful not to poke into the meat. Bring a large pot of water to a boil (the pot needs to be big enough to hold a whole duck with enough water to submerge it completely). Carefully lower one duck into the boiling water and blanch it for 1 minute. Remove it to drain and repeat with the remaining duck. This process helps to open the pores and lets in the marinate. Later, as the ducks cook, the same holes will allow the rendered fat to escape.

When the ducks are cool enough to handle, quarter them. Cutting up a duck is like cutting up an odd-looking chicken: the pieces are in the same places and connected in the same manner, but they are somehow different. It will be easiest if you first remove the legs at the point where the thigh joins the body. Then take off the wing tips and cut out the backbone, reserving both for stock. Split the breast in half from top to bottom. Use a Chinese cleaver or a pair of poultry shears for these tasks, settling on what you can handle most easily. You should end up with four leg-and-thigh pieces and with four half breasts, each with the first joint of the wing attached. If you are unsure, have your butcher quarter the ducks for you, then blanch the pieces. If you're using duck legs only, skip this whole step.

perforated pan set over 1 or 2 inches of water will do. Just make sure that the duck isn't touching water and that the lid fits tightly, or use aluminum foil or a damp cloth to keep in all the steam. Serve the duck with the Tomatoes in Ginger Vinaigrette if tomatoes are in season (don't even try the tomato recipe if you don't have vine-ripe beauties to work with) and wild rice. Other great accompaniments would be a corn and bok choy sauté and steamed basmati rice (page 189). I also like it with grilled whole ears of sweet corn and hot, sweet Chinese-Style Mustard Sauce (page 196). If you're serving wild rice, remember to allow time for it to soak.

To make the salt cure, toast the cloves, cinnamon, star anise, Szechuan peppercorns, and coriander seeds in a dry skillet over high heat until aromatic. This will take 1 to 2 minutes at the longest. Smash them to a coarse powder in a mortar with a pestle, then add the salt, mixing well. Thickly coat the inside and outside of the ducks with this mixture. Refrigerate, uncovered, overnight.

To make the honey glaze, combine all the ingredients in a small bowl and mix well. Set it aside.

To make the steaming broth, combine all the ingredients in the bottom of a steamer. Bring to a boil over high heat until steaming, then reduce the heat to medium. Place the rack in place. Brush the duck pieces with some of the honey glaze, and place them on the rack. Steam for 1 hour, basting with additional honey glaze three to four times during this time, and adding water to the steamer as needed. Be careful not to burn yourself. After about 1 hour, the skin will look darker than when you started and quite a bit, but not all, of the fat will have rendered out of the ducks.

Allow the ducks to cool as you build a base fire in your smoker, continuing to baste them with honey glaze until you are ready to smoke. Longer and slower cooking is better for rendering out more of the fat, so you want a medium charcoal fire. In my testing for this book, I smoked the duck for 2 hours, adding 1/2 cup of the tea smoke mixture whenever the smoker seemed not be putting out a decent amount of smoke, meaning just under what would bring the fire department. It might take longer (up to 4 hours), depending on the weather conditions, equipment, heat of the fire, and so on. The ducks should be glistening, mahogany brown, have tight skin, and most of the fat should be rendered out.

Start cooking the rice about 45 minutes before the duck will be coming out of the smoker. The tomatoes should be prepared just before serving. When you are finished with the smoking process, grill the ducks over a medium-low fire bone side down first, then finish skin side down, for 6 to 8 minutes, enough to crisp the skin and warm the duck through. Watch for flare-ups due to the honey; don't have your ducks too close to the coals. It's best to smoke and grill the birds the same day you steam them.

Just before serving, peel the tomatoes and cut them into thick slabs. Arrange the slices attractively around a large platter. To make the vinaigrette, whisk together the vinegar, ginger, scallions, salt, and pepper in a small bowl, until the salt is dissolved. Gradually whisk in 6 tablespoons of the olive oil, and continue to whisk until fully emulsified. Taste to see if the vinaigrette balances with the acidity of the tomatoes, then whisk in additional olive oil if needed.

Drizzle the vinaigrette over the tomatoes. Sprinkle with the sea salt and with more pepper, if desired.

To serve, mound rice in the center of a large serving platter, and arrange the duck pieces around it. Accompany with the platter of tomatoes.

Half-Slab BBQ Baby Back Ribs with Crispy Yams and Coleslaw

Serves 4 to 6

It's hard to be exact when it comes to barbecuing, as a lot is dictated by the equipment you have. Don't be afraid to experiment. When my doctor tested this recipe, he smoked the ribs in an electric smoker for 5 hours and then, over indirect heat, he slowly smoke-grilled them in his covered kettle-type grill for 30 minutes, with additional grapevine prunings. When we tested one recipe, we used a Brinkman charcoal-fired smoker, which has a water pan between the fire and the grate that keeps the environment moist, catches drips, and reduces flare-ups. It took us 3 hours to smoke the ribs on a moderately warm day. We then "finished" them over a mesquite charcoal grill. Another option is to use a kettle-type grill, which would work if you put the fire on either side of a drip pan and the ribs right over the drip pan. There are several manufacturers making rib racks, which are the most efficient way to hold ribs in your smoker.

3 slabs (1¹⁄₂ to 2 pounds each, 5 to 6 pounds total) pork baby back ribs

BBQ Sauce
2 cups ketchup, purchased or homemade (page 195)
¹⁄₂ cup cider or malt vinegar
2 tablespoons BBQ spice, purchased or homemade (page 213)
1 tablespoon chile powder (a combination of ancho and chipotle is good)

¹⁄₄ teaspoon red chile flakes
¹⁄₄ cup dark molasses
¹⁄₂ to 1 teaspoon Tabasco sauce
1 tablespoon Worcestershire sauce

Crispy Yams (page 174)
Erasto's Coleslaw (page 169) or Sweet-and-Sour Coleslaw (page 168)

If necessary, cut each slab of ribs in half to fit your smoker. Remove the membrane along the inside (bone side) of the ribs. If this membrane is left on, the ribs will only smoke on one side, and the meat will also be too tough to bite through.

To make the sauce, combine all the ingredients in a bowl and mix well. Liberally coat the ribs on both sides with the sauce, cover, and let marinate in the refrigerator for 24 hours.

Prepare your smoker according to the manufacturer's directions. I always wait 20 minutes or so after starting the fire to be sure it has burned down and the coals are nice for the smoking fuel to work on. Once you've started smoking the ribs, resist the temptation to check them more than once every 45 minutes, or they will never get done. When the meat has pulled slightly away from the bones and taken on a rosy pink tone, they have smoked enough. Depending on your equipment, the heat of the fire, the weather, and so on, this could take from 3 to 5 hours. Remember, the wetter your smoking wood, the redder the finished meat will turn out.

Prepare the yams for grilling and make the coleslaw while the ribs are cooking. For that final touch, finish the ribs by lowering the grill grate directly over the fire to caramelize the meat. If you smoke the ribs in advance, when you're ready to serve, finish them on a hot grill, basting them with more BBQ sauce as you go. Put the yams on the grill at the same time.

To serve, cut the slabs of ribs in half if you haven't already done so, and serve them up with the yams and coleslaw and a good supply of napkins.

Grilled Rabbit "Coq au Vin" with Winter Vegetables

Serves 6

You know how some people say rabbit tastes like chicken? The truth, however, is that rabbit has a lot more flavor than your average chicken. I thought I'd convert more people to eating rabbit with this recipe, which got its inspiration from the French standard coq au vin, with a little help from Bruce Le Favour, one of my favorite chefs, who taught me the marinade. I've used Zinfandel for the wine sauce, but any dry red wine will do. The vegetables are wrapped in a foil packet and cooked on the grill.

3 (2½-pound) rabbits
Madeira-Herb Marinade (page 214)

WINE SAUCE
3 to 4 tablespoons butter
1 large shallot, thinly sliced
3 cloves garlic, minced
1 tablespoon chopped fresh thyme
2 tablespoons chopped fresh tarragon
1 cup Zinfandel or other dry red wine
2 tablespoons red wine vinegar
3 cups chicken stock (page 218), or rabbit stock (page 218), or a mixture

WINTER VEGETABLES
12 baby carrots
6 to 8 baby turnips
½ pint pearl onions, or 1 bunch spring onions or scallions
6 to 8 small red or Yukon Gold potatoes
6 tablespoons sliced shallots (3 large)
6 to 8 fresh shiitake mushrooms, stems removed, halved, or whole button, cremini, or wild mushrooms, trimmed
Several thyme, savory, basil, or parsley sprigs
¼ cup extra virgin olive oil
Salt and freshly ground black pepper

6 slices bacon, cut crosswise into narrow pieces

Cut each rabbit into six pieces as follows: Remove the front legs as you would the wings of a chicken. Remove the back legs and bone the thigh. Trim off the neck, and cut the loin in half. (For a fancier presentation, you can bone the two pieces of rabbit loin off the backbone and trim off the belly flap, reserving the bones and flap meat for stock. You would then put the loin pieces on the grill much later than the leg pieces, as they cook quite quickly.) Make the marinade, add the rabbit pieces to it, and marinate in the refrigerator for at least 6 hours, or as long as overnight.

To prepare the wine sauce, melt 2 tablespoons of the butter in a saucepan over medium-high heat. Add the shallot, garlic, thyme, and tarragon and cook, stirring occasionally, for 4 to 5 minutes, until the shallots and garlic are soft and translucent. Add the wine and bring to a boil, then cook until the wine is reduced to ¼ cup. Add the vinegar and reduce again until nearly dry. Add the stock and bring to a boil, skimming off any foam that rises to the surface. Reduce the heat and allow the sauce to simmer for about 1 hour, until reduced by half and thick enough to coat the back of a spoon. Strain through a sieve, cover, and refrigerate until needed.

To prepare the vegetables, peel the carrots, and cut off the tips and tops of the turnips. If the turnips are waxed, peel them off as well. Peel the pearl onions, which is most easily done if you trim off the roots, drop the onions into boiling water for 30 seconds, cool in an ice bath, and drain. When you press each onion gently, the onion will pop out of its skin. Quarter the unpeeled potatoes, then cut the carrots and turnips into the same-sized pieces. Combine all the trimmed vegetables in a bowl and add the shallots, mushrooms, a few sprigs of your favorite herb, and the olive oil. Mix well to be sure everything is evenly coated with oil, then sprinkle with salt and pepper. Lay out a double layer of aluminum foil large enough to form a sturdy grilling pouch for the vegetables. Pour the vegetables onto the foil and form the packet, folding the edges up carefully to create a tight seal. You'll be turning the packet over frequently on the grill, and you don't want to lose any of the steaming juices. This can be set up earlier in the day and refrigerated until needed. Bring to room temperature before grilling.

Fry the bacon in a skillet over medium heat for 3 to 5 minutes, until crisp. Using a slotted utensil, transfer to paper towels to drain. Set aside.

Put the vegetable packet on the grill 8 to 10 minutes before you start grilling the rabbit. Turn the packet over as you hear it sizzle. To cook the rabbit, place the front legs on first. When they are beginning to caramelize on the first side, add the remaining pieces. Cook, turning as needed to get a nice even golden brown, 8 to 10 minutes in all. The timing is similar to grilling chicken. Just remember that you're working with a skinless meat and it can easily dry out, so a lower flame is best. The vegetable will take 15 to 20 minutes. To test for doneness, open a corner of the packet and test with a knife. If they are cooked before the rabbit is done, move the packet off to the side of the grill to keep warm. While the rabbit is grilling, finish the wine sauce, reheating it gently, and whisking in the remaining 1 to 2 tablespoons butter right at the end, until incorporated.

To serve, arrange the rabbit pieces on a large platter and arrange the vegetables nicely around them. Pour the sauce over the rabbit. Sprinkle with the crisp bacon.

Grilled Squab with Dijon Mustard Sauce and Spicy Herb Salad

Serves 6

I love squab, but it's one of the hardest items to sell at the restaurant. Every chef I know and respect loves squab, too, both for cooking and for good eating. But if squab doesn't appeal to you, you can use Cornish game hens, wild duck (domestic would be too fatty), or bone-in chicken breasts instead. In the winter, you could serve this dish with sautéed red or green chard and mashed potatoes. I often serve Grilled Potatoes with Rosemary and Garlic (page 180) with this as well. Between the marinade and the vinaigrette, you need to toast and grind 2¹/₂ teaspoons cumin seeds, so you might as well prepare it for both all at once.

6 squabs
2 cups chicken stock (page 218)

MARINADE
¹/₂ cup coconut milk
¹/₂ cup minced red onion
2 serrano chiles, minced and
    including seeds if you want it hot
2 teaspoons peeled and minced or
    grated fresh ginger
2 teaspoons cumin seeds, toasted and ground
2 tablespoons minced fresh tarragon
2 tablespoons minced fresh mint
2 tablespoons minced fresh cilantro
1 to 1¹/₂ teaspoons salt
¹/₄ cup extra virgin olive oil

SPICY HERB SALAD
1 cup fresh small basil leaves
1 bunch cilantro, leaves and small tender stems only
1 bunch scallions, white and 2 inches of green parts,
    thinly sliced on the diagonal
1 seranno chile, sliced into paper-thin circles
1 cup fresh small mint leaves
1 cup very thinly sliced celery heart, leaves, and stalks
1 lime, peeled and sectioned

HERB SALAD VINAIGRETTE
1 tablespoon mustard seeds
1 shallot, minced
2 tablespoons sherry vinegar
1 tablespoon Dijon mustard
¹/₂ teaspoon cumin seeds, toasted and ground
1 or 2 pinches of salt
Pinch of freshly ground black pepper
¹/₂ cup extra virgin olive oil

Steamed Basmati Rice (page 189)
2 to 3 tablespoons butter
3 tablespoons Dijon mustard

To prepare the squabs, remove the backbone by cutting down through the bird on both sides of the backbone, or by cutting it out with a pair of poultry shears. Split the birds down the breast into two pieces, with half a breast and a leg and a thigh per side. A good whack with a meat cleaver will do it. Trim off the wing tips and add them and the backbone to the chicken stock to increase its flavor. Simmer the stock on low heat for 20 minutes or so, skimming off any foam that surfaces.

While the stock is simmering, prepare the marinade: Combine the coconut milk, onion, chiles, ginger, cumin, tarragon, mint, cilantro, and salt and mix well. Whisk in the olive oil. Thoroughly coat the squab with the marinade and let marinate for at least 4 hours or up to 24 hours in the refrigerator. Strain the stock and chill it until needed to complete the mustard sauce.

Very gently combine all the salad ingredients in a large bowl, cover, and refrigerate until you are ready to serve.

To make the vinaigrette, toast the mustard seeds in a small skillet over medium-high heat, tossing frequently, for about 1 to 2 minutes, until they develop a rich, toasty aroma. Keep a lid handy as the seeds will pop quite a bit. Set them aside to cool. Whisk together the shallot, vinegar, mustard, cumin, salt, and pepper in a small bowl until the salt is dissolved. Gradually whisk in the olive oil, and continue to whisk until fully emulsified. Mix in the toasted mustard seeds. Set the vinaigrette aside until you are ready to serve.

Get the rice going about 45 minutes before you're ready to serve.

To prepare the mustard sauce, put the reserved stock in a saucepan, bring it to a boil, then reduce the heat to maintain a low boil. Skimming all the while, reduce the stock to a glazelike consistency, thick enough so the sauce coats a spoon. The more surface area in your pan, the quicker this will go. Stir in the butter and mustard until well incorporated. Keep warm until needed.

To prepare the squabs, grill them bone-side down over medium coals for 5 to 6 minutes, then turn the pieces over to caramelize the skin and finish cooking, another 5 to 6 minutes, or a total of 10 minutes for rare and 12 minutes for medium. (I prefer my squab rare, but I only know a handful of chefs and hunters who agree with me.)

Dress the salad just before serving. If the dressing has separated, just whisk it until it recombines and becomes smooth. Be very careful not to overdress the herbs, and handle them gently so you don't bruise them. You can drizzle some of the vinaigrette about the plate, too.

To serve, place the cooked squab alongside a mound of the rice on each dinner plate and drizzle with the mustard sauce. Dress the greens and sprinkle them about or place them in a mound off to one side.

Out o the Pan

In the very beginning, we only had six burners and could hardly keep up with preparing the accompaniments to the grilled food, so no entrées came off the sauté station. But as Mustards has grown, so has the number of burners, now twelve, and so have our cooks' skills. Our sauté cooks are the fastest on the planet, producing pastas, risottos, liver, and "mallet" chickens, in addition to all the accompani-

ments, vegetables, and sauces for the grill. I can no longer handle that station on a busy Friday, but our sauté cook Antonio Lopez can run ten to twelve pans on the range top and have both ovens full and not over-cook a single item or even break a sweat. Watching him work is like watching a ballet.

Following is a sampling of some of the wonderful Mustards dishes that come "out o' the pan"—specialties that would fall through the grill grates or dry up over a direct flame if we tried to prepare them any other way.

You'll find everything from simple pastas to such hearty, cold-weather dishes as braised lamb shanks or duck legs.

Butternut Squash and Goat Cheese Risotto

Serves 6

Fresh or aged goat cheeses are ideal for this dish, but for anyone who doesn't like goat cheese (my husband, for instance), a sharp Cheddar, a ripe Taleggio, or a smoked provolone would also work well. Garnished with toasted walnuts and shaved Parmesan, this risotto makes a beautiful vegetarian entrée or side dish. It goes particularly well with braised or grilled lamb. Minced fresh sage makes a nice garnish. If you want to go the extra mile, fry the sage in a tiny bit of olive oil and sprinkle with some black pepper and gray sea salt.

5 to 6 cups chicken stock (page 218) or vegetable stock (page 215)

2 tablespoons butter

1 tablespoon extra virgin olive oil

1 onion, finely diced

1 large carrot, finely diced

1 large leek, white and light green parts only, julienned

1½ pounds butternut, Red Kuri, or other winter squash, peeled, seeded, and diced into ½-inch cubes

3 cloves garlic, minced

2 cups arborio rice

1 cup dry white wine (Sauvignon Blanc or Chardonnay works well)

¼ pound aged goat cheese, such as cabécou

1½ teaspoons salt

Freshly cracked black pepper

Minced fresh sage for garnish (optional)

Heat the stock to bare simmer in a saucepan and keep it hot. Heat the butter and oil in a large skillet over medium heat. Add the onion, carrot, and leek, and cook, stirring, occasionally, for 2 to 3 minutes, until soft. Add the squash, garlic, and rice and cook, stirring, until all the grains of rice are coated with oil. Add the wine and cook, stirring, until it is almost completely absorbed.

Add the hot stock about ½ cup at a time, stirring constantly and allowing the liquid to be absorbed by the rice before adding more. When all of the stock has been added, check the rice for doneness. It should be creamy but slightly al dente at the center. Add more stock or water if necessary to complete the cooking, then add the cheese, and season with the salt and pepper. Stir well.

To serve, spoon into shallow bowls and garnish with sage.

Cauliflower and Sweet Pea Penne

Serves 4 as an entrée or 6 as an appetizer

From start to finish, this dish should take no more than 20 minutes to prepare. You will, however, need to keep two pots going at once, one for the pasta and one for the vegetables. The dish, which is really a fancy macaroni and cheese, brings together produce from the end of winter and the beginning of spring. Be sure to use only one of the herbs listed. Tarragon is my favorite.

1 pound penne or other tube pasta

1 tablespoon plus $^1/_4$ cup extra virgin olive oil for the vegetables plus 1 tablespoon for the pasta

2 or 3 cloves garlic, minced

$^1/_2$ head cauliflower, cut into small florets

2 cups vegetable stock (page 215) or chicken stock (page 218)

2 cups shelled peas

6 to 7 spring onions or scallions, white part only, sliced on the diagonal

Pinch of red chile flakes

$^1/_2$ teaspoon salt

$^1/_4$ teaspoon freshly ground black pepper

$^1/_4$ to $^1/_3$ cup heavy whipping cream

$^1/_2$ cup grated Parmesan cheese

1 to 2 tablespoons butter

2 to 3 tablespoons finely shredded fresh mint, tarragon, or sage leaves

Bring a large pot of salted water to a full rolling boil. When the water comes to a boil, add the pasta, and cook for 8 to 11 minutes until al dente. Drain the pasta, toss with the 1 tablespoon olive oil, and set aside.

While the pasta water is heating up begin making the sauce: Heat the $^1/_4$ cup olive oil in a large, wide sauté pan over medium-high heat. Add the garlic and cauliflower and sauté for 8 to 10 minutes until golden brown. Add the stock and simmer until reduced by half and the cauliflower is tender. Add the peas, onions, chile flakes, salt, and pepper and cook for 6 to 8 minutes, until the peas are almost done. Stir in the cream and the penne, heating it through and reducing the sauce until it coats the noodles nicely. Add the cheese and butter and half of the herb, tossing to let everything mingle and meld together.

To serve, divide the pasta and vegetables among wide shallow bowls and sprinkle with the remaining herbs. Serve at once.

Linguine with Morel Mushrooms, Garlic, and Sage

Serves 4 to 6

Fresh morels are a fleeting springtime phenomenon and seldom easy to come by. That's one good reason to make friends with a mushroom forager. If you do find morels in the market, don't hesitate to buy them. They're well worth whatever price you have to pay. Dried morels are great, too, because they reconstitute well, keeping both their flavor and structure. You will need 2 cups for this recipe. Dried morels should be soaked in hot water to cover for 20 to 30 minutes, until soft. Lift them out of the soaking water carefully, so that all the sand and grit drops to the bottom, then pour the clear liquid off the top to use in this sauce or in mushroom or vegetable stock. If you can't get fresh or dried morels, shiitakes, portobellos, or chanterelles would be tasty, too.

If you can manage it, start the sauce while the pasta is cooking, so that both are done about the same time. If you're feeling ambitious, you can make your own pasta (page 215). Serve with marinated asparagus or tomatoes in vinaigrette for a simple quick supper.

1 pound fresh linguine
2 tablespoons extra virgin olive oil
1 leek, spring onion, or shallot, finely julienned
1 tablespoon minced garlic
$^1/_2$ pound fresh morel mushrooms, carefully cleaned and halved
$^1/_2$ bunch fresh sage, chopped (3 to 4 tablespoons)
$^1/_4$ cup dry white wine
1 cup vegetable stock (page 215), chicken stock (page 218), mushroom soaking liquid, or pasta water
$^1/_2$ cup heavy whipping cream
2 tablespoons butter
Salt and freshly ground black pepper
Grated Parmesan cheese for garnish
Chopped fresh flat-leaf parsley for garnish

Bring a large pot of salted water to a full rolling boil, add the pasta, and cook for 7 to 8 minutes, until al dente. Drain, saving a cup of the water for the sauce, if desired, and set the pasta aside.

To make the sauce, heat the oil in a large deep saucepan over medium heat. Add the leek and garlic and sauté for 3 to 5 minutes, until just tender but not browned. Raise the heat to medium-high, add the mushrooms, and sauté for 3 to 8 minutes, until tender. Add half of the sage and all the white wine. Let the wine reduce by half, then stir in the stock and cream. Reduce again by one-fourth, then stir in the butter, and season with salt and pepper. Remove from the heat.

Add the pasta to the sauce, toss them together, and cook for a moment or so longer to heat the noodles through. Serve in large deep bowls and garnish with Parmesan, parsley, and the remaining sage.

Lemon-Garlic Chicken

Serves 6

In this dish, we use split boneless chickens so that each chicken half will lie fairly flat in the pan. The halves are sautéed briefly on the stovetop, then transferred to the oven, pan and all, to finish cooking. Depending on your equipment, you might need to make some adjustments to this basic scenario, but it is definitely feasible to prepare this dish in any home kitchen. For instance, several of our testers used cut-up bone-in chicken and thought the results were great. So if you can't get a butcher to bone the chicken for you, you can go that route. If you don't have pans with heatproof handles, or if your oven is too small to accommodate enough pans, you could transfer the birds to a roasting pan for the second stage of cooking. We use a convection oven, but a conventional oven works just fine. In case you're wondering, this recipe is an adaptation of an Italian dish called pollo al mattone, in which the chicken is smashed flat with a brick, then roasted or grilled with the brick on top to weight it

LEMON-GARLIC VINAIGRETTE
2 heads garlic
4 lemons, peeled, including all pith
    and membrane, and seeded
2 tablespoons champagne vinegar
2 tablespoons minced mixed fresh herbs such as
    parsley, thyme, tarragon, basil, and savory
1/4 teaspoon salt
1/8 teaspoon freshly ground black pepper
6 tablespoons extra virgin olive oil

1 tablespoon minced fresh rosemary
1 tablespoon minced fresh thyme
2 1/4 teaspoons minced fresh marjoram or oregano
3/4 teaspoon minced fresh sage
2 tablespoons kosher salt
1 1/2 teaspoons freshly cracked black peppercorns
1 1/2 teaspoons minced shallots
1 tablespoon minced garlic
3 (2 1/2-pound) chickens, halved and boned

3 spring garlics, leeks, or scallions
1 1/2 to 2 pounds asparagus spears
3 tablespoons extra virgin olive oil
2 tablespoons butter
4 to 5 tablespoons water
1 tablespoon minced fresh tarragon or chervil leaves
    (no stems)
Salt and freshly ground black pepper

Mustards' Mashed Potatoes (page 178)
Lemon-Garlic Vinaigrette (recipe follows)

To prepare the vinaigrette, pull the heads of garlic apart, peel the cloves, and remove any green sprouts. Put the lemons and garlic in a small saucepan with enough water just to float them. Bring to a boil, reduce the heat, and simmer for about 20 minutes, until the garlic is very tender. Drain, then purée the lemons and garlic in a blender and measure out 1/2 cup for the vinaigrette. Refrigerate any additional purée for use later in the week.

Whisk together the 1/2 cup of lemon-garlic purée with the vinegar, herbs, salt, and pepper, until the salt is dissolved. Slowly whisk in the olive oil in a thin stream, and continue to whisk until fully emulsified.

Combine the rosemary, thyme, marjoram, sage, salt, peppercorns, shallots, and garlic and mix well. Rub the mixture into the chicken halves. Allow them to marinate in the refrigerator for 6 to 12 hours.

To prepare the vegetables, slice the garlic thinly on the diagonal and rinse well. Snap off ends of the asparagus (they will break where the tender part meets the tough stem). Slice on the diagonal up to the tip in 1/4- to 1/2-inch pieces. Set the tips aside.

continued from page 129

down and force all the wonderful juices to permeate the meat. Many Americans don't like the idea of the small bits of bone left in the meat, so we developed this tamer version.

Some advance preparation tips: Allow 6 to 12 hours to marinate the chicken. The vinaigrette can be made up to a day ahead, but make sure not to add the herbs until just before using. Steam the vegetables while the chickens are roasting. We use a combination of two or three vegetables, such as red chard, gold beets, and savoy cabbage in the winter; asparagus, young leeks, and peas in the spring; and roasted red bell peppers, zucchinis, and pattypan squash in the summer. Serve whatever is fresh and tasty in the market.

To prepare the chickens, preheat the oven to 500°. Heat the olive oil in a large ovenproof sauté pan over medium-high heat. Add the chicken halves, skin side down, and brown until nice and crispy. Turn the chickens and sear on the other side. The browning should take 6 to 8 minutes in all. Turn the chicken halves again, so that they are skin-side down, and weight them down with a clean, heavy brick, stone, or ovenproof sauté pan. Place in the oven and roast for about 6 to 10 minutes in a convection oven and a bit longer in a conventional oven. The skin should be crispy and the meat moist, and the juices should just run clear.

While the chickens are roasting, cook the vegetables. Heat 1 tablespoon of the butter in a sauté pan over medium heat. Add the garlic and sweat for 3 to 4 minutes, until soft. Add the asparagus pieces and toss to coat with the butter. Add the water and asparagus tips, cover, and steam for 3 to 4 minutes, until tender but still a bit crisp. Drain off any water that has not evaporated, add the tarragon and the remaining 1 tablespoon butter, and season with salt and pepper.

To serve, place the potatoes and vegetables on either side of the plate, put the chicken in the middle, and drizzle the vinaigrette over all.

Braised Duck Legs

Serves 6

I wanted to put duck confit in this book, but then I wondered how many people would want to melt down several pounds of duck fat. And if they were the type who would do that, they probably already know how to make the confit and wouldn't need me to explain it. So here is a much simpler recipe for braised duck legs that can be served over a pasta or with mashed potatoes for a rib-sticking winter supper.

2 teaspoons salt
2 cloves garlic
Leaves only from 3 thyme sprigs
2 teaspoons freshly ground black pepper
Pinch of red chile flakes
6 duck legs
1 bay leaf
3 tablespoons extra virgin olive oil
1 large onion, diced
1 carrot, diced
2 slices peeled fresh ginger (¼ inch thick)
2 to 3 cups dry red wine
1 cup peeled, seeded, and diced tomatoes
½ bunch parsley
½ bunch thyme
3 to 4 cups chicken stock (page 218) or water
Salt
1 to 2 tablespoons butter

Crush the salt, garlic, thyme, pepper, and chile flakes together with a mortar and pestle. Rub each duck leg on the meat side with the spice mixture and combine with the bay leaf in a covered container. Marinate in the refrigerator overnight.

Heat the olive oil in a large, heavy pot over high heat. Add the duck legs skin side down and sear until nicely browned. Turn the duck legs over and sear on the other side until browned. This should take 10 to 20 minutes in all. Transfer the duck legs to a platter. Pour off all but about 3 tablespoons of the fat, add the onion, carrot, and ginger, and cook over high heat for 8 to 10 minutes, stirring frequently, until browned and tender. Add the red wine, tomatoes, parsley, and thyme and bring to a boil. Lower the heat to a simmer and cook until reduced by half.

Return the duck legs to the pot and add stock to cover. Bring to a boil, skim off any visible fat from the surface, and reduce to a simmer. Cover and cook for 20 to 30 minutes, until very tender.

Remove the duck legs once again, strain the cooking liquid through a sieve, and return the liquid to the pot. Bring the liquid to a boil, skimming off the excess fat, and reduce it to the desired consistency for a sauce. Taste and add salt as needed. Stir in butter to taste to finish the sauce.

Put the duck legs on individual dinner plates or all on a platter. Spoon some of the sauce over and pass the rest at the table.

Louise's Bouillabaisse with Rouille

Serves 6

Louise Branch, who was chef at Mustards several years ago, developed this fish stew to feature our West Coast delicacy, Dungeness crab. It's not absolutely necessary to use Dungeness crab, however. You can use Alaskan king crab, East Coast blue crabs, or even lobster. Let availability be your guide. That's what we do at Mustards. And with the exception of the shrimp, make sure all the seafood is live.

This dish is a showstopper. It always draws oohs and ahs when it's carried from the kitchen to the dining rooms. To eat it, you need to roll up your sleeves and forget about trying to be neat. Have plenty of wet napkins and lemon wedges on hand.

BROTH

2 tablespoons olive oil
3 to 4 cloves garlic, sliced
2 onions, thinly sliced
2 teaspoons fennel seeds
2 tablespoons salt
$\frac{1}{2}$ teaspoon freshly ground black pepper
20 to 25 saffron threads
1 bay leaf
2 to 3 thyme sprigs
1 cup dry white wine
8 to 10 cups fish stock (page 221), vegetable stock (page 215), or bottled clam juice without MSG
1 cup peeled, seeded, and diced tomatoes
$1\frac{1}{2}$ pounds new potatoes, yellow Finns, or Yukon Golds, sliced $\frac{1}{2}$-inch thick

ROUILLE

1 red bell pepper, roasted, peeled, and seeded
1 Fresno chile, roasted, peeled, and seeded
$\frac{1}{4}$ teaspoon ground cayenne pepper
$\frac{1}{4}$ teaspoon hot paprika
1 egg
1 tablespoon freshly squeezed lemon juice
$1\frac{1}{3}$ cups extra virgin olive oil
$\frac{1}{2}$ teaspoon salt
$\frac{1}{4}$ teaspoon freshly ground black pepper

$2\frac{1}{2}$ to 3 pounds whole live Dungeness crabs or 2 or 3 (2-pound) whole live lobsters
18 clams
24 mussels
12 shrimp
2 tablespoons extra virgin olive oil
1 to $1\frac{1}{2}$ pounds firm white fish fillets such as halibut, monkfish, or sea bass, cut into 2- by $2\frac{1}{2}$-inch chunks
Rouille (recipe follows)
6 to 8 thick slices rustic sourdough bread, grilled

To make the broth, heat the olive oil in a large pot over medium-high heat. Add the garlic, onions, and fennel seeds and cook, stirring occasionally, for 10 to 12 minutes, until soft but not brown. Season with the salt and pepper. Add the saffron, bay leaf, and thyme, and cook, stirring occasionally, for 1 to 2 minutes, until the saffron starts to color the onions and fennel. Add the wine and continue cooking, until it is reduced by half. Add the stock, tomatoes, and potatoes, reduce to a simmer, and cook for about 15 to 20 minutes, just until the potatoes are tender. (The broth can be prepared as much as a day ahead.)

To make the rouille, combine all the ingredients in a food processor or blender. Blend until smooth and fully emulsified.

To prepare the crabs, cook them in salted boiling water for 7 minutes. Then pop them into a big bowl of ice water and wait until they are cool enough to handle. Working with 1 crab at a time, remove the back shell by pulling from the back to the front (save the yellow crab butter for other dishes), and remove the feathery lung tissue that lines each side of the body. Break off the legs right where they attach to the body. Split the body in half and then cut each half into three pieces. Gently smash the legs with the side of a cleaver, enough to crack them, but not so much as to uncover the meat and cause the legs to fall apart. Set the crabs aside. Lobsters should be poached as for the crabs, and split into halves or quarters. Scrub the clams and mussels to rid them of any sand or mud. If the mussels have "beards, which are the tough fibrous wisps near the hinge with which they originally attached themselves to rocks or other anchors, you need to pull them off. To devein the shrimp, cut right through the upper part of the shell with a sharp knife and remove the dark, veinlike intestinal tract, leaving the shell on to add more flavor to the stew.

When you are ready to serve, heat the olive oil in a very large sauté pan over high heat. Add the crab or lobster pieces and sauté for 1 to 2 minutes to coat with the oil. (The lobsters could also be seared on a grill, which you would do last, and serve them on top of the bouillabaisse.) Add the clams, mussels, and shrimp, stir, and cook for 1 minute to coat with the oil. Add the broth and cook for 3 to 4 more minutes, until the clams and mussels begin to open. Add the fish chunks and continue to cook for 2 to 3 minutes, until the clams and mussels are completely opened and the fish chunks are just cooked through. Do not overcook.

To serve, divide the shellfish evenly among warmed bowls and ladle the broth over all. Just before serving, put a healthy dollop of Rouille in each bowl. Serve with grilled bread for dunking into the broth and sopping up all the luscious juices.

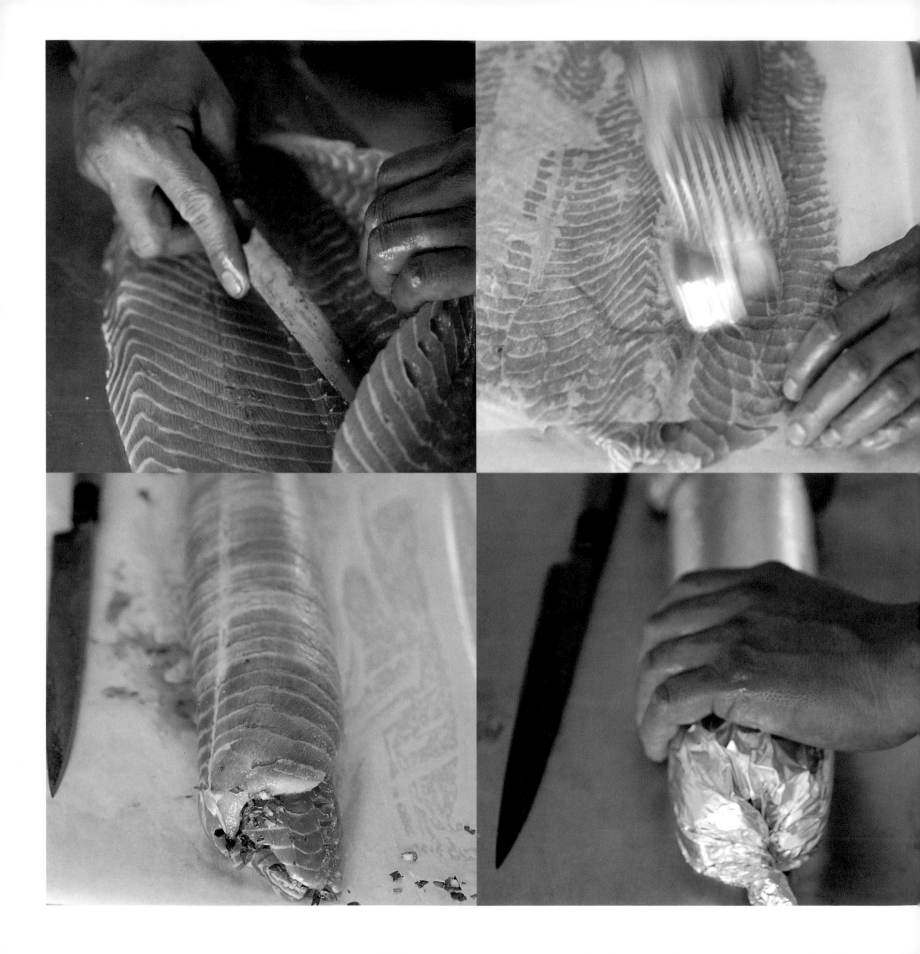

Sean's Salmon Roulade with Kalamata Olive, Orange, and Celery Relish

Serves 8 to 10

Sean Mindrum, a past chef at Mustards, created this elegant dish. It's made like a jelly roll, but here the fish is the cake and the filling is made of garlic and parsley. It's a great party dish, and it is much easier to make than it looks. The trickiest part is butterflying the salmon fillet. If you don't think your hands are steady enough, ask your fish purveyor to do it for you. To impress your guests, you can cook the entire roll in one piece, then unwrap and cut it tableside.

The relish is quite colorful and will brighten up a late winter or early spring dinner. You may use any type of orange, or even mandarin oranges or tangerines. It is also great served with swordfish, tuna, mahi mahi, bluefish, grilled fennel, or roasted bell peppers.

ROULADE
12 to 16 cloves garlic
Leaves from 1 bunch parsley, chopped (1½ cups)
3 tablespoons extra virgin olive oil
1 (3-pound) salmon fillet, skin intact
Salt and freshly ground black pepper

KALAMATA OLIVE, ORANGE, AND CELERY RELISH
Finely grated zest and juice of 1 orange
¼ cup sherry vinegar
1 tablespoon thinly sliced shallots
½ teaspoon salt
¼ teaspoon freshly ground black pepper
½ cup extra virgin olive oil
¼ cup pure olive oil
¼ cup pitted, sliced kalamata olives
1 celery heart, leaves and tender center stalks only, thinly sliced on the diagonal
1½ teaspoons minced fresh thyme or savory
1 tablespoon minced fresh chives

6 to 7 tablespoons pure olive oil
3 tablespoons butter

To make the filling, remove any green sprouts from the garlic cloves and slice. Place the garlic in a small saucepan with cold water to cover, bring to a boil, drain, and cool in an ice bath or place under cold running water. Drain well, pat dry, and place in a bowl along with the parsley and extra virgin olive oil. Mix well and set aside.

Cut a piece of aluminum foil the length of the salmon fillet and 10 to 12 inches wide, large enough to go around the roll with a bit extra. Cut a piece of parchment paper the same size as the foil. Lay the parchment paper on top of the foil, and brush the parchment with enough olive oil to coat lightly. Next, place the salmon skin side down on the parchment paper and carefully butterfly it lengthwise, being sure not to cut completely through the flesh at the end. You want to be able to open it out into a thin double-width fillet. Season the salmon with salt and pepper, and sprinkle the garlic mixture evenly over the surface.

To start the roulade, fold one-fourth of the top (skinless) piece back over and begin to roll from that side so that you end up with the skin on the outside. Just pretend you're making a jelly roll cake or sushi. (You can use the foil-parchment sheet as an aid in rolling up the fish, just as you would a bamboo mat to make sushi, but be careful not to roll any of it in with the fish.) Your roll

continued from page 137

should be in the mid-range of tightness. It cannot be too tight, as it will expand as it cooks, and it cannot be too loose, or it will fall apart. To finish, roll the foil-parchment sheet around the salmon roulade, and twist the ends together nicely. Chill for at least 1 hour to firm the roll.

To make the relish, whisk together the orange zest and juice, vinegar, shallots, salt, and pepper in a small bowl until the salt is dissolved. Gradually whisk in the olive oils, and continue to whisk until fully emulsified. Toss in the olives, celery, thyme, and chives and mix gently.

When you are ready to serve, preheat the oven to 450°. Cut the roulade into 8 to 10 equal slices, each about 1½ to 2 inches thick, cutting right through the foil. Heat the pure olive oil and the butter in a heavy skillet over high heat. Add the slices and sear for 2 minutes per side at most. Transfer the salmon slices to a baking sheet and bake for 3 to 6 minutes. The timing will depend on the thickness of the slices and how well done you like your salmon. For fully cooked fish, the rule is 10 minutes per inch of thickness, but I never cook it more than 6 minutes per inch total, browning time plus baking time.

To serve, divide evenly among dinner plates. Remove the foil wrappers, and spoon the relish on top of the fish.

Mixed Wild Mushroom Risotto with Grilled Chanterelles

Serves 6 to 8

Local farmers' markets are a good source for fresh and dried wild mushrooms, and they are probably your best hope for finding chanterelles — frilly, trumpet-shaped mushrooms with a delightful flavor. Black chanterelles may be more difficult to find than the more common yellow chanterelles. Thinner fleshed and dark black, they will add a wonderful color to this dish. In the spring, morel mushrooms are a good substitute, and it is alright to use cultivated mushrooms in a pinch, but for better flavor, use a combination of them. Chanterelles tend to hold a lot of dirt, pine needles, and the like, so clean them carefully. Split the large ones in half and clean out the core. The mix is best with a combination of mushrooms, even if you have to reconstitute some dried ones.

If you're not using the grill, you can just sauté the large chanterelles along with the other mushrooms, holding some of them out for the garnish. You could also grill the mushrooms ahead of time and gently reheat them when the risotto is ready.

$6^1/_2$ cups mushroom stock (page 220), chicken stock (page 218),
    vegetable stock (page 215), or game stock (page 218)

4 to 6 tablespoons butter

3 to 4 tablespoons extra virgin olive oil

1 leek, all of the white and 2 inches of the light green parts,
    cut in half lengthwise, then thinly sliced crosswise

$^1/_2$ onion, thinly sliced

1 (1- to 2-inch) piece cinnamon stick

2 cups arborio rice

1 cup dry white wine

$^3/_4$ pound mixed fresh chanterelles, hedgehogs, and other
    fresh wild mushrooms, carefully cleaned and sliced

$1^1/_2$ teaspoons minced fresh thyme

$1^1/_2$ pounds large fresh chanterelles, carefully cleaned and
    torn in half if very large

2 teaspoons salt

1 teaspoon freshly ground black pepper

6 ounces Taleggio cheese, cut into small dice

Heat the stock to a bare simmer in a saucepan and keep it hot. Heat 2 tablespoons each of the butter and olive oil in a large sauté pan over medium heat. Add the leek and onion and sauté for 8 to 10 minutes, until tender. Stir in the cinnamon and rice and cook for 2 minutes to coat with the butter and oil. Add the wine and cook, stirring, until it is almost completely absorbed.

Add the hot stock, $^1/_2$ cup at a time, stirring constantly and allowing the liquid to be absorbed by the rice before adding more, until you've used 4 cups of the stock. At this point, heat 2 to 3 tablespoons of the butter in a second sauté pan over high heat. Add the sliced mushrooms and thyme and sauté the mushrooms as you continue to cook the risotto, adding the remaining stock $^1/_2$ cup at a time as before. Remove the mushrooms from the heat when they are done. They should take 12 to 15 minutes.

When the final $^1/_2$ cup of stock goes into the risotto, stir in the sautéed mushrooms and their juices (if any) and remove the cinnamon stick. Check the rice for doneness. It should be creamy but slightly al dente at the center. Add more stock or water if necessary to complete the cooking. Stir in the remaining 1 to 2 tablespoons butter, salt, and pepper. Fold in the cheese and taste for seasoning.

When the risotto is almost done (the total time for the risotto should be about 20 minutes), toss the large chanterelles in the remaining 1 to 2 tablespoons olive oil and season with salt and pepper. Put them on the grill, turning them until they are tender and golden brown. To serve, spoon the risotto into shallow soup plates and top with the grilled chanterelles.

Sweet Potato and Leek Ravioli with Morel Mushrooms and Brown Butter Sauce

Serves 6

It's fun to make ravioli, and a lot eas-ier than you would think. They do take a bit of time, but they're a great Sunday afternoon project to do with the kids. Try it and you'll get wows from your friends and family. It's best to make your own pasta dough (there's a recipe on page 215), but if you're not inclined, or if you don't have a pasta machine, wonton skins or egg-roll skins work fine, although they will not be as rich or sturdy. You can make the ravioli ahead of time, then store them in the refrigerator for several hours on parchment dusted with semolina. You can also freeze them in a single layer and then toss them into resealable plastic bags and tuck them in the freezer until needed.

I prefer to make the ravioli small, about 2 inches square, and serve five or six of them per person. Use a hand masher for the filling, as it makes for a rougher, more interesting texture.

FILLING

1 large sweet potato or yam (about 1½ pounds)
1 tablespoon extra virgin olive oil
1 leek, white and light green parts only, thinly sliced
½ cup grated dry Jack or Asiago cheese
1 teaspoon minced savory or thyme
⅛ to ¼ teaspoon freshly grated nutmeg or ground mace
½ teaspoon salt
¼ teaspoon freshly ground black pepper

1 egg
1 tablespoon water
Fresh pasta (page 215), rolled out into sheets, or 1 to 1½ pounds store-bought pasta sheets
8 to 10 tablespoons butter
2 cups fresh morel mushrooms, carefully cleaned and quartered
1½ teaspoons minced summer savory or thyme leaves
3 shallots, sliced into rings
2 spring onions, sliced into rings
Juice of 2 lemons
6 tablespoons minced fresh parsley
½ to ⅔ cup shredded Parmesan or dry Jack cheese

To make the filling, preheat the oven to 375°. Bake the sweet potato for 30 minutes to 1 hour, until just fork tender. Remove from the oven, let cool, then peel. Meanwhile, heat the olive oil, in a sauté pan over medium heat and sweat the leek for 4 to 6 minutes.

Combine the sweet potato, leek, grated cheese, savory, nutmeg, salt, and pepper in a bowl. Mix well but gently (a potato masher does a good job). Taste and adjust the seasoning.

To make the ravioli, beat the egg with the water until well mixed. Lay out one sheet of pasta and brush it with the egg wash. Leaving enough room for a 1/4-inch edge on all sides, spoon scant tablespoons of filling about 2 inches apart across the pasta sheet. Brush the exposed pasta with water to help create a seal. Lay a second sheet of pasta over the first, and press firmly around each dollop of filling to ensure no air bubbles exist and to seal the pasta together. Cut out the ravioli. If you are going to finish the dish later, store the ravioli as described in the introduction.

To finish the dish, bring a large pot of salted water to a full rolling boil.

While the water comes to a boil, start preparing the sauce: Melt 4 tablespoons of the butter in a sauté pan over medium heat. Add the morels and sauté for several minutes, until they absorb the butter, caramelize, and release their juices. Add the savory, shallots, and spring onions, and cook for several minutes more. Remove the mushrooms from the heat.

Add the ravioli to the pot of water and cook for 5 to 7 minutes, while finishing the sauce. When the ravioli have about 4 minutes left to cook, scoop out 1 cup of the pasta-cooking water. Add 1 cup of the pasta water to the mushrooms and cook over medium heat until the mushrooms are tender and the pan is almost dry.

When the ravioli are tender, scoop them out of the pot, drain, and coat with 2 tablespoons of the butter. Gently combine the ravioli with the mushrooms and arrange on warm plates.

To make the brown butter, heat the remaining 2 to 4 tablespoons butter in a large saucepan over high heat until the butter browns. (How much butter you use depends on how rich you want the dish.) Add the lemon juice to stop the browning. Drizzle the butter over the ravioli, sprinkle with the parsley and Parmesan cheese, and serve.

Liver Diablo with Applewood-Smoked Bacon and Polenta

Serves 6

When I was a little kid and my mom would ask me what I wanted for dinner, I always said liver. It must have been all that bacon, ketchup, and onions that got me addicted. This is a lot fancier than my mom's liver dinners, but it's still very easy to prepare. Since we are a grill, we do keep true to our name and grill the liver most of the time, but this panfried version is on our menu now, too, and I love it the best of all our variations.

Applewood-smoked bacon has so much flavor that it's worth the search. Out here we use Hobbs's brand. In the Midwest, there is a company called Nueskies that makes it, and I have seen their product here in California at the local grocery store on occasion.

Caramelized Onions (page 200)
Sharp Cheddar Polenta Cakes (page 187) or Stilton Polenta (page 186)

DIABLO SAUCE
$^1/_4$ cup Tomato and Apricot Chutney (page 205)
$^1/_4$ cup firmly packed brown sugar
$^1/_4$ cup ketchup, Heinz or homemade (page 195)
$^1/_4$ cup red wine vinegar
1 tablespoon Worcestershire sauce

$2^1/_2$ to 3 pounds calf's liver
12 slices applewood-smoked bacon
3 to 5 tablespoons butter
2 tablespoons extra virgin olive oil
Salt and freshly ground black pepper
3 tablespoons minced fresh parsley

Liver cooks very quickly, so you want to get everything else heated up and ready to go before you start cooking it. Make the onions and polenta first, and then the sauce. To make the sauce, combine the chutney, brown sugar, ketchup, vinegar, and Worcestershire sauce in a saucepan. Bring to a boil, lower the heat to a simmer, and cook for 10 to 15 minutes, until the sauce is thick enough to coat a spoon. Keep warm until needed.

When you are ready to serve, trim the liver of any membranes or veins, cut it into six equal slices, and set it aside. Cook the bacon in a frying pan over medium-high heat for about 3 minutes, until crisp. Transfer to paper towels to drain. Keep it warm in a low oven until needed. Reheat the onions in 1 tablespoon of the butter in a small saucepan over medium heat. When hot, stir in the sauce and cook for 1 or 2 minutes, until the sauce has reduced somewhat. Finish with 2 or 3 more tablespoons of the butter, if desired.

To cook the liver, select a sauté pan large enough to hold all the slices in a single layer, or use 2 pans if necessary. Heat the olive oil and 1 tablespoon of butter over medium-high heat, until foamy. Dust the liver with salt and pepper, and sear quickly on both sides. Liver is best cooked medium-rare, 1 to 2 minutes per side.

To serve, put the polenta on one side of the dinner plate with a slice of liver alongside. Top each serving with some of the sauce combined with the onions and 2 strips of the bacon, and sprinkle the parsley all over. Pass any remaining sauce on the side.

I get annoyed when I read some menus because it's obvious that the chefs who created them look down on sandwiches. There are too few choices, and the compositions they do offer are uninteresting. It seems like these chefs only do sandwiches because they have to, not because they have any real passion or fire about things between bread. To them, sandwiches are something you just slap together and toss on a plate with a few chips, an olive, and a sprig of parsley.

In my view, sandwiches are as deserving of attention as any other dish on a menu, and are actually one of the hardest items to make perfect. For one thing, there's the bread. You might think that the critical part of a sandwich has to do with the stuff that goes inside. The fact is, the outside—the bread—is what can make or break a sandwich. I am always on the lookout for a better hamburger bun, a softer hot-dog roll to heighten the pop and snap of a crisp sausage skin, a bread with just the right sweetness to complement the sour relish and the heat and spice of the mustard, a whole-grain bread that isn't so heavy that the vegetable stuffing squishes out the back as you take your first bite. You have to have the right bread, the right crumb, crust, or tang of sour to work with the ingredients inside, in order to arrive at the perfect sandwich.

Grilled Eggplant and Zucchini Sandwiches with Muffuletta Mix

Serves 6

New Orleans is the home of a sandwich known as the muffuletta. Traditionally, the "muff" consists of deli meats and cheeses and an olive relish piled into partially hollowed-out loaves of Italian bread. What makes a muffuletta different from your average deli sandwich is the olive relish. The Central Grocery in the French Quarter, which is world-famous for its muffulettas, even sells their special relish mix by the jar. When I made up our muffuletta mix, I had only ever read about a New Orleans muffuletta. Years later, when I finally visited there and got a chance to try the real thing, I found out that my relish is quite different. But it's tasty nonetheless, and I still call it a muffuletta mix. We serve it on this vegetarian sandwich, but it would be excellent on cheese, ham, or rare roast beef, too. Use rolls with a thin, crisp crust, or a loaf of ciabatta, a soft Italian bread. The loaf option is fun for a family party, or when you're traveling or picnicking: Wrap the whole thing up and cut it up when you get where you're going.

1 large globe eggplant, or 3 to 4 small Asian
    eggplants
3 small zucchinis
¼ cup extra virgin olive oil
1 teaspoon salt
½ teaspoon freshly ground black pepper
1 red onion

MUFFULLETA MIX
½ red onion or 2 scallions, white and a bit
    of the green parts, minced
2 cloves garlic, smashed and finely minced
1 tablespoon capers, well drained
1 tablespoon chopped cornichons, dill, or other pickles
1 tablespoon chopped red Fresno or
    serrano chile
6 tablespoons chopped green or oil-cured black olives
2 tablespoons extra virgin olive oil
½ teaspoon freshly ground black pepper

6 crusty white rolls, or 1 loaf ciabatta
6 tablespoons Aioli (page 201)
2 red bell peppers, roasted, peeled, and diced
6 tablespoons grated Parmesan cheese

Trim off the ends of the eggplant, and cut it crosswise into ½-inch-thick slices. (Cut Asian eggplants on the diagonal.) Trim off the ends of the zucchinis and slice them lengthwise ¼ inch thick. Spread the eggplant and zucchini slices out on baking sheets, drizzle with olive oil, and sprinkle with salt and pepper. Set them aside for 30 minutes to 1 hour. Cut the onion into 6 thick rounds, then carefully brush the slices with olive oil so that they don't break up.

Grill the eggplant, zucchini, and onion slices over medium to low heat for 2 to 3 minutes per side, until just tender. This can be done the night before, using up the dying embers on the grill. Or you can roast the vegetables in a 450° oven, turning them once.

To make the muffuletta mix, combine all the ingredients, mix well, and set aside. This can be made as much as a week ahead and stored, covered, in the refrigerator. If refrigerated, bring to room temperature before serving.

To assemble the sandwiches, split the rolls, toast the cut sides, and smear with the aioli. Layer the bottoms with the eggplant, zucchini, and onion slices and the diced bell pepper. Sprinkle each sandwich with 1 tablespoon of the Parmesan, top with about 1 tablespoon of the muffuletta mix. Close up the sandwiches and serve.

For the whole loaf, slice off the center of the top, leaving the sides intact to support the goodies to come. Hollow out the loaf a bit, and toast the loaf and the lid lightly over the grill or under the broiler. Smear both the top and bottom with aioli, and start layering the zucchini, eggplant slices, and diced bell pepper inside the loaf. Sprinkle with the Parmesan cheese, add the muffuletta mix, and top off with the onions. Put the lid back on the bread and press gently before cutting and serving.

Wild Mushroom "Burgers" with Apple-Jicama Slaw

Serves 5

At least four times a year, we do a "formal" food tasting to help us change the printed menu in accordance with the seasons. It is always a stressful time for both the chef and I. One of our former chefs, Louise Branch, invented these burgers for one of her tastings. When it was added to the menu, her husband, Phillip Claypool, claimed it was all his idea.

This is great for vegetarians. It looks just like a burger, although it's quite a bit more tender, and the combination of meaty sautéed mushrooms held together with cream cheese is very satisfying both in richness and color. You can substitute whatever mushrooms are available in your area at the time. A small amount of reconstituted dried mushrooms will add interest and flavor, if all you can get are domestic button mushrooms. Be sure to use fresh soft buns, or the burger will squirt out the edges at the first bite. I also like these on thick slices of toasted brioche (a rich egg bread), served open-faced, with the

APPLE-JICAMA SLAW
$1/4$ cup rice vinegar
$1^1/4$ teaspoons cumin seeds, toasted and ground
$1/4$ teaspoon salt
$1/8$ teaspoon freshly ground black pepper
$3/4$ cup extra virgin olive oil
1 or 2 jalapeño chiles, seeded and minced
2 or 3 scallions, cut on the diagonal
2 cups battonne-cut apples
2 cups peeled and battonne-cut jicama

2 pounds mixed fresh portobello, shiitake, and cremini mushrooms, carefully cleaned
2 tablespoons exta virgin olive oil
3 to 4 tablespoons butter
1 teaspoon salt, plus more to taste
$1/4$ teaspoon freshly ground coarse black pepper, plus more to taste
Several gratings of nutmeg
1 head roasted garlic (page 5)
2 tablespoons cream cheese
2 tablespoons grated Asiago cheese
$1^1/2$ tablespoons Dijon mustard
3 tablespoons minced fresh parsley
3 to 6 tablespoons toasted bread crumbs
6 slices red onion, cut $1/4$ inch thick

5 tender-crusted burger buns, or 5 thick slices brioche or challah
$3/4$ cup Roasted Garlic Aioli (page 194)
2 tablespoons Basil Pesto (page 194) or Mint-Tarragon Pesto (page 204)
2 to 3 cups arugula, tough stems removed, washed, torn into pieces if large, and spun dry
Turmeric Pickles (page 200) or store-bought bread-and-butter pickles

To make the slaw, combine the vinegar, cumin, salt, and pepper in a small bowl, whisking until the salt has dissolved. Gradually whisk in the oil, and continue to whisk until fully emulsified. Stir in the jalapeños and scallions. Prepare the apples and dress them lightly so they don't darken. Next, mix in the jicama and add additional dressing as needed.

You can use the stems of all the mushrooms, except for the shiitakes, which are too tough. Those you can cut off and use in stocks. Finely chop one-fourth of the mushrooms in a food processor or by hand. Thinly slice the remaining mushrooms. (The combination of chopped and sliced mushrooms gives the burger the appearance and feel of a real burger.)

continued from page 151

*onion on the bottom and the arugula
on the top.*

*The slaw is especially good served
alongside sandwiches that are fairly
rich. It's also quite refreshing on its
own, or served on a bed of lightly
dressed arugula or radicchio. The
jicama and apples are cool and
crunchy. Use a crisp, sweet eating
apple, such as a Braeburn or McIntosh. No need to peel them. We
always cut the jicama and apples in
longish sticks that resemble french
fries so we can say that our mushroom "burger" comes with "fries."*

Heat 1 tablespoon of the olive oil and $1^{1}/_{2}$ teaspoons of the butter in a very large sauté pan until hot
and almost brown. Add half of the mushrooms, spreading them out as thinly as possible, and cook
for about 5 minutes, until golden brown. (Their juices will need to be released and evaporated
before they will brown.) Season with the 1 teaspoon salt, $^{1}/_{4}$ teaspoon pepper, and nutmeg. Transfer
the mushrooms to a bowl and repeat with the other half of the mushrooms, the remaining olive oil,
and $1^{1}/_{2}$ teaspoons butter. Chill uncovered.

Squeeze the pulp from the cloves of roasted garlic and chop it. When the mushrooms are cool, add
the garlic, cream cheese, Asiago cheese, mustard, parsley, and 3 tablespoons of the bread crumbs,
and mix well. Add more bread crumbs if needed to hold the mixture together. Portion out the
mixture into 5 patties (you could use an ice cream scoop for easier measuring).

Heat the remaining 2 or 3 tablespoons of butter over medium to medium-high heat in a nonstick
skillet or on a griddle. When it is hot and bubbly and before it begins to brown, season the patties
with the salt and pepper, add to the pan, and gently sauté until golden brown on the first side.
Turn the patties and cook on the other side until brown and hot through. It should take 4 to 5
minutes in all. Sauté the onion slices alongside the mushroom patties until golden and tender.
Meanwhile, toast the buns and combine the aioli with the pesto and mix well.

To make the sandwiches, spread the buns with the aioli-pesto mixture. Place the arugula and
onions on the bottoms, followed by the mushroom burgers, and then the tops. Serve with the pickles and the slaw.

Soft-Shell Crab Club Sandwiches

Serves 6

I used to gorge myself on these sand-wiches every May, when soft-shell crabs from the East Coast started making their way to market, but then I became allergic to shrimp, crab, and lobster and had to give them up. We only use live crab at Mustards. The frozen ones may be easier to get, but they are watery and disappointing and not worth the effort. Soft-shell crabs are blue crabs that are in the middle of molting. If they're har-vested before the new shell has hard-ened, you can eat the whole crab, shell and all. They are sweet and tasty and have a satisfying crunch.

If you don't want to deep-fry the crabs, you can coat them with olive oil and grill them, and they'll be equally delicious. Aimee, my niece, who began testing recipes toward the end of this project, couldn't find crabs, so I asked her to test the recipe with shrimp. Her tester's notes said it all: "Yum, yum, yum! Fabulous!" The sandwiches are good with the Heirloom Tomato Salad (page 73).

6 live jumbo soft-shell crabs
1/2 cup buttermilk
Mustards' Secret Coating (page 214)
Peanut or vegetable oil for deep-frying crabs
12 slices applewood-smoked bacon
6 sesame or poppyseed rolls, split, or 12 slices brioche
Aioli (page 201)
2 heads butter lettuce, leaves separated, washed, torn into pieces if large, and spun dry
3 or 4 large vine-ripened tomatoes, sliced
Salt and freshly ground black pepper

Clean the crabs by snipping off the eyes and lifting the backflaps over the bodies and removing the fibrous lungs. Put the buttermilk in a bowl, and put the coating in another fairly large bowl. This way you can liberally dust the crabs and shake off the excess without making a mess. Dip the crabs into the buttermilk and let the excess drain off, then coat with the coating. If you use one hand for the buttermilk and the other for the coating, it will keep your fingers from becoming glued together.

Pour the oil to a depth of 2 inches into a deep sauté pan or pans and heat to 365°. Deep-fry 1 or 2 crabs at a time, depending on the size of your pan(s) and how big the crabs are. Cook them for $3^{1}/_{2}$ to 4 minutes until golden brown. Make sure not to crowd the pan and to let the oil return to 365° before frying each batch. Meanwhile, fry the bacon slices in a skillet over medium heat for 3 to 5 minutes, until crisp. Transfer to paper towels to drain.

To assemble the sandwiches, toast the cut sides of the rolls lightly and smear with a little aioli. Layer the lettuce, tomatoes, a crab, and 2 pieces of bacon (crossed over the crab) on each bottom half. Season with salt and pepper and close up the sandwiches.

Ahi Tuna Sandwiches

Serves 6

Here's a perennial favorite that's easier to fix than your basic burger. I like to dress these sandwiches up with Japanese pickled ginger, which you can find in Asian markets (look for it in small plastic tubs in the produce section or in the refrigerator). If you want to make your own, there's a recipe for it in the Fog City Diner *Cookbook.*

6 (¼-pound) ahi tuna steaks, each ¾ inch thick
6 slices red onion, cut ¼ inch thick
Salt and freshly ground black pepper
1 tablespoon extra virgin olive oil
6 poppyseed buns, preferably made with brioche dough
1 to 2 tablespoons Basil Pesto (page 194)
4 to 5 tablespoons Aioli (page 201) or mayonnaise
Japanese pickled ginger
Arugula, tough stems removed, washed, torn into pieces if large, and spun dry

Sprinkle the tuna and onion slices with salt and pepper and brush with olive oil. Split the buns and toast the cut sides lightly on the grill. Combine the pesto and aioli, and spread the mixture on the buns.

Grill the tuna and onions. Plan on 1½ to 2 minutes per side for medium-rare to medium for the tuna.

Assemble each sandwich with a piece of tuna, a slab of onion, several slices of pickled ginger, and some arugula. Close up the sandwich and serve.

Ahi Tuna and Shiitake Mini Burgers

Makes 16 to 18 tiny sandwiches

I always have a few pieces of tuna left that are too small for a sandwich or an entrée, but big enough to combine with something else to make an appetizer or "buff" plate. (A buff plate is a small taste that we send out when a few friends or employees from other restaurants come by, and we want to say welcome.) These tiny burgers are just right for that. One year we made two thousand of these bite-sized "sliders" for the Napa Valley Wine Auction. After that project, I thought I would never be able to face a cutting board again! We served them with shoestring potatoes and a Thai "ketchup'" to complete the burger-and-fries image.

You can find kaffir lime leaves in Asian markets, sometimes in the frozen foods section. These leaves give off a wonderful flowery lemony aroma. I was actually able to acquire a kaffir lime tree recently, and, touch wood, have kept it growing so far—further proof that Northern California is chef heaven.

THAI KETCHUP
$1/4$ cup peanut oil
$3/4$ cup sliced onions (cut crosswise, not in rings)
1 red bell pepper, seeded and finely diced
$1^1/2$ red Fresno chiles, cut into rings with seeds intact
$2^1/2$ serrano chiles, cut into rings with seeds intact
1 fresh pasilla or bird chile, julienned
$2^1/2$ cloves garlic, sliced
2 tablespoons peeled and grated fresh ginger
3 cups peeled and diced fresh or drained canned tomatoes
$1/2$ cup sugar
$1/3$ cup fish sauce

$2^1/2$ pounds tuna fillet
$1/2$ to $3/4$ pound fresh shiitake mushrooms, carefully cleaned
$1/4$ cup sesame oil
3 to 4 tablespoons peanut oil
1 leek, white and light green parts, thinly sliced
1 tablespoon minced garlic
$2^1/2$ tablespoons peeled and minced young ginger or finely grated old ginger
3 kaffir lime leaves or very finely grated zest of 1 lime
$1/2$ cup cooked short-grain white rice (arborio or Calrose)
$1^1/2$ to 2 tablespoons tamari soy sauce
$1/4$ cup mirin or sake
1 teaspoon salt
$1/4$ teaspoon freshly ground black pepper
16 to 18 sesame buns, $1^1/2$ inches in diameter

To make the ketchup, use a large, flat sauté pan to speed up evaporation and shorten overall cooking time. Heat the peanut oil over medium-high heat. Add the onions, bell pepper, chiles, garlic, and ginger and sauté for 3 to 4 minutes, until tender and caramelized. Add the tomatoes, sugar, and fish sauce and cook on high heat for 15 to 20 minutes, until thick and rich. Let cool before serving.

Remove any skin from the tuna, and trim off any blood veins or tough sinewy pieces. You can mince the tuna by hand or grind it in a food processor. Using a food processor, cut the tuna into large dice, then pulse it into a clean, fine mince. Don't let the machine get too hot, or it will start to "cook" the fish, and don't purée the fish, as you do want some texture. In fact, you could grind half the tuna and finely mince the rest for better effect. Refrigerate the tuna.

The Thai-style ketchup came about due to an overabundance of Thai bird chiles in our garden one summer. It's a pretty hot sauce, maybe 8 on a scale of 10, so if you're not into spicy, trim the seeds and membranes off the chiles, and cut the chiles into strips rather than circles. Leftover ketchup, which keeps refrigerated for up to 3 weeks, is great on regular beef burgers, grilled tuna steak, or turkey breast.

Cut the stems off the shiitake mushrooms, reserving them for stock, and mince the caps. Heat the sesame oil and 2 tablespoons of the peanut oil in a large sauté pan over medium-high heat. Add the leek, garlic, and ginger and sweat for 5 minutes, until soft but not caramelized. Raise the heat to high, add the mushrooms, and cook for 5 to 6 minutes, until tender and all the liquid has cooked away. Spread the mushrooms out on a plate to cool.

Heat another 1 tablespoon or so of peanut oil and frizzle the kaffir lime leaves. (This releases the oils and makes them more aromatic. If using lime zest skip this step.) Remove them from the pan to cool. When all the cooked ingredients are cool, mix them together gently with the tuna, cooked rice, soy sauce, mirin, salt, and pepper. Unless you are going to make the burgers immediately, put the mixture back in the refrigerator.

To make the burgers, form the tuna mixture into patties about 2 inches in diameter and about $1/2$ inch thick. Brush them lightly with peanut oil, so they don't stick to the cooking surface. If you don't want to use an outdoor grill, a ridged or smooth cast-iron griddle works well. Split the buns and toast the cut sides lightly on the grill. Grill or griddle the burgers, turning them once, for 1 to $1^1/_2$ minutes per side. They should be light golden brown and slightly springy to the touch. Serve tucked in the buns, with a dab of ketchup.

WARNING:

Preoccupation with Government (City, State or Federal) Required Precautionary Notices is Known to the Proprietors to Make You Paranoid, Boring and No Fun at All.

Smoked Turkey, Bacon, and Grilled Apple Sandwiches with Guacamole

Serves 6

On our first menu, we had a simple smoked turkey sandwich. Much later, chef Sean Mindrum invented a great grilled apple and smoked turkey salad. I married the two, and this is the result. The apples add a little moisture and sweetness to the turkey. We use our own smoked turkey breasts at Mustards, but high-quality smoked or roasted turkey from your local deli or butcher shop is fine. There are two schools of sandwich-making thought: one is the paper-thin, deli-style-slices school and the other is the hand-sliced school, in which the meat is not quite as thin. As long as the meat is very tender and you can bite through it easily without tearing the sandwich apart, hand-cut wins for me. Use any good eating apple, such as Gala, Braeburn, or McIntosh.

This is how we do our turkeys for our smoked turkey sandwiches. The recipe makes about twice as much smoked meat as you'll need for the sandwiches, but it's so good you'll have no trouble using it up.

SMOKED TURKEY BREAST
4 quarts water
1 cup kosher salt
1 cup sugar
10 whole cloves
20 black peppercorns
1/2 bone-in turkey breast (about 3 pounds)

2 large apples, cored and sliced into 1/4-inch-thick "donuts" (unpeeled looks best)
1 large red onion, sliced 3/8 inch thick
Extra virgin olive oil
Salt and freshly ground black pepper

GUACAMOLE
2 avocados, pitted, peeled, and finely diced
Juice of 1 lemon or 2 limes
1 jalapeño chile, seeded and minced
1/4 red onion, minced
2 tablespoons minced fresh cilantro leaves
1 1/2 teaspoons extra virgin olive oil
Salt and freshly ground black pepper

8 to 12 slices thick-cut applewood-smoked bacon
6 light, crusty sandwich rolls, split
3 tablespoons mayonnaise
3 tablespoons Dijon mustard
Arugula or watercress, tough stems removed, washed, torn into pieces if large, and spun dry

Pour the water into a nonreactive container large enough to hold the turkey breast. Dissolve the salt and sugar in the water, then add the cloves and peppercorns. Add the turkey breast, weighting it down with a plate to keep it submerged. Refrigerate for 36 to 48 hours.

Drain and rinse the turkey breast. Place it on a rack that will fit in your smoker and let it dry a bit while you get your smoker hot. Smoke over a water pan at 250° to 300°, until an internal temperature of 140° is reached. It should take about 2 hours, stoking the fire about 4 times. Chill the turkey breast before slicing if you are using it for sandwiches. If you want to serve it hot, cover it with aluminum foil and let it rest for 10 to 15 minutes before slicing, to allow the juices to set.

Lightly coat the apple and onion slices with olive oil and salt and pepper, then marinate for 10 to 20 minutes.

To make the guacamole, combine the avocados, lemon juice, jalapeño, onion, cilantro, and olive oil in a small bowl, mashing them together with a fork. Season to taste with salt and pepper.

Grill or sauté the apple and onion slices over medium-high heat until light golden brown and tender but not falling apart, 2 to 3 minutes at most for the apples. As you grill the apple and onion slices, give them a quarter turn to get nice crosshatch marks on both sides. A cast-iron skillet with raised grill strips works well for small tasks such as this. Set the onions and apples aside. Cook the bacon in a skillet over medium heat for 3 to 5 minutes, until crisp. Transfer to paper towels to drain. Toast the rolls.

To assemble the sandwiches, mix together the mayonnaise and mustard and spread it on the bottom halves of the rolls. Layer the turkey, apple, onion, bacon, and greens. Spread the guacamole on the bun tops and close up the sandwiches. Cut them in half and serve.

Smoked Beef Tri-Tip Sandwiches with Horseradish Cream and Watercress

Serves 6

This was one of our most popular sandwiches in the beginning, but I haven't run it in years. When I made some for testing, the staff devoured them all before any customers had a chance to try them.

I have smoked the meat at home in a covered kettle-type grill and in a stack-style water smoker, and I tested it in a convection oven, too. The stack smoker definitely turns out the best meat, but it doesn't matter. Work with whatever equipment you have.

Tri-tips come from the bottom sirloin butt, and they generally have no more than $^1/_4$ inch of fat on them. You can get them fat-free, but the meat would probably dry out completely during the smoking and taste like sawdust. Serve the meat warm, fresh from the smoker, or smoke it when you're smoking something else, and eat it later in the week.

After you've tried the basic sandwich, try some other tasty additions, such as roasted red peppers, roasted garlic (page 5), Aioli (page 201), cheese (mozzarella, fontina, or white Cheddar), or Onion Jam (page 206) .

1 teaspoon minced garlic
$1^1/_2$ teaspoons brown sugar
1 tablespoon chile powder
$1^1/_2$ teaspoons salt
$1^1/_2$ teaspoons freshly ground black pepper
1 ($2^1/_2$ to 3-pound) beef tri-tip roast
1 onion, thinly sliced (if oven roasting)
2 or 3 tablespoons extra virgin olive oil (if oven roasting)
Bacon slices (if oven roasting; optional)
Beer or wine for basting (if oven roasting; optional)

Horseradish Cream (page 18)
6 crusty sandwich rolls, preferably with poppyseeds, split and toasted
Watercress, arugula, or lettuce, tough stems removed, washed, torn into pieces if large, and spun dry
$^1/_2$ red onion, thinly sliced
6 tablespoons Dijon or coarse-grain mustard

Mix together the garlic, sugar, chile powder, salt, and pepper. Rub the spice mix thoroughly into the beef and let it marinate in the refrigerator for at least 2 to 3 hours to allow the flavors to permeate the meat. For an even tastier result, let it marinate for 24 hours.

Smoke the meat for $1^1/_2$ to 2 hours, until it reaches an internal temperature of 140°.

To roast the meat in a convection oven, spread the onion slices on the bottom of a roasting pan. Lightly coat the marinated meat with the olive oil, set it on the onions, and roast it at 450° for 30 to 35 minutes. If you want to get fancy, you can lay several slices of bacon on the meat to add a little smoky flavor, and baste the meat occasionally with beer or wine, whichever is handy.

When the meat is done, allow it to rest for about 20 minutes, then slice it as thinly as possible. If you prefer a paper-thin cut, chill the beef thoroughly before slicing. While the meat is resting, make the horseradish cream. Cover and refrigerate until needed.

To assemble the sandwiches, spread the bottom halves of the rolls with the horseradish cream, pile on a generous layer of sliced beef, and add some greens and onion slices. Spread the tops with the mustard and close up the sandwiches.

Slow-Smoked BBQ Pork Sandwiches with Ooo-Eee! Sauce

Serves 6

One of our former cooks, Jeff, who I believe was from Texas, developed the original recipe for this pork. As with all good things, it has evolved over time, until now it has reached a state of near perfection. It has been on the menu for a long time, and it seems to stay in the number two slot for sales year after year, coming in after the cheeseburger, which is always on top. We go through tons of this pork, but that could be due in part to the fact that all the chefs, sous chefs, and cooks start snacking on the meat as soon as it comes out of the smoker. Yes, that juicy, smoke-flavored shredded meat is great, but what sends this sandwich over the top is the Ooo-Eee! Sauce that goes on it, so don't take any shortcuts there. The sauce is modeled after a Carolina-style vinegar BBQ sauce. Keep a shaker jar of it on the table to sprinkle on all sorts of grilled meats and poultry and egg dishes. Refrigerated, it will keep well for several months.

1 (2¹/₂ to 3-pound) pork butt roast
1 tablespoon finely ground dried orange peel
1¹/₂ tablespoons freshly ground black pepper
1¹/₂ teaspoons ancho chile powder
¹/₄ cup kosher salt
3 tablespoons sugar
1¹/₂ teaspoons hot paprika

OOO-EEE! SAUCE
¹/₂ cup BBQ Sauce (page 112) or your favorite barbecue sauce
1 cup cider vinegar
¹/₄ cup apple cider
¹/₄ cup sugar
³/₄ cup water

6 soft, seeded poor boy rolls
¹/₂ red onion, very thinly sliced
Sweet-and-Sour Coleslaw (page 168)

Cut the pork into 3 or 4 manageable pieces, trimming off most of the exterior fat and any tissue (you need to leave some fat to keep the meat moist throughout its long, slow smoke). Combine the orange peel, black pepper, chile powder, salt, sugar, and paprika and mix thoroughly. Liberally coat all the surfaces of the pork with the spice mix, rubbing it in well. Cover and refrigerate for at least 4 hours and up to 24 hours.

To make the sauce, combine all the ingredients in a bowl, stirring well to dissolve the sugar. No cooking required.

Smoke the pork until it is tender enough to pull apart into tasty shreds. The longer and slower you go, the better the meat. When we used a home-style water smoker and placed the meat on the bottom rack, it took 6 hours, but it was a cold, windy day. Another time we tried it on a hot, sunny day and it took 5 hours, so try to keep the smoker out of the wind. The meat should be crispy on the outside and soft within. Shred the meat as soon as you can handle it, picking out the big pieces of fat that didn't render out in the smoking process. Try not to eat all the crusty, crisp edges while doing this so everyone else will get some. The meat should have taken on a rich pink hue, which is the effect of the smoking the meat. If it's not all rosy, you roasted it rather than smoking it, and next time you need to use more green or soaked chips and to keep your fire or heat lower.

If you don't have a smoker, you can roast the pork in a conventional oven. Follow the recipe below, but to give the meat a smoky flavor, substitute Spanish pimentón or chipotle chile powder for some of the ancho chile powder (remember, the chipotle is a lot hotter). Roast the meat on a rack over water at about 225° for 5 to 7 hours, or even overnight.

When you're ready to serve, heat the sauce in a large skillet over high heat until slightly thickened, toss in the pork, and stir to coat the meat with the sauce and heat it through. As the pork is heating up, toast the rolls. Portion the pork and sauce evenly among the buns, and stuff in the onion slices and coleslaw. Serve with additional sauce.

Herb-Cured Chicken Breast Sandwiches with Eggplant Relish and Romesco Sauce

Serves 6

Boneless, skinless chicken breasts, the mainstay of America's low-cholesterol regime, are also a great medium for those of us who love flavorful marinades and spicy condiments. In this dish, the chicken will be infused with gingery basil flavors. The romesco sauce is a nut-enriched chile-and-bell-pepper sauce from Spain. It's a bit on the spicy side and is a rusty red color. It is often served with grilled fish, such as tuna or swordfish, and is also good on mahimahi, mackerel, and bluefish. It keeps well refrigerated, so feel free to make it ahead, but bring it to room temperature before serving.

3 tablespoons Basil Pesto (page 194)

$^3/_4$ cup dry white wine

1 tablespoon peeled and grated fresh ginger

3 boneless, skinless whole chicken breasts

ROMESCO SAUCE

5 almonds

2 ancho chiles, stemmed and seeded

1 tablespoon water, or as needed

1 or 2 cloves garlic

1 tomato, peeled, seeded, and chopped

1 red bell pepper, roasted, peeled, seeded, and chopped

1 slice rustic country bread, 1 inch thick, toasted and broken into pieces

$^1/_4$ to $^1/_2$ teaspoon salt

$^1/_8$ to $^1/_4$ teaspoon freshly ground black pepper

3 tablespoons extra virgin olive oil

1 $^1/_2$ teaspoons sherry vinegar

$^1/_2$ red onion, thinly sliced

6 crusty country rolls, split

Eggplant Relish (page 207)

Arugula or watercress, tough stems removed, washed, torn into pieces if large, and spun dry

Combine the pesto, wine, and ginger, and coat the chicken breasts with the mixture. Allow them to marinate for 1 hour.

Meanwhile, make the sauce: Toast the almonds in a 375°oven for 7 minutes until fragrant. Toast the chiles in the same oven for 1 minute, then put them in a small pan with enough water to cover and bring to a boil. Turn off the heat, cover the pan, and let the chiles soften for 5 minutes. Put the chiles, almonds, and 1 tablespoon water in a food processor or blender and purée until smooth adding a little more water if needed to ease the processing. Add the garlic, tomato, bell pepper, bread, and salt and pepper to taste and purée again. The sauce should be thick and a bit coarse at this point. Blend in the olive oil and vinegar. Refrigerate the sauce until needed, but allow it to come to room temperature before serving.

When you're ready to serve, grill the chicken breasts over a medium fire for 2 to 3 minutes on each side until firm, giving them a quarter turn to get nice crosshatch marks on both sides. Grill the onion slices at the same time for 1 to 2 minutes on each side and lightly grill the cut sides of the rolls. Layer the bottoms with the grilled onions, chicken breasts, the relish, and arugula. Spread the tops with the sauce and close up the sandwiches. You can serve additional sauce on the side.

Smoked Ham and Jarlsberg Cheese Sandwiches with Basil Mayonnaise and Tomato and Apricot Chutney

Serves 4

I think my husband married me for this sandwich. Actually, I'm sure of it. Years ago, he used to come to the bar all the time and order a Heineken and one of these sandwiches, which is how I met him. When I made them at home recently for the recipe testing, he looked as though he had died and gone to heaven. It had to be the sandwich.

The chutney makes a big difference, but if you're not up to making your own, see what your local market or specialty foods store has to offer. Other than the chutney, this sandwich comes together in a snap, since the slicer at the deli counter does all the work. This sandwich is at its best with potato chips and the Turmeric Pickles.

2 tablespoons Basil Pesto (page 194)
$^1/_3$ cup mayonnaise or Aioli (page 201)
8 slices rye bread
8 tablespoons Tomato and Apricot Chutney (page 205)
8 slices Jarlsberg cheese
$^3/_4$ pound thinly sliced honey-smoked or pepper-cured ham (12 to 16 slices)
Butter
Potato chips (optional)
Turmeric Pickles (page 200, optional)
Assorted mustards

Mix together the pesto and mayonnaise and spread a thin layer of the mixture on each slice of bread. Working with four slices of the bread, spread with a thicker layer of the chutney, add a slice of cheese, the ham, and another slice of cheese. Close up the sandwiches.

Heat a griddle to medium, smear it with butter (or smear the outsides of the sandwiches with the butter), and toast the sandwiches slowly to a nice golden brown, making sure the cheese is melting before turning the sandwiches over.

To serve, cut the sandwiches on the diagonal and serve with pickles, chips, and your favorite mustards.

Some dishes seem to go together naturally, but maybe that's just a matter of habit. Who's to say you couldn't serve a side of black beans instead of potatoes with that steak or grilled polenta instead of onions with the liver? Every dish in this chapter was designed to complement some other menu item, but there's no reason you couldn't borrow a piece from one dish to use with another if you think it will work. Experiment with the sides in this chapter, and look in other parts of the book for ideas, too.

There's one area where you should not compromise, though. When it comes to vegetables, let the seasons dictate what you do. It is always best to use fresh ingredients that are in season versus buying produce when it's out of season, tasteless, and exorbitantly priced.

Sweet-and-Sour Coleslaw

Serves 6

This slaw is great with any grilled meat, but particularly with BBQ pork. It's the version you want to use when you're after a lighter slaw. Our recipe testers used all different vinegars. Some used cider vinegar, some used champagne vinegar, and one person used rice vinegar, and all were happy with the results. (I would not recommend red wine or balsamic vinegar.) Celery seeds are traditional, but I really like the ground cumin for a change of pace.

$^{1}/_{2}$ to $^{3}/_{4}$ head green cabbage, thinly sliced
1 red bell pepper, seeded and thinly sliced
2 carrots, grated

DRESSING
$^{1}/_{3}$ cup sugar
$^{1}/_{2}$ teaspoon celery or cumin seeds, toasted and ground

1 teaspoon dry mustard powder
1 to 1$^{1}/_{2}$ teaspoons salt
$^{1}/_{4}$ teaspoon freshly ground black pepper
$^{1}/_{3}$ cup cider or distilled vinegar
$^{2}/_{3}$ cup extra virgin olive oil

Put the cabbage, bell pepper, and carrots in a large bowl and mix well.

To make the dressing, combine the sugar, celery seeds, mustard, salt, and pepper in a small saucepan. Gradually whisk in the vinegar and olive oil to avoid lumps. Bring to a boil over high heat and cook for 1 minute.

Pour the hot dressing over the slaw and toss, mixing well. Cover and refrigerate until needed.

Carrots with Onion and Cumin

Serves 6

I like the smokiness the toasted cumin adds to the sweetness of the carrots. This dish would be nice with veal chops, halibut, or mahimahi.

2 to 2$^{1}/_{4}$ pounds large carrots or 2 to 3 bunches baby carrots
1 red onion, or 1 leek, white part only, julienned
$^{1}/_{2}$ to $^{3}/_{4}$ cup water
1 teaspoon cumin seeds, toasted and coarsely ground
1 teaspoon salt
$^{1}/_{2}$ teaspoon freshly ground black pepper
1 teaspoon sugar (optional)
3 tablespoons butter
1 tablespoon chopped fresh mint (optional)

If you're using full-sized carrots, peel them and cut into short sticks or half-moons. Baby carrots should be peeled and left whole. Combine the carrots, onion, $^{1}/_{2}$ cup water, cumin, salt, pepper, sugar, and butter in a saucepan, cover, and bring to a boil. Lower the heat to low and simmer for 3 to 5 minutes until the carrots are just tender, 3 to 5 minutes. Add more water as needed.

When the carrots are done, all the water should be absorbed and the carrots should be nicely glazed. If not, remove the cover, increase the heat, and, while shaking the pan, continue cooking until all the water has evaporated and the carrots are well glazed. Stir in the mint just before serving.

Erasto's Coleslaw

Serves 6

Erasto Jacinto started with us at Mustards as a dishwasher, way back when we were all young. Now he's a sous chef, and he knows more about the place than I do because he never went off to open other restaurants. Through the years we've added many of his original recipes to our menus. This creamy, tangy slaw is one of them. Serve it with really spicy BBQ meats to cool the palate.

1/2 cup sour cream
1/2 cup mayonnaise
2 1/2 tablespoons Dijon mustard
2 teaspoons honey
2 teaspoons champagne vinegar

6 tablespoons dried currants
1/2 head green cabbage, chopped
1 carrot, grated or shredded
1 apple, quartered, cored, and thinly sliced (no need to peel)
Salt and freshly ground black pepper

Combine the sour cream, mayonnaise, mustard, honey, vinegar, and currants in a large bowl. Mix well. Add the cabbage, carrot, and apple and toss to combine. Season to taste with salt and pepper.

Braised Red Cabbage

Serves 6

This dish is super easy to make. It is delicious with Mongolian Pork Chops (page 99) or with smoked duck or grilled squabs.

1 large head red cabbage (about 1 pound)
1 tablespoon butter
1/2 large red onion, julienned
1/2 cup red wine vinegar or cider vinegar

1/3 cup firmly packed brown sugar
3/4 teaspoon cumin seeds, toasted and ground
3/4 teaspoon salt
3/4 teaspoon freshly ground black pepper

Cut the cabbage in half lengthwise and cut out the core. Cut each half in half again lengthwise, then cut each quarter crosswise into 3/4- to 1/2-inch cubes.

Melt the butter in a large saucepan over medium heat. Add the onion, and cook, stirring occasionally, for 10 to 15 minutes, until soft and golden brown. Add the cabbage and sauté, stirring now and then, for 25 minutes or so, until tender. Add the vinegar, sugar, and cumin. Mix well, lower the heat to medium-low, and simmer for about 20 minutes more, until the juices are syrupy and the cabbage appears shiny. The cabbage should be tender but not mushy.

Remove from the heat and season with salt and pepper. You can make this ahead and reheat it when needed.

Sautéed Greens

Serves 6

You can use a single type of green in this recipe, or you can mix a couple of different kinds. If you're using spinach, however, you should use all spinach and increase the amount to 3 pounds. Leftovers of any kind can be stirred into a minestrone soup or chopped up and mixed in with a dish of macaroni and cheese. For lemony greens, add the grated zest and juice of half a lemon at the very end.

2 bunches coarse greens, such as Swiss or red chard, turnip, kale, or mustard, or 3 pounds spinach
2 tablespoons extra virgin olive oil
2 cloves garlic, finely chopped
$^1/_2$ teaspoon salt
$^1/_4$ teaspoon freshly ground black pepper
1 scant tablespoon balsamic vinegar or freshly squeezed lemon juice
Finely grated zest and juice of $^1/_2$ lemon (optional)

Wash the greens, and then trim off any coarse stems or simply tear the tender leaves away from the stems. Heat the olive oil and garlic in a large saucepan over medium heat until the oil is bubbly and hot but not browning. Add the greens, sprinkle with the salt and pepper, and then with the vinegar. Cook, stirring occasionally, until the greens are tender. Different greens require different cooking times, so it's best to sample as you go along. Spinach is probably the quickest to cook, while mustard greens and collard greens take longer. When the greens are tender to the bite, scoop them out of the pan and put them in a serving dish, leaving the liquid in the saucepan.

Continue cooking the liquid over medium-high heat until reduced to a thick and syrupy consistency. Stir in the lemon zest and juice. Drizzle the sauce over the sautéed greens and serve.

Baby Zucchinis with Garden Herbs

Serves 6

When you pick young zucchinis and grill them very quickly, they are wonderfully tender and sweet. Just be sure you select squashes that are no more than 4 to 5 inches long. Sugar snap peas, pencil-thin asparagus spears, bell peppers, or other varieties of summer squash are also wonderful grilled, and they make great appetizers as well as side dishes. Just sprinkle with Maldon flake salt or gray sea salt as they come off the grill. See right for directions on grilling scallions.

2 pounds baby zucchinis
1 tablespoon fresh oregano or savory leaves, minced
1 tablespoon fresh thyme or parsley leaves, minced
2 tablespoons extra virgin olive oil
Salt and freshly ground black pepper
2 tablespoons butter
Coarse sea salt, preferably French gray sea salt or Maldon flake salt

Trim off the tough ends and split the zucchinis in half lengthwise (or leave whole if small). Mix the oregano and thyme with the olive oil. Season the zucchinis with salt and pepper, then brush with the oil mixture.

Grill over medium coals, cut side down first, then turn and grill the other side until tender. It should take about 2 minutes per side.

To serve, brush with the butter and sprinkle with sea salt.

GRILLED SCALLIONS: Figure on 2 to 4 scallions per person. Trim off the root and green parts. Omitting the herbs, brush the scallions with olive oil and sprinkle with salt and pepper. Grill, turning often, until lightly charred and hot through. To serve, stack zucchini and scallions, alternating, on a platter.

Summer Succotash

Serves 6

The testers split down the middle on this recipe—half took our lead and made their own corn stock, and they raved about the dish, while the other half used chicken stock instead and will never know what they missed. If you're going to make the corn stock, be sure you use fresh, juicy, in-season corn, or it won't be worth the work. This succotash is excellent with grilled halibut, Achiote-Marinated Chicken Breasts (page 97), or, my favorite, rabbit.

1 to 1^1/$_2$ cups green and/or yellow wax beans, trimmed and cut on the diagonal into 1-inch pieces
2 tablespoons extra virgin olive oil
1 tablespoon butter
^{3}/$_4$ cup minced scallions, white and light green parts only, or thinly sliced sweet onions
1 zucchini, diced
1 yellow or orange bell pepper, roasted, peeled, seeded, and diced
1^1/$_2$ cups fresh corn kernels
^{3}/$_4$ cup corn stock (page 220), chicken stock (page 218), or fish stock (page 221)
^{1}/$_4$ cup heavy whipping cream
Salt and freshly cracked black pepper

Blanch the beans in boiling salted water for 5 to 7 minutes until crisp-tender. Drain and run under cold water to stop the cooking.

Heat the olive oil and butter in a large skillet over medium-high heat. Add the scallions and cook gently for 1 minute, until slightly soft. Add the zucchini, pepper, and corn kernels and cook for 3 minutes, stirring frequently. Stir in the beans, corn stock, and cream and simmer for 2 to 3 minutes, until the liquid is reduced to a thick, creamy consistency. Season to taste with salt and pepper and serve.

Fava Bean Succotash

Serves 6

Fava beans are popular in Northern California. They came in with the Mediterranean food craze that swept through in the 1990s. Favas take a little more work to prepare than other beans, as you must first shell them, blanch them, and then peel off the outer skin of each bean. If you can't get fava beans, you can substitute young, tender green beans, fresh lima beans, or cooked white beans.

2 to 2^1/$_2$ pounds fava beans or 1 to 1^1/$_2$ pounds young, tender green beans
2 tablespoons butter
^{1}/$_4$ cup minced onion
2 cups fresh corn kernels
2 to 3 tablespoons water
Salt and freshly ground black pepper
1 tablespoon minced fresh cilantro, oregano, or basil

Shell the fava beans and blanch them in boiling water for about 30 seconds. Drain and plunge them into an ice bath to stop the cooking and set the color. Peel off the skins and discard any beans that are not bright green. (If you are using green beans, trim the ends but leave them whole. Blanch for 2 to 3 minutes.)

Put the butter into a sauté pan large enough to hold all the vegetables in a shallow, even layer and place the pan over medium-high heat. Add the onion and cook for about 1 minute, until just tender. Add the corn and cook for 1 to 2 minutes, stirring until well coated with butter. Add the fava beans and water, raise the heat to high, and cook for 1 to 2 minutes, until all the vegetables are hot through and the water has evaporated. Season to taste with salt and pepper, toss in the cilantro, and mix well. Serve hot or warm.

Crispy Yams

Serves 6

Darker-fleshed varieties, such as the Garnet and Jewel yams (actually simpler varieties of the sweet potato rather than true yams), are sweeter and more flavorful than the lighter-fleshed sweet potatoes, but you can use either. Bake them ahead, keep them refrigerated, then fry or grill them when you're ready to serve.

3 large yams (about 3 pounds)
2 to 3 tablespoons extra virgin olive oil
Salt and freshly ground black pepper

Preheat the oven to 375°. Wash the yams well, rub them with some of the olive oil, and sprinkle with salt and pepper. Prick the yams with a fork, then bake for 35 to 45 minutes, until a skewer can just barely go to the center. Allow the yams to cool until you can handle them. Then, without peeling them, cut crosswise into ^{1}/$_2$- to ^{3}/$_4$-inch-thick rounds.

When you're ready to serve, heat the remaining oil in a nonstick skillet over medium heat. Add the yam slices and fry until crisp on both sides and hot through. This will take no more than 1 to 2 minutes per side. To grill the yams, brush them with oil and grill them over a low fire to keep them from burning. Serve them while they are hot and crisp.

Winter Squash Gratin

Serves 6 to 8

We use French Cinderella pumpkins for this gratin, but any of the hard winter squashes would do. I love growing those pumpkins, both the white and orange varieties. They look wonderful in the field (you can just imagine one turning into Cinderella's coach), and they cook up rich, creamy, and flavorful. This is super with roasted chicken, veal chops, or grilled swordfish or tuna.

2 pounds winter squash, peeled, halved, seeded, and thinly sliced
2 tablespoons butter
2 cups thinly sliced red onions
$^1/_2$ to 1 teaspoon salt
$^1/_2$ teaspoon freshly ground black pepper
3 cups chicken stock (page 218)
$^1/_2$ cup heavy whipping cream
2 tablespoons finely minced fresh parsley

Preheat the oven to 375°. Butter a large baking dish, arrange the squash in it, and set it aside.

Heat a large pot or sauté pan over medium-high heat and add the butter. When it has melted, add the onions and cook, stirring occasionally for 5 to 8 minutes, until soft and caramel colored. Season with the salt and pepper (add the smaller amount of salt if you're using canned stock). Add the stock, bring to a boil, and pour the stock and onions over the squash. Bake for about 35 minutes, until the squash is tender and the top of the gratin is caramelized. Pour the cream evenly over the top and continue to bake for 10 to 12 minutes, until golden brown.

Serve the gratin, making sure everyone gets a bit of the crusty top. An offset spatula is the best tool for getting nice, even edges. Sprinkle with the parsley.

Grilled Yams and Yukon Gold Potatoes with Harissa

Serves 6 to 8

The original version of this dish was put on our menu years ago by Peter Hall, one of our sous chefs at the time. I think it changed after Alice Waters's vegetable book came out, as we then started using a variation of her harissa recipe. (Harissa is a fiery-hot Moroccan condiment.) Both the vinaigrette and the harissa can be done well in advance, making this a dish that can go on the table quickly. The leftover harissa is great on grilled tuna and swordfish, toasted bread for sandwiches, and scrambled eggs.

HARISSA
8 serrano chiles
2 teaspoons cumin seeds, toasted and ground
4 cloves garlic, finely minced
2 tablespoons hot paprika
1 teaspoon ground cayenne pepper
$^1/_2$ cup extra virgin olive oil
2 tablespoons freshly squeezed lemon juice
Salt

2 large yams (orange-fleshed sweet potatoes; about 2 pounds)
6 small to medium Yukon Gold potatoes, halved lengthwise
2 tablespoons pure olive oil
Salt and freshly ground black pepper

VINAIGRETTE
Grated zest and juice of $^1/_2$ lemon
1 shallot, minced
Pinch of salt
Pinch of freshly ground black pepper
3 to 4 tablespoons extra virgin olive oil

$^1/_4$ cup plain yogurt
3 tablespoons minced fresh parsley
3 tablespoons coarsely chopped fresh cilantro
3 scallions, white parts only, cut on the diagonal

To make the harissa, remove the seeds from the serranos if you want a milder sauce. Mince them and place in a small bowl with all the remaining ingredients, including salt to taste.

Mix well, cover, and refrigerate until needed. Warm gently before serving, so that it can be drizzled easily.

Preheat the oven to 375°. Wash the yams and potatoes well and rub them with some olive oil. Prick the yams with a fork. Place on a baking sheet and bake for 35 to 45 minutes, until a skewer can just barely go to the center. Allow the yams and potatoes to cool until you can handle them. Then, without peeling them, cut on the diagonal into $^1/_2$-inch-thick slices.

Brush the slices lightly with olive oil, season with salt and pepper, and place on a grill (an oak fire is good). Rotating a quarter turn on each side to get nice crosshatch grill marks, grill until heated through. This should take no more than 2 minutes per side.

To make the vinaigrette, whisk together the lemon zest and juice, shallot, salt, and pepper in a small bowl, until the salt is dissolved. Gradually whisk in the oil, and continue to whisk until fully emulsified.

To serve, arrange three slices of yam alternately with three slices of potato on individual plates. Drizzle with 1 or 2 teaspoons of vinaigrette, and sprinkle on a few drops of harissa. Top with a drizzle of yogurt and a scattering of chopped parsley, cilantro, and scallions over all.

Mustards' Mashed Potatoes

Serves 6

Of all the mashed potato recipes in the world, this one and the goat cheese variation below are my favorites. My husband likes the non-goat cheese potatoes so well, he'll have some as an appetizer and then have a second helping with his main course.

4^1/$_4$ pounds russet or Yukon Gold potatoes, peeled and cut into 2- to 3-inch chunks
1^1/$_2$ teaspoons salt plus more as needed
^{3}/$_4$ to 1 cup milk
1 cup butter, cubed
^{1}/$_2$ teaspoon minced garlic
^{1}/$_2$ teaspoon freshly ground black pepper

Put the potatoes in a large pot along with 1^1/$_2$ teaspoons salt and water to cover. Bring to a boil, reduce the heat to a strong simmer, and cook for 15 to 20 minutes, until the potatoes are tender when poked with a fork but not mushy.

Drain the potatoes and transfer them to a mixer fitted with the paddle attachment (or, if you prefer a lumpier finish, you can mash them with a potato masher). Add ^{3}/$_4$ cup milk, the butter, garlic, and pepper. Mix on low speed to combine, then increase the speed to medium to mix thoroughly. Add more milk if the potatoes seem too thick. Taste and adjust the salt if needed.

GOAT CHEESE MASHED POTATOES: Prepare the mashed potatoes according to the above recipe, reducing the butter by half and mixing in ^{1}/$_2$ pound fresh goat cheese (we use Laura Chenel's chèvre) and 1 tablespoon minced fresh thyme at the end.

Celery Root Mashers

Serves 6

Louise Branch, one of our former chefs, was famous for all her flavored mashed potatoes. She would flavor them with shrimp, mushroom, lobster . . . just about anything, but she only used one flavoring at a time. They're all good, but I think I like these mashers the best.

4 large russet potatoes, peeled and cut into 2-inch chunks
1 celery root, peeled and cut into 2-inch chunks
2 to 4 teaspoons salt
2 tablespoons extra virgin olive oil
1 leek, white part only, minced
2 tablespoons butter
1 teaspoon freshly ground white pepper

Put the potatoes and celery root in a large pot along with 1 teaspoon of the salt and water to cover. Bring to the boil, reduce to a strong simmer, and cook for 15 to 20 minutes, until both vegetables are fork tender but not mushy. Meanwhile, heat the olive oil in a sauté pan over low heat, add the leek, and sweat for about 8 minutes, until soft. Do not allow the leek to brown. Remove from the heat and set aside.

Drain the potatoes and celery root and transfer them to a mixer fitted with the paddle attachment (or, if you prefer a lumpier finish, you can mash them with a potato masher). Add the butter and 1 teaspoon of the salt and mix on low speed to combine, then increase the speed to medium to mix thoroughly. Season with the pepper and additional salt if needed.

Stir in the reserved leek and serve hot.

Grilled Potatoes with Rosemary and Garlic

Serves 4 to 6

Two pounds may sound like a lot of potatoes, but I cook up that amount all the time, and I have never had leftovers in my family of two. The potato varieties that I prefer for grilling (and roasting) are yellow Finns, Yukon Golds, Banana fingerlings, and Purple Peruvians. How small you need to cut the potatoes depends on how large they are when whole and how hungry you are—the larger the cut, the longer the cooking time. On a perfect day, all the potatoes will be 1¹/₂ inches in diameter and need only be cut in half.

2 pounds small roasting potatoes, washed and cut (see left)
1¹/₂ teaspoons salt
2 tablespoons extra virgin olive oil
¹/₄ teaspoon freshly ground black pepper
2 or 3 rosemary, sage, or thyme sprigs
4 or 5 cloves garlic, smashed

Combine all the ingredients in a large bowl and toss well to ensure that the potatoes are well coated with oil and evenly seasoned. Lay out double the amount of foil that you need to cover the potatoes. Usually I need to seam two pieces together lengthwise to have a piece large enough. Place the potatoes on one end of the foil, and fold the other half over them. Leave yourself enough foil at the edges to double or triple roll the edges, as the packet has to be sturdy enough to keep the potatoes from sliding out when you flip it over.

Grill the packet over a medium-hot fire, turning it after 10 minutes. How long it takes to cook the potatoes depends on the heat of the grill and the size potato chunks, but 20 to 30 minutes should do. After 20 minutes, test for doneness with a bamboo skewer.

The potatoes will probably take longer than the other food you're grilling, but since they're wrapped in foil, you don't need to wait until the coals are perfect, either, so you can put them on first. Just be careful not to puncture the foil. You can move the potatoes off to the side when you want to grill other items.

Mashed Potato Pancakes with Jarlsberg Cheese

Serves 6 to 8

These are great with grilled or roasted meats and poultry. We have served them with ribs, skirt steaks, hanger steaks, and BBQ chicken.

2^1/$_2$ pounds russet potatoes (6 to 8), well scrubbed

1 or 2 scallions, white and green parts, chopped

^{3}/$_4$ cup grated Jarlsberg or Emmentaler cheese

2 tablespoons sour cream

^{1}/$_2$ teaspoon salt

^{1}/$_2$ teaspoon freshly ground black pepper

Pinch of ground cayenne pepper

1 tablespoon butter

Oil or butter for frying

Preheat the oven to 375°. Prick the potatoes all over with a fork and bake for about 1 hour, until fork tender. If you want to peel the potatoes, do it while they are still hot. Using an electric mixer fitted with the paddle attachment on low speed, or by hand with a potato masher, mash the potatoes until they are well broken up. Add the scallions, cheese, sour cream, salt, black and cayenne peppers, and 1 tablespoon butter and mix on medium speed or by hand until thoroughly combined. Allow the mixture to cool.

To make the pancakes, out ^{1}/$_2$-cup portions and, with wet hands, shape them into patties about ^{3}/$_4$ to 1 inch thick and 3 to 3^1/$_2$ inches in diameter. Heat a griddle or large sauté pan over medium-high heat and spread with oil. (A nonstick pan is great, if you have one.) Cook until golden brown, turn and cook until the second side is nicely browned. This will take 10 to 15 minutes in all, depending on how thick you've made the patties and how hot your pan is. Opt for longer and slower cooking in order to heat them through, as it guarantees a nice crisp outside crust.

Cumin Potato Salad

Serves 6

For this dish, I recommend such heirloom potatoes as Yukon Golds, Banana fingerlings, Rose Firs, and Purple Peruvians, as they have the best flavor. This dish improves if, when cooking the potatoes, you use French gray sea salt, which has a wonderful affinity for them. You can find the salt through mail-order or specialty stores. You may end up with a bit more dressing than you will need, but some batches of potatoes absorb more than others, so make the whole amount. Leftover dressing keeps well in your refrigerator and makes a good dressing for salads, a sauce for grilled fish, or a marinade for a steak before it hits the grill. This salad is great with grilled fish such as sturgeon, tuna, swordfish, or mahimahi.

5 pounds small heirloom or red potatoes, washed
Sea salt, preferably French gray sea salt
1 teaspoon cumin seeds, toasted and ground
1 red bell pepper, roasted, peeled, seeded, and chopped
1 clove garlic, minced
3 tablespoons sherry vinegar
3 tablespoons extra virgin olive oil
6 tablespoons pure olive oil
$^1/_4$ teaspoon table salt
$^1/_8$ teaspoon freshly cracked black pepper
3 scallions, white and light green parts, minced

Generously sprinkle the potatoes with sea salt and place on a steamer rack over boiling water. Cover and steam until fork tender. Allow the potatoes to cool just enough so that you can handle them, then peel, if desired, and cut into $^1/_3$-inch-thick slices. Place in a bowl.

While the potatoes are cooking, make the dressing: Combine the cumin, bell pepper, garlic, vinegar, olive oils, table salt, and pepper in a blender or food processor. Blend until smooth.

While the potatoes are still hot, toss them with enough of the dressing to coat them well. As they chill and absorb the dressing, add more as needed. Just before serving, stir in the scallions.

Erasto's Chile and Orange Black Beans

Serves 6

Served with steamed rice and warm corn tortillas and salsa, this makes a great vegetarian meal. To toast cumin seeds, shake them over a hot fire in a dry skillet (I prefer cast iron) until aromatic and lightly toasted. Dried epazote can be ordered from Penzeys Spices, but keep an eye out for epazote seeds. This herb grows like a weed; plant some and then you can have your own supply of fresh and dried epazote.

1 pound black beans ($2^{1}/_{2}$ cups), picked over and well washed
2 to 3 bay leaves
1 epazote sprig (2 to 3 inches) or 1 tablespoon dried epazote leaves or dried Mexican oregano
3 tablespoons extra virgin olive oil
$1^{1}/_{3}$ cups diced onion
3 or 4 cloves garlic, minced
1 pasilla chile or 1 Anaheim chile (if you prefer less heat), diced
1 red bell pepper, seeded and diced
Grated zest and juice of 1 orange
Grated zest and juice of $^{1}/_{2}$ lemon or lime
$^{1}/_{2}$ teaspoon cumin seeds, toasted and ground
$1^{1}/_{2}$ teaspoons red chile flakes
$^{1}/_{2}$ teaspoon freshly ground black pepper
Salt

Put the beans in a large pot and add water to cover by 3 times their depth. Add the bay leaves and epazote and bring to a boil. Skim the surface of any foam that rises and reduce the heat to low. Cover and cook for about 1 hour, until tender. Drain, reserving half of the liquid for the finished dish and discarding the rest.

Select a pot large enough to hold everything. Heat the olive oil in the pan over medium-high heat. Add the onion and garlic and sauté for 2 to 3 minutes, until translucent. Add the diced chile and bell pepper, and cook, stirring, for 5 to 8 minutes, until tender. Stir in the citrus zests, cumin, chile flakes, black pepper, and salt to taste. Add the beans and the reserved cooking liquid, stir well, and simmer for 15 to 20 minutes, adding more water as needed to keep the beans moist, tender, and slightly saucy, but not watery. Add the cirtus juices, taste for seasoning, and add salt if needed.

Crispy Black Bean-Rice Cakes

Serves 6

These crispy cakes are great with grilled fish and a simple salsa for a quick dinner. They also make a nice center point for a vegetarian meal: Surround the cakes with grilled veg-etables and serve with several of the salsas in the book. My friend and pot-tery teacher Sherry made these with garbanzo beans instead of the black beans and she liked the result—a lighter flavor and a more elegant look. You need cooked black beans for this. To cook your own, see Erasto's Chile and Orange Black Beans (page 183). If you use canned beans, you'll need two 16-ounce cans. You will have some leftover beans, which you can use in salads.

2 cups well-drained cooked black beans
³/₄ cup cooked basmati rice
¹/₂ cup finely chopped red onion
¹/₂ bunch scallions, white and a bit of the green parts, minced
1 to 1¹/₂ jalapeño chiles, minced
Leaves from ¹/₄ bunch cilantro, minced
¹/₂ teaspoon salt
¹/₄ teaspoon freshly ground black pepper
1 to 2 tablespoons butter
Sour cream
Freshly squeezed lime juice or salsa

Put half of the beans and half of the rice in a food processor and pulse several times until coarsely chopped and well mixed. Combine the onion, scallions, chiles, cilantro, salt, and pepper in a large bowl, add the processed beans and rice, and stir well. Alternatively, eliminate the food processor step and mash up everything with a potato masher or strong whisk.

To cook the cakes, scoop out ¹/₂-cup portions and, with wet hands, shape them into six patties about ³/₄ inch thick and 3 inches in diameter. Use a griddle or a heavy pan big enough to hold all the cakes and with room to get a spatula around them. Melt 1 tablespoon of the butter over medium heat. When the butter is foamy and begins to brown, add the cakes. When the bottoms are nice and crispy, flip the cakes over and cook the other side until nice and crispy, adding more butter if needed. This should take 5 to 6 minutes in all. Serve warm, topped with a dollop of sour cream and a squeeze of lime juice or salsa.

Polenta

Serves 4 to 6

Most Americans would never touch a menu item called cornmeal mush, but call it by its Italian name, polenta, and its popularity soars. Polenta makes a great side dish for meat or poultry coming off the grill, or for braised dishes with lots of gravy. It also makes an excellent vegetarian dish when prepared with vegetable stock or water and topped with Roasted Red Bell Pepper and Black Olive Relish (page 89), or grilled vegetables. You can experiment with other cheeses or combinations of cheeses if you like: Asiago or Gruyère, for instance, works well, or try the baked Stilton cheese version or the Cheddar cheese version on pages 186 and 187.

Polenta can be served soft, out of the pan, in which case it will have the consistency of mashed potatoes. You can also grill or griddle the cooked polenta (directions follow).

4 cups chicken stock (page 218), vegetable stock (page 215), or part stock and part water
1 cup milk
1 teaspoon salt
1 cup polenta
2 teaspoons minced fresh thyme
$^1/_2$ teaspoon minced fresh rosemary
$^1/_4$ cup grated Parmesan cheese
$^1/_4$ cup grated fontina cheese
Several gratings of nutmeg
$^1/_2$ teaspoon freshly ground black pepper

Combine the stock, milk, and salt in a saucepan and bring to a boil over high heat. Add the polenta in a thin stream, whisking constantly to prevent lumps. Reduce the heat to medium and cook, stirring often, for 45 to 50 minutes, until the polenta pulls away from the sides of the saucepan and is creamy and no longer gritty.

Add all the remaining ingredients, mix well, and taste for seasoning. Serve warm, one generous scoop per serving.

For grilled or griddled polenta, spread the cooked polenta out evenly on an oiled 9-inch square baking pan with 2-inch sides, cover with parchment paper or plastic wrap, and refrigerate until firm. Cut the polenta into 3-inch squares, and cut each square into two triangles. Brush both sides of each triangle with olive oil and grill for 1 to 2 minutes on the first side. Brush again on the top and turn to finish grilling for 1 to 2 minutes. The polenta should be nicely browned and crispy. You can also brown it on a lightly oiled hot griddle, 1 to 2 minutes per side.

Stilton Polenta

Serves 6

In this dish, the polenta is first cooked on the stovetop, then baked with Stilton and Asiago cheeses. This is a good way to prepare polenta in the winter; in the summer, I would probably use lighter cheeses, like a goat cheese or mascarpone mixed with some Parmesan. One of my friends, Kathy Dennett, loves to serve this topped with spicy Italian sausages.

5 cups water
1 cup polenta
2 to 3 ounces Stilton cheese, crumbled
³/₄ cup grated Asiago cheese
2 to 3 tablespoons butter
1¹/₂ teaspoons salt

Bring the water to a boil over high heat. Add the polenta in a thin stream, whisking constantly to prevent lumps. Reduce the heat to medium and cook, stirring often, for 45 to 50 minutes, until the polenta pulls away the sides of the saucepan and is creamy and no longer gritty. Mix in half of the Stilton cheese, all of the Asiago cheese, the butter, and the salt. Transfer the polenta to a baking dish.

About 20 minutes before the polenta is ready, preheat the oven to 375°. Bake the polenta for 10 to 12 minutes. Crumble the remaining Stilton over the surface, return the dish to the oven, and bake for 15 to 20 minutes until golden brown and bubbly.

To serve, cut the polenta into 6 portions. You may want to make it ahead to the point of baking it. If you refrigerate it, allow it to return to room temperature before baking.

Sharp Cheddar Polenta Cakes

Serves 6

This polenta recipe is a bit richer than other ones in this chapter, as it calls for cream plus an egg. You'll need to cook the polenta ahead of time, to give it time to cool, then pan-fry or griddle the cakes shortly before serving. These go especially well with the Liver Diablo on page 144.

4 cups water
1½ teaspoons salt
1 cup heavy whipping cream
2 tablespoons butter
1 cup polenta
½ cup grated sharp Cheddar cheese
1 egg

Combine the water, salt, cream, and 1 tablespoon of the butter in a saucepan and bring to a boil over high heat. Add the polenta in a thin stream, whisking constantly to prevent lumps. Reduce the heat to medium and cook, stirring often, for 45 to 50 minutes, until the polenta pulls away the sides of the saucepan and is creamy and no longer gritty. Remove from the heat and whisk in the Cheddar cheese and egg. Transfer the polenta to a bowl or loaf pan to cool. If cooled in a bowl, shape into 6 equal-sized cakes about ¾ to 1 inch thick and 3 to 3½ inches in diameter. If cooled in a long pan, invert onto a cutting board and cut into 6 equal slices. Keep refrigerated until needed.

Heat the remaining 1 tablespoon butter in a skillet or on a griddle over medium heat. Add the cakes and cook until golden brown on the first side. Turn and cook until golden brown on the second side and heated through. It should take about 5 to 7 minutes in all.

The cakes hold their heat fairly well and may be kept warm for 4 or 5 minutes as you finish the rest of the meal.

Steamed Basmati Rice

Serves 6

Basmati rice, a particularly fine variety of long-grain rice, originated in India but is now grown in Texas and California's Central Valley. You should be able to find it in your local markets. If you cannot, it's okay to use any other long-grain rice. Steamed rice is probably the best accompaniment for any Asian-style dish. You can also jazz the rice up, as we often do, with star anise, cinnamon stick, and cloves. Some people flavor their rice with a fresh herb sprig or lemon zest as well.

2 cups basmati rice

4 cups water

2 teaspoons salt, preferably sea salt

3 or 4 whole star anise (optional)

1/2 cinnamon stick (optional)

2 whole cloves (optional)

Rinse the rice well under cold water until the water runs clear. Place it in a saucepan with a tight-fitting lid and add the water, salt, star anise, cinnamon, and cloves. Cover and bring to a boil over high heat. Immediately reduce to the lowest possible level and let the rice "steam" for about 20 minutes, until all the water has been absorbed and the rice is tender.

Remove from the heat and fluff with a fork. Covered, it will keep warm for 20 to 30 minutes. Remove the spices before serving.

Roasted Potatoes

Serves 6

These potatoes remind me of the ones my mom used to make for all the kids, grammas, and the occasional bachelor uncle at our Sunday family suppers. Mom always peeled her potatoes, but you can leave the skins on if you'd rather.

12 small- to medium-sized yellow Finn, fingerling, or Yukon Gold potatoes

1/2 head garlic, cloves peeled and halved

3 or 4 thyme sprigs

1/2 teaspoon salt

1/2 teaspoon freshly ground black pepper

2 scant tablespoons extra virgin olive oil

Preheat the oven to 400°. Peel the potatoes, if desired, and quarter them. Combine all the ingredients in a large bowl and toss well to ensure that the potatoes are well coated with oil and evenly seasoned. Spread the potatoes out in a single layer in a roasting pan. Roast, stirring once or twice, for 40 to 50 minutes, until golden brown, crisp on the edges, and tender inside. Pick out the thyme sprigs before serving, if desired.

Wild Rice

Serves 6 to 8

When I was growing up in Minnesota, this was my favorite part of our fall family meals. My mom would begin soaking the rice when my dad, brother, and uncle left to go deer or duck hunting. As I recall, I was the only girl who had seconds of the wild game, but we all had seconds of the rice. Most people only know the long-grain wild rice, but it is actually available in three colors (black, brown, and blond) and three lengths (long, medium, and "broken"). Many different varieties are boat-harvested in Minnesota, Wisconsin, and North and South Dakota; long-grain is grown mostly in Canada, and the northernmost parts of Minnesota and North Dakota. The rice varies in processing as well as in length. Black wild rice has most of the bran layer attached and cooks in 45 to 60 minutes. Brown has some bran layer and cooks in 30 to 45 minutes. Blond has very little of the bran and cooks in 15 minutes.

2 cups long-grain brown wild rice
3 to 5 tablespoons butter
2 shallots, minced
2 tablespoons peeled and grated fresh ginger
1 carrot, minced
$^{1}/_{2}$ fennel bulb, finely minced, or 2 to 3 tablespoons chopped fennel leaves
1 cup dry white wine
6 cups chicken stock (page 218) or vegetable stock (page 215)
$1^{1}/_{2}$ to 2 teaspoons salt
1 teaspoon freshly ground black pepper
3 tablespoons chopped fresh parsley

Rinse the wild rice thoroughly in hot tap water until the water runs clear. When the rice is clean and dust-free, soak it for at least 1 hour or even as long as overnight generously covered by hot tap water. This will cause the grains of rice to swell, which makes for more even cooking. Pour off the water when it cools, and replace it with more hot water. Repeat until the water runs clear, then drain the rice.

To cook the rice, melt 3 tablespoons butter in a saucepan with a cover over medium heat. Add the shallots, ginger, carrot, and fennel and cook, stirring occasionally, for 3 minutes, until the vegetables soften. Add the rice and cook for several minutes, stirring to coat the grains with butter. Add the wine and cook until reduced. Add the stock, salt, and pepper, reduce the heat to a simmer, cover, and cook for 30 to 45 minutes, until the liquid is absorbed and the rice is tender.

Remove from the heat and fluff with 2 forks as you stir in the chopped parsley and the remaining 1 to 2 tablespoons butter. Leftover wild rice reheats quite well.

I've had a lifelong love for condiments, and running my own restaurants has given me the chance to indulge myself. Some of my experiments (like the House-Made Ketchup) have been successful, and some (like a mushroom ketchup that I try  again every few months and always end up tossing out) have not. My original plan was to make everything in house, but as we became busier, I had to give up.

We make our own pickles, mayonnaise, curry spices, barbecue sauce, and yes, off and on we have made our own mustards.

Condiments can dress up a simple cheese-toast supper or lift a meat loaf from the mundane. If you're an avid vegetable and fruit gardener, as I am, you're always looking for ways to use up that second bushel of tomatoes, peppers, or plums. Here are my favorite hits.

Roasted Garlic Aioli

Makes about 2 cups

Since the early 1980s, people have gone bonkers for any item with "roasted garlic" in its title. I do like it, but only when used with discretion and not in or on everything. Here, it adds its unmistakable flavor to an aioli that would be especially good for making garlic bread, but try it on grilled peppers or roasted potatoes or grilled fish, too. Rare roast beef sandwiches and french fries also come to mind.

1 large head roasted garlic (page 5)
2 egg yolks
1 clove garlic, mashed to a paste
Juice of 1 small lemon
$^{1}/_{4}$ cup water
$^{1}/_{4}$ teaspoon salt
Pinch of ground cayenne pepper
$1^{3}/_{4}$ cups extra virgin olive oil

Squeeze the pulp out of the roasted garlic into a food processor or blender and add the egg yolks, garlic, lemon juice, water, salt, and cayenne pepper. Purée until smooth. With the motor running, add the oil in a slow, steady stream and continue processing until emulsified.

Basil Pesto

Makes about $^{3}/_{4}$ cup

Here is a very simple way to use a whole bunch of basil, and the result has multiple uses. It is good on pasta or mashed potatoes, or to dress up a soup. Fold a little into some mayonnaise or aioli to use as a sandwich spread or to top grilled fish. Or, try working a bit of pesto into a vinaigrette for a different flavor. It's a must for the ham and cheese sandwich on page 165.

2 cups loosely packed fresh basil leaves (about 1 bunch)
4 or 5 cloves garlic
$^{1}/_{3}$ cup grated Parmesan or aged dry Jack cheese
$^{1}/_{4}$ teaspoon salt
$^{1}/_{8}$ teaspoon freshly ground black pepper
$^{1}/_{2}$ cup olive oil plus 1 to 2 tablespoons (optional)

Combine the basil, garlic, cheese, salt, and pepper in a blender or food processor and process briefly. With the motor running, add $^{1}/_{2}$ cup oil in a slow, thin stream. Continue processing until the pesto is the texture you prefer. If you plan on keeping this for a while in the refrigerator, float a tablespoon or so of oil across the surface to keep the top from turning dark, then cap tightly. It should keep until it's all used up. Serve at room temperature.

CILANTRO PESTO: Use fresh cilantro leaves in place of the basil leaves, and prepare as described above.

House-Made Ketchup

Makes about 6 cups

If you have been blessed with an abundance of tomatoes, double the recipe, as the ketchup keeps well in the refrigerator or makes a wonderful gift. It is delicious with liver and onions (page 144) or meat loaf, as well as burgers and fries. This is one of the few times it's okay to use canned tomatoes.

2 tablespoons extra virgin olive oil
1 1/2 cups diced onions
1 tablespoon minced garlic
1/4 bunch thyme
3 1/4 pounds tomatoes, peeled and diced
1/2 cup sugar
1/2 cup cider vinegar
1/4 cup tomato paste
1 bay leaf
3/4 teaspoon dry mustard powder
1/8 teaspoon ground cayenne pepper
1/4 teaspoon ground allspice
1 tablespoon salt

Heat the olive oil in a large saucepan over medium heat. Add the onions and garlic and cook, stirring occasionally, for 10 to 15 minutes, until soft. Tie the thyme sprigs up with kitchen string and toss the bundle into the pan along with all the remaining ingredients. Bring to a boil, lower the heat to a simmer, and cook stirring occasionally, for about 35 minutes, until slightly thickened. Fish out and discard the thyme, then purée the ketchup, in batches, in a blender or food processor. (Be careful when blending hot foods, and only fill the blender half full. Otherwise, whatever is inside may end up on your ceiling.)

Strain the ketchup through a medium-mesh sieve, return it to the pan, and simmer, stirring frequently, for 25 to 35 minutes, until reduced to the desired thickness. Let cool, cover tightly, and refrigerate until needed. It will keep for up to a month refrigerated.

Chinese-Style Mustard Sauce

Makes about 2 cups

This mustard sauce is delicious on grilled meats or as a dipping sauce for chicken wings. Some people swear by it as the perfect burger condiment. It's my favorite on hot dogs.

$^1/_2$ cup sugar
$^1/_4$ cup Colman's mustard powder
2 egg yolks
$^1/_2$ cup red wine vinegar
$^3/_4$ cup crème fraîche or sour cream

Put the sugar and mustard in the top of a double boiler and mix with a whisk. When well combined, whisk in the egg yolks and vinegar. Cook over simmering water, stirring occasionally, for 10 to 15 minutes, until it is thick enough to form ribbons when drizzled from the spoon. Remove from the heat and allow the mixture to cool. When cool, fold in the crème fraîche. Keep refrigerated until needed.

Lime Crème Fraîche

Makes about 1 cup

Use this quick garnish on gazpacho, tostadas, or a bowl of steaming-hot black beans. Depending on the time of year and size of your limes, you may have to double the amount of limes to get enough zest and juice to make this sufficiently flavorful.

1 cup crème fraîche
Finely grated zest and juice of 2 to 4 limes ($1^1/_2$ to 2 tablespoons juice)
Tiny pinch of salt
Tiny pinch of freshly ground black pepper

Combine all the ingredients in a small bowl, mixing well. Cover and chill until needed.

LIME SOUR CREAM: Substitute 1 cup sour cream for the crème fraîche.

Salsa Ranchera

Makes about 1 to 1½ cups

Serve this spicy salsa with any South-western-inspired dish (we use it with the grilled pasilla chiles on page 30). It would also be great with scrambled eggs and spicy black beans for a quick breakfast, or, some hot, lazy Sunday afternoon, try it with chips and guacamole and maybe a margarita. This is a good salsa to make when tomatoes are in season: Grill them in advance to give yourself a head start. If you prefer, you can roast them on the stovetop in a heavy pan. You could use the broiler, too, although the flavor would not be as good.

2 dried chipotle chiles
2 pounds tomatoes, cored
2 tablespoons extra virgin olive oil
¼ cup chopped red onion
2 teaspoons minced garlic
1 cup water
2 teaspoons fresh oregano leaves
2 tablespoons plus 2 teaspoons minced fresh cilantro
2 teaspoons champagne vinegar
1½ teaspoons salt

To prepare the chiles, stem them and remove the seeds. Toast the chiles in a dry skillet over high heat for about 2 minutes, until lightly toasted. Transfer to a bowl, add warm water to cover, and let soak for 5 to 6 minutes, until pliable.

To grill the tomatoes, put them over medium-low fire and grill, turning to color evenly, until the skins blacken. It may be a bit messy, as the tomatoes will get soft and juicy, but it shouldn't take too long, no more than about 5 minutes. To griddle them, put the tomatoes in a heavy, dry sauté pan or skillet over medium-high heat, and roast them, turning them often, until the skins are black and blistered. Allow the tomatoes to cool, then peel them.

Heat the oil in a saucepan over medium-high heat. Add the onion and garlic and sauté for 4 to 5 minutes, until golden. Add the tomatoes, chipotles, and water and simmer for 10 minutes. Remove from the heat and let cool, then transfer to a blender along with the oregano and cilantro, adding enough of the chile-soaking water to loosen the mixture. Purée until smooth and thick, but not watery. Season with the vinegar and salt, then cover and refrigerate. This salsa will keep for up to 3 days. Serve chilled or at room temperature.

Turmeric Pickles

Makes about 4 cups

These are the house-made bread-and-butter pickles we've been serving with our burgers for what seems like forever. They go great with any kind of sandwich, and if you're out of cornichons, they are pretty good chopped up in a tartar sauce. You can make these with zucchinis or with pickling cucumbers that are about 1 inch in diameter. Kirby is a good variety.

6 to 8 small (3-inch-long) zucchinis or
   12 to 16 pickling cucumbers
1 white onion
1 tablespoon kosher salt
2 cups champagne vinegar

1 cup sugar
$^1/_4$ teaspoon ground turmeric
$^1/_4$ teaspoon yellow or brown mustard seeds
$^1/_2$ teaspoon celery seeds
1 generous slice fresh ginger, peeled

Cut the zucchinis crosswise into $^1/_8$-inch-thick slices (peeling is not necessary). Slice the onion lengthwise into $^1/_8$-inch-thick slices. Place the zucchini and onion slices in a colander over a large bowl and sprinkle with the salt. Allow to sit for 2 hours. Rinse with cold water, drain, and gently squeeze dry. Transfer the slices to a large bowl.

To prepare the pickling brine, combine the vinegar and sugar in a saucepan, stirring to dissolve the sugar. Add the turmeric, mustard seeds, celery seeds, and ginger and bring to a boil. Lower the heat to a simmer and cook for 8 to 10 minutes. Remove the ginger and pour the brine over the zucchinis and onion. Place a plate on top of them to keep them submerged. Allow the pickles to sit in the brine for 24 hours before using. Keep refrigerated thereafter.

Caramelized Onions

Makes about 1$^1/_2$ cups

You can make the onions ahead and reheat them in a sauté pan. To turn them into French onion soup, deglaze the pan with 2 tablespoons brandy, cook until it has evaporated, then add 4 cups veal stock (page 219) or chicken stock (page 218) and simmer briefly. Top jumbo croutons or baguette slices with grated Jarlsburg, Parmesan, or Comté cheese, and broil until bubbly and golden brown. Float the cheese-topped breads on the soup and voila!

2 tablespoons butter
3 onions, julienned
Pinch of sugar
2 tablespoons water
$^1/_2$ teaspoon salt
$^1/_2$ teaspoon freshly ground black pepper

Heat the butter in a heavy pan over medium-low heat. Add the onions and sweat, stirring occasionally, for about 30 minutes, until soft and translucent. Add the sugar and water and continue cooking, stirring more often now, for 10 to 12 minutes, until the water has evaporated and the onions are golden brown. Season with salt and pepper.

Aioli

Makes about 1 cup

My first experience with aioli took place years ago at a grand aioli celebration on Bastille Day in Minneapolis, Minnesota. The street was closed off, and there were strolling accordion players and a band. A restaurant called New French Café, when I once worked, had set up picnic tables and loaded them with steamed salt cod, tons of steamed and raw vegetables, and huge bowls of aioli, for using as a sauce. I've been addicted ever since.

This aioli is good for general use. We use it on most of our sandwiches, for instance. But it also makes a good sauce, dip, or condiment. If you don't have time to prepare the aioli, use a good-quality mayonnaise instead. If you're not fond of garlic, leave it out. If you are fond of garlic, try the Roasted Garlic Aioli (page 194). There is also a tarragon version on page 12, and a lemon version below.

1 egg yolk
1 to 2 tablespoons ice water
2 or 3 cloves garlic, smashed into a paste
Pinch of sea salt
Tiny pinch of freshly ground black pepper
$^{1}/_{4}$ cup extra virgin olive oil
About $^{3}/_{4}$ cup pure olive oil

Combine the egg yolk, 1 tablespoon water, garlic, salt, and pepper in a bowl and whisk until thick and light. Slowly add the extra virgin olive oil in a steady stream, whisking all the while. Then whisk in as much of the pure olive oil as the egg yolk will hold. If it begins to break, add a few more drops of cold water. This can be made in a blender, too, if desired.

LEMON AIOLI: Prepare the aioli as directed. After whisking in the olive oil, whisk in 1 tablespoon freshly squeezed lemon juice and the grated zest of 1 or 2 lemons.

Avocado and Pumpkin Seed Salsa

Makes about 2 to 2¹/₂ cups

This salsa was made to go with the Grilled Beef Tenderloin con Tres Salsas (page 92) and the Morel Mushroom and Green Corn Tamales (page 24), but it is also very, very good on just about anything off the grill, including swordfish, tuna, or chicken breast, and with scrambled eggs and warm corn tortillas. I don't know why, but pasilla chiles are called poblano chiles in just about every state other than California. Look for them under either name. You will also need raw shelled pumpkin seeds, which you can find in health food stores or in Latin markets. In the latter, they may be sold as pepitas.

2 tablespoons peanut or safflower oil
¹/₂ cup pumpkin seeds
2 ripe but firm Hass avocados

VINAIGRETTE
¹/₄ cup freshly squeezed lime juice
¹/₄ teaspoon salt
Pinch of freshly ground black pepper
¹/₄ cup extra virgin olive oil

3 tablespoons minced fresh cilantro
1 tablespoon minced fresh chives
1¹/₂ tablespoons roasted, peeled, and minced pasilla chile

Heat the oil in a skillet over medium-high heat. Add the pumpkin seeds and sauté, shaking often, for about 3 minutes, until they begin to pop and smell nice and toasty. Alternatively, roast the seeds in a 375° oven, shaking the pan occasionally, for 7 to 10 minutes, until nice and toasty. Pour onto a plate and let cool.

Cut the avocados in half and remove the pits. Holding an avocado half in your hand, cut the flesh into 1-inch strips with a paring knife, being careful not to cut through the skin. Make 1/2-inch crosswise cuts, then scoop the dice out into a bowl. Repeat with the remaining avocado halves. Place in a bowl.

To make the vinaigrette, whisk together the lime juice, salt, and pepper in a small bowl until the salt is dissolved. Gradually whisk in the olive oil, and continue to whisk until fully emulsified.

Pour the vinaigrette over the avocados. Add the cilantro, chives, pumpkin seeds, and chile and mix gently so as not to break up the avocado. You don't want to make guacamole.

Mango Salsa

Makes about 2 to 2¹/₂ cups

Serve this salsa on all kinds of grilled poultry and on BBQ pork, or use it to dress up a vegetarian menu of black beans and rice. It is a good one with which to experiment. If mangoes are unavailable, ripe papaya or pineapple may be substituted. If you don't have lime juice, try rice vinegar or champagne vinegar instead. And if you don't care for cilantro, chervil or chives would be nice.

1 red bell pepper, roasted, peeled, seeded, and minced
1 jalapeño chile, roasted, peeled, seeded (if desired), and minced
2 ripe mangoes, peeled, pitted, and diced
1 tablespoon minced red onion
1¹/₂ tablespoons minced fresh cilantro
1 tablespoon minced fresh mint
2 tablespoons minced scallions, white and 2 inches of the green parts
¹/₂ teaspoon red chile flakes
1 tablespoon freshly squeezed lime juice
3 tablespoons extra virgin olive oil

Combine all the ingredients in a bowl and mix gently to keep from smashing the mangoes. Cover and refrigerate for up to 2 days. Do not keep longer, as the fruit will get mushy. Serve chilled.

Black Olive Relish

Makes about ³/₄ cup

You could use kalamata or niçoise olives for this, but my personal favorite are oil-cured black olives. They look all shriveled up, but their flavor is both intense and sweet. This relish goes with the grilled tuna sandwich (page 154).

¹/₂ cup oil-cured black olives, minced
¹/₄ cup extra virgin olive oil
¹/₄ cup minced fresh parsley
1¹/₂ teaspoons freshly squeezed lemon juice
¹/₈ teaspoon freshly ground black pepper

Combine all the ingredients in a small bowl and mix well. The relish can be stored, covered, in the refrigerator for up to 4 weeks.

Tomato Chutney

Makes about 4 cups

We thin this chutney with a little rice vinegar and olive oil, and use it as a sauce for the Curry Chicken Skewers (page 6). It also goes with grilled lamb chops, or swirl some into a beef stew or braised lamb shanks. Or, toast a slab of good bread, spread with cream cheese and then a generous layer of this chutney. Makes a perfect snack.

$^1/_4$ teaspoon fenugreek seeds
$^1/_4$ teaspoon cumin seeds
$^1/_4$ teaspoon fennel seeds
$^1/_4$ teaspoon aniseeds
3 tablespoons extra virgin olive oil
$^1/_4$ teaspoon brown mustard seeds
6 cloves garlic, minced into a fine paste

$^3/_4$ cup red wine vinegar
$^3/_4$ cup cider vinegar
$1^1/_2$ cups sugar
2 pounds tomatoes, peeled, seeded, drained, and coarsely chopped
3 tablespoons raisins
$1^1/_2$ teaspoons salt

Combine the fenugreek seeds, cumin seeds, fennel seeds, and aniseeds in a small bowl, mixing well. With all the ingredients at hand, heat the olive oil in a deep saucepan over medium heat. Add the mustard seeds and cook until they begin to pop. (Cover the pan if you're the nervous sort.) Add the garlic and cook for 1 minute, then add the bowl of combined seeds. Cook for 30 seconds or so, until aromatic. Add the vinegars, sugar, tomatoes, raisins, and salt, and bring to the boil. Lower the heat and simmer for 40 minutes to 1 hour, until the chutney is thick, dark, and unctuous. Let cool and store tightly covered in the refrigerator for up to 1 month. Serve chilled.

Mint-Tarragon Pesto

Makes about 2 cups

We use this on our mushroom burger (page 151), but it's also quite nice on grilled swordfish or lamb chops. Ig Vella, a Sonoma cheesemaker extraordinaire, makes a great aged dry Jack under the Bear Flag label. He coats it with cocoa, black pepper, and oil and ages it 3 years to develop a rich, nutty taste.

$^3/_4$ cup loosely packed fresh mint leaves (about $^1/_2$ bunch)
$^3/_4$ cup loosely packed fresh tarragon leaves (about $^1/_2$ bunch)
6 to 8 cloves garlic, smashed
$^3/_4$ cup pure olive oil
$^1/_2$ cup grated aged dry Jack or Parmesan cheese
Salt
Extra virgin olive oil for coating surface (optional)

Combine the mint, tarragon, garlic, pure olive oil, and cheese in a blender or food processor and blend until smooth. Taste and add salt if needed (this will depend on the saltiness of the cheese). If you plan to keep this for a while in the refrigerator, float a tablespoon or so of olive oil across the top to keep the surface from turning dark, then cap tightly. It should keep until it's all used up. Serve at room temperature.

Tomato and Apricot Chutney

Makes about 3 cups

I love this smeared all over a nice juicy cheeseburger or, even better, a lamb burger. Thinned with a bit of stock, it also makes a great topping for meat loaf, and it takes the Smoked Ham and Jarlsberg Cheese Sandwich (page 165) to world-class status. I think that Robert Cubberly developed this chutney when he was chef at Fog City Diner.

2¹/₂ tablespoons extra virgin olive oil
1¹/₂ tablespoons peeled and grated fresh ginger
³/₄ teaspoon red chile flakes
³/₄ teaspoon brown mustard seeds
¹/₄ teaspoon ground cumin
¹/₄ teaspoon fennel or cardamom seeds
¹/₈ teaspoon fenugreek seeds

2¹/₄ pounds tomatoes, peeled and chopped
9 cloves garlic, smashed into a paste
¹/₃ cup sugar
1¹/₂ teaspoons salt
2 or 3 jalapeños chiles
9 dried apricots, diced

Heat the olive oil in a large saucepan over medium-high heat. Add the ginger and cook for 1 minute. Add the chile flakes, mustard seeds, cumin, fennel seeds, and fenugreek seeds and stir for a few seconds. Stir in the tomatoes, garlic, sugar, and salt. Bring to a boil, lower the heat, and simmer, stirring occasionally, for 25 to 30 minutes, until the mixture starts to thicken.

Cut a slit in the side of each jalapeño (use only 2 chiles if you do not want the chutney as hot), then add them and the apricots to the pan. Simmer, stirring frequently, for 15 to 20 minutes more, until the mixture is jamlike. I like to remove the jalapeños after the chutney has finished cooking, and serve them on the side later. Those of you who like more spice might want to try this. Store tightly covered in the refrigerator for up to 1 month. Serve chilled.

Smoked Tomatoes

Makes 2 to 3 cups

Simple to make, delicious to eat. Try some tucked into scrambled eggs, stirred into a salsa, or smashed on a grilled steak with some Gorgonzola and caramelized onions. They keep refrigerated for several days for use later in the week. Try half a batch with the cumin and half without, to see which you like best.

4 pounds ripe plum tomatoes, cut in half
2 tablespoons extra virgin olive oil
1 teaspoon ground toasted cumin
   (optional)

2 teaspoons salt
Freshly ground black pepper

Put the tomatoes in a large bowl, add all the remaining ingredients, and toss gently until mixed but not broken up. Lay the tomatoes cut-side up on a rack or mesh square. Put them in the smoker or on the grill and close the lid (if you don't have a covered grill, make a tent with some foil for a temporary cover). On dying coals, I would toss in some fresh rosemary or thyme to get the embers smoldering, and smoke the tomatoes for 45 minutes to 1 hour. On a hot fire, I would add fresh chips or green wood and smoke the tomatoes for 20 to 30 minutes. Depending on the heat, the tomatoes will reduce somewhat as their juices evaporate. They should be smoky smelling and somewhat caramelized, slightly shriveled, and have nicely blackened edges.

Cool the tomatoes enough so that they are easy to handle, then peel off the skins. Use them as they are or dice them up for sauces, soups, or whatever you fancy.

Onion Jam

Makes about 1 cup

This versatile jam can be made ahead and kept in the refrigerator for up to 2 weeks. I've often swirled a couple of tablespoons into a red wine steak sauce to enrich it, tucked it between the ham and cheese in a grilled sandwich, or spread some over just-grilled chicken breasts. It looks best if you use large onions and cut them lengthwise into $1/4$-inch wedges, rather than rings.

1 tablespoon extra virgin olive oil
2 cups sliced onions
2 tablespoons sugar
$1/2$ teaspoon soy sauce
2 tablespoons balsamic vinegar
2 tablespoons red wine
2 tablespoons water

Heat the olive oil in a skillet over medium heat. Add the onions and cook for 5 to 8 minutes, until tender and translucent. Add the sugar and cook, stirring occasionally, for 15 to 20 minutes, until golden brown. Add all the remaining ingredients and cook, stirring often to avoid scorching, for 20 minutes or so, until thick and jamlike. The slower you cook it, the richer the jam will become. Store tightly covered in the refrigerator for up to 1 week. Serve chilled.

Ginger Butter

Makes about $1/3$ cup

Serve this butter on baked potatoes, grilled tuna, swordfish, chicken breasts, and steaks—the possibilities are endless. Make extra and have it on hand. If you can find young ginger, which has a very thin skin and is pink around the edges, use it. It has a sweeter and brighter flavor, more juice, and less fiber than standard fresh ginger.

6 tablespoons butter, at room temperature
$2^1/2$ to 3 tablespoons peeled and grated fresh ginger
1 small clove garlic, minced
$1/2$ shallot, minced
$1/4$ teaspoon salt
$1/8$ teaspoon freshly ground black pepper

Combine all the ingredients in a bowl and mix with an electric mixer, or by hand with a fork or wooden spoon, until thoroughly combined. To serve, heat gently in a small pan just enough to melt it without browning it. Refrigerate any leftovers.

Eggplant Relish

Makes about 1¹/₂ cups

You can use any kind of eggplant for this relish, but I find that the slender Chinese type, which has light purple skin, is less bitter than globe or Japanese eggplant, both of which have dark purple skin. Chinese eggplants are so mild, in fact, that you can almost eat them raw. We serve this peppery relish with the Curry Chicken Skewers (page 6), but I also like it with a simple grilled chicken breast or spread on grilled bread, as an appetizer (drizzle a little olive oil on the bread before grilling). The eggplants need to be grilled, so plan ahead: Next time you fire up the grill for another meal, throw some eggplants on and make the relish for another day. It will keep for at least 1 week.

EGGPLANT
3 or 4 Chinese eggplants
Pure olive oil for brushing
Salt and freshly ground black pepper

VINAIGRETTE
3 tablespoons rice vinegar
1¹/₂ teaspoons minced garlic
2 teaspoons salt
1 tablespoon freshly cracked black
    pepper
6 tablespoons extra virgin olive oil

3 tablespoons minced fresh parsley
2 tablespoons minced scallions

To prepare the eggplants, cut them in half lengthwise and score a crosshatch pattern on the cut surfaces. Brush with pure olive oil and sprinkle with salt and pepper. Grill over medium coals, turning once, until tender throughout and nicely caramelized. It should take about 1 or 2 minutes per side depending on how hot the fire is. Cut the eggplant into small dice.

To make the vinaigrette, whisk together the vinegar, garlic, salt, and pepper in a small bowl until the salt is dissolved. Gradually whisk in the extra virgin olive oil, and continue to whisk until fully emulsified.

Combine the eggplant, parsley, and scallions in a bowl and toss with just enough vinaigrette to coat liberally. The relish can be made ahead and refrigerated, but be sure to bring it to room temperature before serving.

Thyme and Parsley Beurre Blanc

Makes about 1¹/₂ cup

*A beurre blanc is a simple white but-
ter-and-wine sauce, ideal for serving
with fish, chicken, or vegetables. It
will hold for up to an hour while you
are preparing the rest of your meal.
When I'm cooking at home, I keep
my beurre blanc hot in one of those
large, insulated coffee cups that are so
popular now.*

2 shallots, minced
¹/₄ cup champagne or rice vinegar
¹/₄ cup dry white wine
6 black peppercorns
1 bay leaf
1¹/₂ cups butter, at room temperature, diced
Pinch of salt
Pinch of freshly ground black pepper
2 teaspoons minced fresh thyme
1 tablespoon minced fresh parsley

Put the shallots, vinegar, and white wine in a blender and blend until smooth. Pour into a nonreactive saucepan and add the peppercorns and the bay leaf. Cook over high heat for about 5 minutes,
until most of the liquid has evaporated and you have a thick paste of shallots.

Over very low heat, or off the heat, whisk in the butter, bit by bit, until all of it has been absorbed.
(I go back and forth between having the pan on a burner and not, but it's probably safer off the
heat, because if you let the sauce come to a boil, the butter will separate.) Strain the sauce through a
fine-mesh sieve and season with the salt and pepper. Keep warm over the lowest possible heat or
in a thermos. Just before serving, strain out bay leaf, and then stir in the thyme and parsley.

COARSE-GRAIN MUSTARD BEURRE BLANC: Proceed as directed, omitting the peppercorns, thyme,
and parsley. Stir 2 tablespoons coarse-grain mustard into the sauce after it has been strained.

Erasto's Oaxacan Mole

Makes about 4 cups

Moles, which have complex, rich flavors, are usually poured over poached chicken or meats, but they are also good with grilled rabbit. Prepare the mole a couple of days ahead, as its flavor seems to improve with a little age.

Many years ago, my English friend Sara Kemp was dining at Mustards and saw the mole on the menu. She asked her dining companion how we cooked the moles. Were they babies? Were they fried? Her friend laughed so hard he almost fell on the floor.

2 tablespoons white sesame seeds

3 corn tortillas

2 or 3 dried chiles negros

5 ancho chiles

$^{1}/_{4}$ cup peanut oil

1 apple, cored and diced

$^{1}/_{2}$ banana, peeled and chopped

$^{1}/_{3}$ large onion, diced

2 cloves garlic

1 plum tomato, quartered

6 oregano sprigs

1 or 2 allspice berries

$^{1}/_{4}$ cup golden raisins

2 to $2^{1}/_{2}$ cups chicken stock (page 218)

$1^{1}/_{2}$ ounces semisweet or Mexican chocolate, chopped

Preheat the oven to 350°. Toast the sesame seeds in a small, dry skillet over medium heat, tossing constantly, for 3 minutes, until golden and aromatic. Grind the sesame seeds in a blender or spice grinder to a fine powder and set aside. Toast the tortillas in the oven, directly on the rack, for 7 to 8 minutes, until golden brown and crisp, then crumble them and set aside.

To prepare the chiles, remove the stems, then split them open and remove the seeds and membranes. Place the chiles on a baking sheet and toast in the oven for 3 to 5 minutes, until fragrant. Do not let them darken too much, or the sauce will be bitter. Soak the chiles in warm water to cover for 5 to 10 minutes, until soft and pliable. Combine the chiles and their soaking liquid in a blender and purée until smooth. Set aside.

Heat the peanut oil in a saucepan over high heat until almost smoking. Add the apple and cook, stirring for 4 to 5 minutes, until caramelized. Add the banana, and continue to cook until the banana is golden brown on all sides. Next add the onion and garlic and cook until golden brown. Add the tomato, puréed chiles, ground sesame seeds, oregano, allspice, and raisins and stir for 1 minute. Add the stock and crumbled tortillas and bring to a boil. Lower the heat to a simmer and cook for 15 to 20 minutes, until thick. Add the chocolate and stir until melted.

Transfer the mixture to a blender and purée until smooth. Strain through a fine-mesh sieve. The mole can be made up to a day ahead. Reheat gently to avoid scorching the chocolate.

My editor tried to get me to lump all the recipes in this chapter in with the condiments and sauces, but I resisted because these odd little numbers have earned their own place. I guess you might call them basics—they certainly are basic to me and essential to my cooking—although some would find it a curious collection of odds and ends. I certainly don't think home cooks need to make everything from

scratch the way we do in the restaurant, but once you make your own croutons or stock, for example, the store-bought ones will never again seem good enough. For many of these recipes, do what I do when I'm cooking at home: Make a double batch and store the extra. A freezer full of homemade stock or a jar of hand-mixed curry paste tucked away in the 'fridge is like money in the bank.

Those Nuts

Makes 2 cups

My Uncle John had a nut-roasting company, and when we were kids, he always gave us pistachios for Christmas. They were wonderful, but these candied pistachios are even better. We use them as garnishes on many of our salads and sometimes on desserts. Although the recipe calls for pistachios, almonds, pecans, peanuts, and walnuts are also fantastic done this way. Don't try it with Brazil nuts, cashews, or macadamia nuts, though. They have a higher oil content and, consequently, go rancid quickly.

2 cups raw shelled pistachios
$^{1}/_{2}$ cup confectioners' sugar
Peanut oil or vegetable oil for deep-frying
Sea salt
Ground cayenne pepper

Blanch the nuts in boiling water for 2 minutes. Drain and toss immediately with the confectioners' sugar, mixing well to coat the nuts evenly.

Pour the oil into a deep, heavy pan to a depth of 1 to $1^{1}/_{2}$ inches and heat to 375°. Add the nuts in batches, and fry for 1 or 2 minutes, until crisp and golden brown.

Using a slotted spoon, transfer the nuts to a rack or fine-mesh screen to drain (don't use paper towels or the pistachios will stick!). Allow the oil to come back to temperature between batches.

Sprinkle the nuts with salt and cayenne to taste while still hot. Now, see if you can keep from eating them all up before company comes.

Croutons

About 1 dozen

Croutons can really be any shape or size you like—in my book, that's what makes the handmade ones so irresistible.

Preheat the oven to 375°. Cut a baguette on the diagonal into $^{1}/_{4}$-inch-thick slices. For extra-large croutons, cut the bread at a severe angle. Brush the slices with the olive oil. Bake for 10 to 12 minutes, until golden brown.

BLUE CHEESE CROUTONS: In a small bowl, mix together 3 ounces Maytag blue or Roquefort cheese, 2 tablespoons butter, a pinch of salt, and a pinch of freshly ground black pepper. Prepare the croutons as described above, then spread the blue cheese mixture on them as they come out of the oven. The mixture can be made ahead and kept refrigerated, but remove it in time to soften, so that you can spread it without breaking the croutons.

Curry Paste

Makes about ¹/₂ cup

The first step in making a curry paste is to make a curry powder, a blend of chiles and toasted spices. The curry powder is then fried in a neutral oil until it is aromatic and bubbling. I use a combination of small, fiery-hot dried chiles in this blend. If you want your curry paste hot, include the seeds of the chiles; if not, remove them. Stored covered and in the refrigerator, the curry paste will keep indefinitely.

15 dried árbol, cayenne, or dundicut chiles, stemmed

4 white cardamom pods

6 tablespoons coriander seeds

4 tablespoons cumin seeds

3-inch piece cinnamon stick

1 tablespoon black peppercorns

1¹/₂ teaspoons whole cloves

1¹/₂ teaspoons fenugreek seeds

4 allspice berries

3 tablespoons turmeric powder

2 tablespoons grated fresh ginger

¹/₂ cup peanut oil or safflower oil

Toast the chiles in a dry skillet over high heat for about 2 minutes, until lightly toasted. Set them aside. In single-layer batches, toast the whole spices (the next eight ingredients) by shaking them in the skillet over high heat until aromatic.

Put the toasted spices and the chiles together in a coffee grinder, spice grinder, or blender and process them to a fine powder, or smash them with gusto in a mortar and pestle. Stir in the turmeric powder and the ginger.

Heat the oil in a skillet over medium heat until almost smoking. Add the curry powder and cook, stirring, for 2 to 3 minutes, until fragrant, bubbling, and thick. Let cool before using. Keep any extra refrigerated.

House-Made BBQ Spice

Makes about 1¹/₂ cups

This BBQ spice is used in our BBQ sauce for baby back ribs (page 112). It is also very good on burgers, chicken breast, french fries, and pop-corn. Heck, make a lot and use it as holiday gifts. If you can't find the ancho and New Mexico powders, you can substitute any pure chile powder.

¹/₂ cup firmly packed light brown sugar

2 tablespoons salt

2 tablespoons celery seeds

2 tablespoons garlic powder

2 tablespoons paprika

1¹/₂ teaspoons New Mexico chile powder

1¹/₂ teaspoons ancho chile powder

5 teaspoons freshly ground black pepper

5 teaspoons freshly ground white pepper

1¹/₂ teaspoons ground cayenne pepper

¹/₂ teaspoon ground cloves

¹/₄ teaspoon ground cumin

¹/₄ teaspoon dried marjoram

¹/₄ teaspoon dried oregano

¹/₄ teaspoon freshly grated nutmeg

¹/₄ teaspoon dry mustard powder

¹/₄ teaspoon ground coriander

Combine all the ingredients and mix well. Run the mixture through a coarse-mesh sieve several times for an even mix. Keep dry in a tightly closed container.

Mustards' Secret Coating

Makes about 1¹/₂ cups

This coating gives a nice crispy finish to deep-fried soft-shell crabs and cala-mari. Try it on shrimp, too, and on squash blossoms.

¹/₂ cup all-purpose flour
¹/₂ cup cornstarch
¹/₄ cup semolina flour
2 tablespoons cornmeal
³/₄ teaspoon toasted and ground cumin seeds
³/₄ teaspoon salt
¹/₂ teaspoon freshly ground black pepper

Sift together all the ingredients into a bowl large enough to use for coating the foods.

Madeira-Herb Marinade

Makes about 1¹/₄ cups

I learned how to make this marinade from Bruce Le Favour, one of my favorite chefs. It's a very tasty indeed, wonderful on rabbit, chicken, Cor-nish game hens, and squab. Use the marinade soon after making it, as the brightness of the herbs dissipates when stored.

3 tablespoons finely chopped fresh parsley
2 tablespoons finely chopped fresh chives
1 tablespoon finely chopped fresh chervil
2 small shallots, finely chopped
2 tablespoons brandy
6 tablespoons Madeira
6 tablespoons extra virgin olive oil
¹/₂ teaspoon salt
¹/₂ teaspoon freshly ground black pepper

Combine all the ingredients in a bowl. Pour it over the prepared poultry or rabbit, making sure everything is well coated and turning occasionally to distribute the flavors evenly.

Fresh Pasta

About 1 pound fresh pasta

This dough is quick to make and produces a very tender dough. You can use it to make pasta sheets for ravioli, or any size flat pasta noodles. Let the leftovers dry on baking sheets and store them for another meal. Even little scraps are good: Dry them, too, then toss some into a rich chicken broth with fresh ginger and basil for a great quick lunch. Note: Even "dried" homemade pasta cooks up in 2 or 3 minutes, so keep an eye on it.

3 cups all-purpose flour, plus extra for rolling out the pasta
Pinch of salt

2 jumbo eggs
6 jumbo egg yolks
2 tablespoons extra virgin olive oil

Combine the flour and salt in a large bowl. Make a well or bowl-shaped indentation in the center. Mix the eggs, egg yolks, and oil together in a small bowl, and pour the mixture into the well. Stir to combine, turn the dough out onto a smooth, cool surface, and knead for about 2 to 3 minutes, just until smooth. Cover the dough with a damp kitchen towel and let it rest for 1 to 1½ hours.

Roll the dough through a pasta machine according to the manufacturer's instructions, dusting it with flour as needed. For ravioli, keep rolling the dough until you get it to the thinnest setting that doesn't tear the sheet. For noodles, you may want to stop one notch sooner. If you will be rolling the dough out by hand, you may want to add a tablespoon or two of water to the dough to make working with it easier. It depends on the eggs and flour you use; with smaller eggs or very dry flour, you may need the water, but don't increase the oil.

Vegetable Stock

Makes about 4 quarts

You can alter the ingredients as the season or your supplies dictate, but this seems to be the best overall combination. I always cook all my stocks uncovered, which makes it easier to skim off the impurities that rise to the surface. It's important to skim frequently as the stock is cooking, or the impurities will cook back into the stock, making it cloudy.

1 tablespoon extra virgin olive oil
3 onions, chopped
3 carrots, chopped
2 celery stalks, chopped
5 cloves garlic, smashed
1 cup chopped cabbage
1 head romaine lettuce, chopped
1 leek, white part and small amount of green, chopped

1 potato, peeled and chopped
2 tomatoes, chopped
Several parsley sprigs
Several thyme sprigs
Several basil or sage sprigs
1 tablespoon freshly cracked black pepper
1 teaspoon salt
6 to 8 quarts cold water

Heat the oil in a stockpot over medium heat. Add the onions, carrots, celery, and garlic and cook, stirring occasionally, for 8 to 10 minutes, until caramelized. If your pot is on the small side, you may want to brown the vegetables in several batches so you don't end up steaming them. Add all the remaining ingredients and bring to a boil. Reduce the heat to a simmer and cook, skimming often, for 45 minutes to 1 hour. Strain through a fine-mesh sieve and chill until needed.

Light Chicken Stock

Makes 4 to 6 quarts

The two most important steps in making a good stock are to begin with cold water and to skim often. If at all possible, include some chicken feet in the stock. They will add flavor and richness. Chinese and Latin American markets are great sources for chicken feet, but most butchers can get them for you with some advance warning. If you can't get chicken feet, turkey wings will also make a difference. You don't need to separate and peel the garlic cloves for the stock. Just break the head of garlic in half as best you can, pull off any loose skin, and give the garlic a good whack with the flat of your knife.

3 to 5 pounds chicken bones, including feet and some meatier bones if possible
Water
2 carrots, chopped
2 to 3 celery stalks, chopped
1/2 head garlic, loose skin removed and cloves cracked open
1 large onion, chopped
2 whole cloves, stuck into 2 of the onion pieces
3 bay leaves
1/4 bunch parsley, stems only
3 or 4 thyme sprigs
1 tablespoon black peppercorns

Remove as much visible fat from the bones as possible. Place the bones in a stockpot and add cold water to cover. Bring to a full rolling boil, skimming off any foam as it rises to the surface. Add all the remaining ingredients and reduce the heat to a simmer. Simmer uncovered, skimming as needed, for 3 hours. Strain through a fine-mesh sieve and reduce further, if desired, for storage.

DARK CHICKEN STOCK: To make a dark stock, preheat the oven to 400°. Place the bones in a roasting pan large enough to allow you to stir them and roast for 30 to 40 minutes until very brown. Turn the bones occasionally to ensure that they all are evenly browned. Transfer the bones to a stockpot, leaving the fat in the roasting pan. Put the carrots, celery, garlic, and onion in the roasting pan and stir to coat with the fat. (If you want to add more color to the stock, leave the onion skin on, but cut off the roots, which can be bitter.) Roast the vegetables, stirring occasionally, for 15 to 20 minutes, until golden brown. Using a slotted spoon, transfer the vegetables to the stockpot, draining off as much fat as you can. Add the herbs and spices and finish cooking as described above.

DUCK STOCK: Proceed as directed for the dark chicken stock, substituting duck bones and feet for the chicken.

RABBIT STOCK: Proceed as directed for the dark chicken stock, substituting rabbit bones for all or part of the chicken bones.

GAME STOCK: The bones of wild game birds make the most flavorful stocks, so befriend a hunter. Proceed as directed for dark chicken stock, substituting the bones of the game birds for the chicken.

Veal Stock

Makes about 6 quarts

When choosing the bones for stock, get a few meaty ones, as they will produce a richer stock. If you can get a calf's foot, it will increase the gelatin quality of your stock. Just have your butcher split it and cut it crosswise into manageable-sized pieces. People often fail to roast their bones and vegetables long enough, ending up with a light, somewhat brothy stock, which is fine as long as you're not trying to make French onion soup. If you want to impart a nice rich color to the stock, use yellow onions and leave the skins on (trim off the roots, though, as they will make the stock bitter). If you are going to reduce the stock to a concentrate, or at least to double strength for easier storage, strain it first, then reduce it quickly over high heat, skimming thoroughly as it reduces.

5 pounds veal shank bones, cut into 2- to 3-inch pieces
2 onions, skins on and roots trimmed off, chopped
3 carrots, chopped
2 to 3 celery stalks, chopped
1/2 head garlic, loose skin removed and cloves cracked open
2 tablespoons tomato paste
1/2 cup dry red wine
8 quarts cold water
1 or 2 bay leaves
1/2 bunch thyme
2 whole cloves
1 tablespoon black peppercorns

Preheat the oven to 400°. Place the bones in a roasting pan large enough to allow you to stir them and roast for 30 to 45 minutes, until very dark brown. Turn the bones occasionally to ensure that they all are evenly browned. Add the onions, carrots, celery, and garlic and roast for 30 to 40 minutes more, until they are nicely caramelized. (If you want to add more color to the stock, leave the onion skin on, but cut off the roots, which can be bitter.) Stir in the tomato paste and roast for 10 to 15 minutes more, stirring as you go. Transfer the bones and vegetables to a stockpot. Drain off any fat in the bottom of the pan.

Place the roasting pan on the stovetop over high heat, add the wine, and deglaze the pan, scraping up all the golden brown bits that are clinging to the bottom. Scrape all this into the stockpot. Add the water and bring to a boil, skimming off any impurities that rise to the surface. Toss in the bay leaves, thyme, cloves, and peppercorns, reduce the heat to a simmer, and cook uncovered, skimming frequently, for 5 to 6 hours. Strain through a fine-mesh sieve and reduce further, if desired, for storage.

Corn Stock

Makes about 4 quarts

This is the quickest and most flavor-ful vegetable stock around. So don't serve corn on the cob; instead, cut the kernels off and cook them separately, then use the corn cobs as the "bones" for a stock.

6 to 10 corn cobs (save kernels for something else)
1 onion, chopped
1 leek, white part only
2 cloves garlic

1 whole clove
2 thyme sprigs
4 quarts cold water

Combine all the ingredients in a stockpot and bring to a boil. Reduce the heat to a simmer and cook, skimming often, for 45 minutes. Taste and, if flavorful, remove from the heat and strain through a fine-mesh sieve. If the flavor is not strong enough for you, continue cooking for an additional 15 to 20 minutes before straining.

Mushroom Stock

Makes about 1¹/₂ quarts

This is a great vegetarian stock which can be made vegan by sautéing the vegetables in olive oil or vegetable oil.

2 to 3 tablespoons butter
1 onion, diced
¹/₂ head garlic, loose skin
   removed and cloves cracked
2 or 3 carrots, diced
1 or 2 parsnips, peeled and diced (optional)

2 pounds fresh mushrooms and trimmings,
   carefully cleaned
1 ounce dried mushrooms
6 to 8 thyme sprigs
6 to 8 parsley stems
Water
1¹/₂ teaspoons peppercorns

Melt the butter in a stockpot over medium-low heat. Add the onion, garlic, carrots, and parsnips and sweat, stirring often, for 8 to 10 minutes. Add the mushrooms and cook, stirring, for 1 or 2 minutes more. Add the thyme, parsley, and cold water to cover. Increase the heat to medium-high and bring to a boil, skimming off any impurities that rise to the surface. Reduce the heat to medium-low, add the peppercorns, and simmer, skimming frequently, for 1 hour. Taste and simmer for an additional 30 minutes or so, until reduced and flavorful. Strain through a fine-mesh sieve.

Fish Stock

Makes about 3 quarts

I like to use bones from the least oily white fish, such as sole, cod, halibut, sturgeon, or monkfish. Tuna, salmon, and mahimahi are too strong, unless that's what you're serving anyway. Salmon, for instance, would make a nice stock for a salmon chowder. You may also use fish heads (gills removed) and tails and/or shrimp, crab, or lobster shells. The shellfish shells produce a stronger stock, which is interchangeable for the fish stock. Be sure to simmer this stock over a very low heat, and avoid stirring it, or it will turn cloudy.

3 pounds fish bones
$^1/_4$ cup butter
2 onions, diced
3 or 4 cloves garlic
2 leeks, white and small amount of green, chopped
2 cups dry white wine
Water
2 or 3 thyme sprigs
2 or 3 bay leaves
3 or 4 parsley stems

Rinse the bones of any blood or scales, and break or chop them up into manageable-sized pieces. Melt the butter in a large stockpot over low heat. Add the onions, garlic, and leeks and cook, stirring occasionally, for 10 to 15 minutes, until tender. Be careful not to brown the vegetables. Add the fish bones and cook, stirring, for 3 to 5 minutes, until the bones are opaque and no longer look raw. Again, do not allow to brown. Add the wine, increase the heat to high, and bring to a boil. Immediately reduce the heat and simmer, skimming frequently, until reduced by half. This will take 10 minutes.

Add enough cold water to cover by 2 inches, then increase the heat again until bubbles just begin to break the surface. Reduce the heat to medium-low, skim the stock, and add all the remaining ingredients. Simmer gently for 1 hour, then taste for flavor. If necessary, continue to simmer for another 15 to 30 minutes to intensify the flavor. Turn off the heat and let the stock sit for 10 to 15 minutes to cool and settle. You could add 1 cup of ice to help it along.

Skim once more, then transfer the stock to a storage container, carefully ladling it from the top and disturbing it as little as possible to keep the broth from getting cloudy. Fish stock will not keep long, so refrigerate it and use it within a day, or freeze it for future use.

Desserts

I've never been one of those "Oh, I'll just have some fresh fruit for dessert" people. Chocolate cake? Boysenberry pie? Vanilla ice cream? Boysenberry pie with vanilla ice cream? I'll take it! As a child I coveted those other-worldly desserts on the pages of *Good Housekeeping* and the Softasilk cake flour box—perfectly textured, mile-high layer cakes with mounds of white frosting, flaky-crusted wedges of juicy apple pie, delectable cookies whose chocolate chips seemed to have been organized by some higher power.

The desserts at Mustards aren't always so symmetrical or organized, but they are always products of the best ingredients— the freshest seasonal fruits, delicious butter, silky Belgian chocolate, exotic vanilla beans. In summer, it's peach and berry cobblers; in the fall, we bake apple tarts; come winter, citrus puddings reign; and when spring arrives, so do the strawberry shortcakes. You can tell what season it is by what's on our specials board. There's always an option for the chocoholics among us, too, as well as smooth, fruity sorbets for a slightly more virtuous finale.

We're quite spoiled here in Northern California with our ideal growing climate and convenient access to organic produce from some of the best growers in the country. At Mustards, I can take full advantage of the eight or so tangerine varieties from the Central Valley, the juicy, marble-sized Sebastopol blueberries, and fresh Italian prunes that grow on the trees right in Mustards' garden. But I realize that not every part of the country is as fortunate, so I've tried to adapt these dessert recipes to ingredients that can be found in stores nationwide. A good indicator of what should be the starring fruit in your dessert is what is cheapest and most plentiful at the market. If, in December, you discover that strawberries are $4.99 a pint, and appear to be suffering jet lag from their recent flight from New Zealand, perhaps a poached pear would be a more appropriate choice for dessert. Frozen fruits, such as blueberries and raspberries, are acceptable substitutes for fresh, particularly if they are going to end up in a sauce. But you will be happier with your desserts if you are using the ripest and freshest fruit in season.

Other standard dessert ingredients, such as eggs, butter, and chocolate, can vary widely and therefore affect your results markedly. Using high-quality ingredients will generally produce better desserts, and I encourage trying different brands of basic ingredients in your quest for the best-tasting and best-behaving ones. You will have better results if you use the following guidelines in choosing your ingredients for these recipes.

Ingredients

BUTTER: Unsalted butter is specified for all the dessert recipes in this book. It is generally better for baking since salted butter can be too salty for baked goods. Margarine should not be substituted for pure sweet dairy-cream butter, as its taste and texture are unacceptable.

CHOCOLATE: European chocolate is, in general, of a higher quality than most American chocolates, owing to strict, often government-controlled production standards. Good-quality Belgian, Swiss, Italian, or French chocolate is made with cocoa butter and is of a silky grain, while many American brands are made with other tropical oils (coconut or palm) and are noticeably coarser. European brands to look for in your supermarket's imported food section, or at your local gourmet shop, are Lindt (Swiss), Callebaut (Belgian), Perugina (Italian), and Valrhona (French). There are also two San Francisco Bay Area companies, Scharffenberger and Guittard, that produce European-style chocolate. All chocolate desserts in this chapter were tested using Valrhona, Guittard, or Callebaut, but any of the other brands listed is acceptable. Just make sure to buy the variety of chocolate called for in a particular recipe (for example, semisweet versus bittersweet), as the sugar content can affect the performance of your dessert's other ingredients.

COCOA: In the making of chocolate, after the cocoa butter has been extracted from the cocoa beans, part of the chocolate liquor is dried and ground to form unsweetened cocoa powder. If the cocoa powder is further processed with alkali, it is called Dutch-process cocoa. The "Dutching" process reduces the acidity and increases the solubility of the cocoa, so it is generally a better product for baking. You can find Dutch-process cocoa in the international sections of many supermarkets. If you are unable to locate it in your area, Ghirardelli and Hershey are acceptable substitutes.

CREAM, HALF-AND-HALF, AND MILK: If you can find it, use heavy whipping cream that has not been ultrapasteurized. The ultrapasteurization process makes the cream less delicious and slightly harder to whip. To whip cream for dessert garnishes, chill your bowl and beaters or whip in the freezer, and make sure the cream is very cold. Whip the cream on medium speed, adding confectioners' sugar to taste as it whips. Whip the cream until it will just hold in mounds, then stir in vanilla extract or seeds to taste.

Half-and-half can be made by combining equal parts whole milk and heavy whipping cream, if necessary. Where milk is called for in these recipes, whole milk was used. Any lower-fat substitutions you choose to make will be at your own risk!

EGGS: All recipes in the chapter were made with Grade AA large eggs. Brown, white, cage-free, vegetarian diet—you decide, but make sure they're large to ensure the desired results.

FLOUR: Recipes in this chapter calling for all-purpose flour were tested with the unbleached variety, which I recommend over bleached, if you have the option. Cake flour, which is made from a soft wheat, is bleached to denature the grain further and make your baked goods ultra-tender and light. Be sure to use regular, rather than self-rising, cake flour, and do not substitute cake flour for all-purpose or vice versa. To measure flour, spoon it into your measuring cup and level the flour off with a knife. Unless specified in the recipe, do not sift flour before measuring.

NUTS: Buy unsalted raw nuts and store them in the freezer to maintain freshness. A reliable source of fresh nuts in bulk can be invaluable. Check the stock at your local health food store.

SPICES: If possible, buy small amounts of fresh spices frequently from a reliable source. Spices purchased in the supermarket, especially the less commonly used ones, may have been sitting on the shelves for a long time, which generally results in a certain feebleness of flavor. Store your spices in well-sealed containers in a cool area of your kitchen. For truly fresh spices (they clear out their inventory at year's end!), check out Penzeys Spice's wonderful catalog.

SUGAR: In recipes calling for sugar, use the granulated white variety. Light brown sugar was used in all recipes calling for brown sugar, and I do not recommend substituting the darker varieties, as they have a higher molasses content that can affect the moistness and flavor of your baked goods. To measure brown sugar, pack it firmly into the cup and level it with your finger or a knife. If you live in a dry climate in which brown sugar petrifies before the second use, try keeping it in a resealable plastic bag with a slice of fresh white bread—the moisture from the bread keeps the sugar soft.

VANILLA BEANS AND VANILLA EXTRACT: The vanilla "bean" is the long, leathery seedpod of an orchid plant that grows in the South Pacific, Mexico, and Madagascar. The pod and its millions of tiny seeds attain their seductive aroma and flavor through an elaborate curing and fermentation process. Both of them impart vanilla flavor, but the pod is inedible, so it is generally used only for infusing flavor into liquids, such as custards, and is then discarded. To use a whole vanilla bean, slit it lengthwise with a small, sharp knife. Holding the end of the bean, scrape the seeds from the pod with the knife. If a recipe calls only for seeds, you can store the unused pods tightly wrapped in the freezer or refrigerator, and use them for your next ice cream or custard recipe. You can also store the beans in sugar in a tightly covered jar. The pods will impart a heavenly aroma to the sugar that will add depth to nearly any dessert recipe. Vanilla beans are wonderfully aromatic and a bit extravagant but well worth the investment. You can order reasonably priced vanilla beans from Penzeys Spice's excellent catalog and store them, tightly wrapped, in the freezer. The bean gives a subtler, more delicate vanilla flavor than vanilla extract, which can often have an undesirable marshmallowlike sweetness.

In recipes calling for vanilla beans, vanilla extract can be substituted if necessary: Use 2 to 3 teaspoons for each half bean. Try a few different brands of vanilla extract to determine which one has the best flavor. I recommend Nielsen-Massey brand, which can be found in some supermarkets and gourmet stores, or you can order it through the King Arthur Flour Baker's Catalog. If you live in a Trader Joe's part of the world, their house brand is quite good. By no means should you use anything labeled "imitation vanilla flavoring" or other such blasphemy.

EQUIPMENT: Part of your success with these recipes depends on your having a few key pieces of equipment and gadgets. I wouldn't expect anyone to run out and buy the latest, state-of-the-art pie weights when a bag of beans would serve the same purpose, so spend your equipment dollars wisely! Here are some good basic toys with which to start.

GRADUATED STAINLESS-STEEL MIXING BOWLS: Heatproof, sturdy, light, and nonreactive, you'll find a million uses for these, from melting chocolate to mixing up a batch of cookies. The best thing about metal bowls: you can pick them up—full—with one hand!

KNIVES: Only three basic knives are necessary to make most recipes: a chef's knife, a paring knife, and a serrated knife, all sharp. Invest in good knives and treat them well, and you will probably never have to replace them.

OFFSET PALETTE KNIFE (ICING SPATULA): Indispensable for leveling batters, frosting cakes, and prying brownies loose from a sticky pan, you can find this plastic- or wooden-handled metal spreading tool in many sizes at kitchenware or craft stores, or often in the housewares section of your hardware store. The most versatile size is 8 inches long and $1\frac{1}{2}$ inches wide, but since they are rather inexpensive, you might as well get a half-sized one for smaller jobs.

PASTRY BRUSH: Spend a little more to get one with tightly bound bristles, so you don't end up with lost bristles baked into your pie crust!

PEELER: Handy for taking off citrus zest, and much quicker than a knife for peeling pears and apples. You can still get one at the grocery store for under two dollars.

RUBBER SPATULA/SCOOPULA: A sturdy rubber spatula is your friend in the folding, scraping, and gentle-stirring departments. The "scoopula" is a sturdy, versatile, spoon-shaped rubber spatula. I wouldn't enter a kitchen without one.

And last, but not least—

KITCHENAID MIXER: This seemed pure extravagance to me, as a home cook, until I found out how fast it is! It is efficient, incredibly versatile, virtually indestructible, and aesthetically superior to any other electric mixer. It's a considerable investment but worth every last dime.

Cindy's Tapioca Pudding with Bourbon Cream

Serves 4

Brigid hates tapioca pudding, so this is the one dessert recipe that is not hers. Basically, it's an adult version of the tapioca pudding my mom made when I was a kid. (Some of her other specialties were unbelievable Christmas cookies, lemon meringue pie made with only one lemon, and angel pie, a wonderful chocolate mousse in a meringue crust.) I put this pudding on our opening menu and it sold well for years. But then the novelty wore off, plus I got a real pastry chef who wanted to snazz things up. So now it's off the menu. But I still love the stuff. Serve it with fresh berries or figs smashed with a bit of sugar and lemon.

PUDDING

$2^2/_3$ cups milk

$1/_2$ vanilla bean, split and scraped, or 1 teaspoon vanilla extract

Tiny pinch of salt

$1/_3$ cup granulated sugar

3 tablespoons quick-cooking tapioca

1 egg, beaten

$1^1/_2$ to 2 tablespoons butter

1 tablespoon bourbon or rum

BOURBON CREAM

1 cup heavy whipping cream

$1/_4$ cup confectioners' sugar

$1/_2$ teaspoon vanilla extract

1 to 2 tablespoons Maker's Mark, Jack Daniel's, or other bourbon

To make the pudding, combine the milk, vanilla bean, and salt in a small saucepan (if you're using vanilla extract, add it at the end with the bourbon and butter). Stirring occasionally to keep the bottom of the pan clear, bring the milk just to a boil and remove it from heat. Whisk together the sugar, tapioca, and egg in a small bowl. Slowly stir a small amount of the hot milk into the egg, then pour the entire egg mixture back into the pan and cook over medium heat, stirring, until thick and the tapioca is tender. (Don't put the egg mixture directly into the hot milk or you will end up with scrambled eggs.) Remove from the heat and add the butter and bourbon (and vanilla extract, if you are using it), mixing well. Pour into a bowl and cover with plastic wrap, pressing it directly onto the surface of the pudding to keep a skin from forming (unless, of course, you're like me and like the skin).

To make the bourbon cream, combine the cream, confectioners' sugar, and vanilla in a bowl and whip until thick. Stir in the bourbon.

Serve the pudding warm or chilled, as you prefer, with a healthy dollop of the bourbon cream.

Vanilla Bean Crème Caramel

Serves 6 to 8

Elegant, sinfully creamy, yet quite simple, this custard is packed with vanilla flavor. It is delicious by itself, or served with fresh berries, whipped cream, and candied pistachios (use the recipe for Those Nuts on page 212, but omit the salt). When working with caramel, always wear oven mitts, as the hot sugar can cause serious burns. Also, be careful not to touch the custard cups after you pour the caramel into them—they'll be blazing hot!

1¹/₂ cups heavy whipping cream
1 cup milk
1 vanilla bean, split and scraped
1¹/₂ cups sugar
¹/₄ cup water
3 eggs
3 egg yolks

Preheat the oven to 325°. Combine the cream, milk, and vanilla bean in a heavy saucepan and bring to a boil. Remove from the heat and allow to steep for 20 minutes.

Meanwhile, make the caramel. Put six 4- or 5-ounce custard cups or ramekins in a baking dish with 2-inch sides and place near the stove. Combine 1 cup of the sugar and the water in a skillet, mixing until evenly combined. Brush the sides of the skillet down with a clean, wet pastry brush, and continue brushing the sides if the crystals form. Cook the mixture over high heat, without stirring, for about 5 minutes, until the sugar starts to caramelize. Now stir the caramelized sugar as necessary to cook evenly, but avoid getting sugar on the sides of pan. When the sugar is a deep amber, after about 15 minutes, remove from the heat and very carefully and quickly pour the caramel into the custard cups, dividing evenly. Swirl the caramel up the sides of the cups, holding them by the rim and carefully tilting them with a circular motion.

To make the custard, whisk together the eggs, egg yolks, and the remaining ¹/₂ cup sugar in a bowl. Add a small amount of the hot cream mixture, whisking quickly. Add the remaining hot liquid, whisking until combined, then strain the mixture through a fine-mesh sieve into a pitcher or large measuring cup. Pour the custard into the caramel-lined custard cups and place the baking dish in the oven. Pour hot water into the baking dish to reach halfway up the sides of the custard cups.

Bake for 20 to 30 minutes, rotating the dish 180° halfway through the baking time. When done, the custards will be set around the edges but still a little jiggly at the center. Remove the baking dish from the oven and allow the custards to cool enough to remove them from the water. Refrigerate for at least 3 hours (or even overnight).

To unmold, run a butter knife around the edges of each custard cup and turn out onto individual plates. Each custard should have a nice glaze of caramel. To make cleanup easier, I soak the empty custard dishes in hot, soapy water right away in order to melt the hardened sugar off the bottoms.

Chocolate-Anise Pots de Crème

Serves 6 to 8

A truly sophisticated and delectable combination, chocolate and anise perfectly complement each other's sexy, floral, earthy notes. These delicious little custards are simple to prepare and can be made a day ahead, needing only a dollop of whipped cream and perhaps a crispy cookie to complete the elegant finale. Using 6-ounce ramekins will give you 6 servings; you'll get 8 servings using 5-ouncers.

2³/₄ cups heavy whipping cream
1¹/₂ tablespoons aniseeds
5 ounces semisweet chocolate
5 egg yolks
¹/₄ cup sugar
3 tablespoons anisette liqueur
Whipped cream, for garnish

Preheat the oven to 325°. Place the six or eight ramekins or custard cups (see introduction) in a large baking dish with 2-inch sides. Combine the cream and aniseeds in a large saucepan and bring to a boil over high heat. Remove from the heat and whisk in the chocolate until it is completely melted. Allow to steep for 20 minutes.

Whisk together the yolks and sugar in a bowl until smooth. Add the hot cream in a thin stream, whisking constantly, then whisk in the anisette. Strain through a fine-mesh sieve into a pitcher or large measuring cup. Pour the custard into the ramekins, filling them almost to the top. Place the baking dish in the oven. Pour hot water into the baking dish to reach halfway up the sides of the ramekins.

Bake for about 25 minutes, rotating the baking dish 180° halfway through the baking time. When done, the custards should be set around the edges but still slightly jiggly at the center. Remove the baking dish from the oven and allow the custards to cool enough to remove them from the water. Refrigerate for at least 4 to 6 hours (or even overnight).

Serve the custards cold with a dollop of whipped cream.

Caramel Apple Bread Pudding

Serves 6

Few desserts are more comforting than bread pudding. This version, with its vanilla custard and juicy caramelized apples, is a big winter favorite at Mustards. For an extra special presentation, bake the puddings in individual 6- or 8-ounce ramekins or custard cups (reduce the baking time to 45 minutes). Or serve it with Whiskey Crème Anglaise (page 257). If you don't have vanilla beans, you can substitute vanilla extract, using 2 to 3 teaspoons per half bean.

BREAD PUDDING
1½ cups milk
1½ cups heavy whipping cream
½ vanilla bean, split and scraped
5 egg yolks
½ cup sugar
6 cups brioche or white bread cubes
    (1-inch cubes from about
    1½ large loaves, crusts removed)

CARAMELIZED APPLES
¼ cup unsalted butter
½ vanilla bean, split and scraped
8 Pippin, Granny Smith, or other apples, peeled, halved, cored, and sliced ⅛-inch thick
1 cup sugar
¼ cup apple brandy or whiskey
½ cup heavy whipping cream

Whipped cream, for garnish

To make the pudding, combine the milk, cream, and vanilla bean (seeds and pod) in a saucepan. Bring the mixture to a boil and remove from the heat. In a medium-sized bowl, whisk together the yolks and sugar until smooth. Add the hot milk to the egg yolks, a little at a time, whisking constantly. Strain the mixture through a fine-mesh sieve placed over a pitcher and discard the vanilla bean. Pour the custard over the bread cubes in a bowl, and allow the bread to soak while you prepare the apples.

Heat the butter and vanilla bean in a large sauté pan or skillet over medium-high heat. When the butter is melted, add the apple slices and increase the heat to high, stirring frequently. When the apples begin to give off some liquid, add ½ cup of the sugar and stir, distributing the sugar evenly among the apples. Cook over medium-high heat, stirring occasionally, for about 15 minutes, until the apples are very brown and soft. If the apples dry out or stick, add a small amount of water to the pan. When the apples are well caramelized and the liquid is syrupy, remove half of them for the bread pudding.

To make a sauce, add the apple brandy and the remaining ½ cup sugar to the apples remaining in the pan. Cook over medium-high heat, stirring constantly, until the apples begin to break up and the mixture is a caramel color. Large bubbles will form in the liquid after 5 to 7 minutes. Remove the pan from the heat and carefully stir in the cream (it will bubble up and steam, so watch out). Keep the sauce warm until you are ready to serve.

Preheat the oven to 325°. To assemble the pudding, butter a 9- or 10-inch glass or ceramic baking dish of any shape that is 2 to 3 inches deep. Distribute half of the bread cubes in the bottom of the pan. Layer the caramelized apples over that, followed by the remaining bread pudding. Place the pudding dish inside a slightly larger baking pan, and pour hot water into the larger pan so that it reaches up about halfway the sides of the pudding pan.

Place the pudding, sitting in its water pan, in the center of oven, and bake for about 1 hour, until the center feels set and the top has some golden brown spots. Serve warm with whipped cream and the warm apple-caramel sauce.

Lemon-Lime Meringue Pie

Makes one 11-inch tart or 9-inch deep-dish pie and serves 10 to 12

When an order of this pie makes its way through the Mustards dining room, diners inevitably gawk, point, and pledge to leave room for that billowing mountain of meringue. The pie was on the Mustards menu when Brigid started working here, and it's one of the standbys that even she couldn't improve. She receives more requests for this recipe than just about any other, and tells how she is held captive by her sister at family holiday gatherings until she produces the fabled mountain for dessert (and breakfast, and lunch).

As far as timing goes, you need to prepare pie crust dough, roll it out, line the pan, and freeze it ahead of time. Then figure on 50 minutes to prebake the crust. The filling will go directly into the prebaked crust and bake for another 35 to 40 minutes.

1 prebaked 11-inch tart or 9-inch deep-dish pie crust (page 238)

FILLING
6 large eggs
1¹/₂ cups granulated sugar
¹/₂ cup freshly squeezed lime juice (4 to 6 limes)
¹/₄ cup freshly squeezed lemon juice (about 2 lemons, zested before juicing)
1 cup heavy whipping cream
1 tablespoon grated lemon zest

MERINGUE
³/₄ cup egg whites (about 6 large)
¹/₄ teaspoon cream of tartar
1¹/₂ cups firmly packed brown sugar

Prepare the pie crust as directed and place in the oven to bake.

About 15 minutes before the crust will finish baking, make the filling: Whisk the eggs and granulated sugar together in a bowl until smooth. Whisk in the lime juice and lemon juice, until smooth. Whisk in the cream, then strain the filling through a fine-mesh sieve into a large measuring cup and stir in the lemon zest. The filling will be quite liquid at this point.

Without removing the crust from the oven, pour the filling into the crust (it's easier to do it this way than to juggle the full pie shell from counter to oven). Reduce the oven heat to 325°and bake the pie for 35 to 40 minutes, until the center is just set. Cool the pie on a rack, then refrigerate until cold.

To prepare the meringue, place the egg whites and cream of tartar in an electric mixer fitted with the whip attachment. Place the brown sugar in a small, heavy saucepan, add water to cover, attach a candy thermometer to the pan, and turn the heat on high. When the sugar is at about 240°, start whipping the whites on high speed (they should be foamy and starting to thicken before you add the sugar). When the sugar is at the high soft-ball stage (245°), remove the thermometer from the sugar and, with the mixer still running, carefully avoiding the whip, pour the sugar into the egg whites in a thin stream. When steam starts to come off the whites, add the sugar more quickly. When all sugar has been added, continue whipping until firm but soft peaks form. The meringue should still be quite warm. Quickly spread the meringue on top of the pie, shaping it with a rubber spatula to form a high, smooth dome. With the back of a soup spoon, make decorative waves, working quickly because as the meringue cools it will become stiff and difficult to shape. Preheat the broiler and place the pie on a lower oven rack to brown, turning every few seconds to brown evenly. Store the finished pie in the refrigerator, but plan on serving it within 3 to 5 hours, as the meringue may start to weep.

Apple Pie with Cheddar Cheese Crust

Makes one 9-inch pie (serves 8 to 12)

Apple pie with Cheddar cheese is the American answer to the European after-dinner cheese and fruit course. This pie has the cheese built right into the crust, so you get the apple-cheese tastiness in every bite. The very best pie apple is the Cortland, a firm red apple with smooth, dense flesh and a complex tart-sweet, almost floral flavor. It holds up very well in pies, and it is Brigid's first choice for this pie. The tart green Pippin is next best. If neither of these varieties is available where you live, a respectable substitution can be made by using half Granny Smith (tart and firm but not that flavorful) and half McIntosh (flavorful, but lacking optimum texture). If you want a very juicy pie, add only 1 tablespoon flour to the filling; add an extra tablespoon for a little sturdier texture.

CRUST
2¹/₂ cups all-purpose flour

1 teaspoon salt

2 tablespoons sugar

6 tablespoons cold unsalted butter, cut into small pieces

6 tablespoons vegetable shortening, frozen and cut into small pieces

1 cup grated extra-sharp white Cheddar cheese

6 to 7 tablespoons ice water

FILLING
8 large apples (see introduction), peeled, halved, cored, and sliced ¹/₄-inch thick

2 tablespoons freshly squeezed lemon juice

2 teaspoons vanilla extract

1 cup sugar

¹/₄ teaspoon salt

1 or 2 tablespoons flour

2 tablespoons unsalted butter, cut into bits

1 egg

1 teaspoon water

Sugar for sprinkling (optional)

Vanilla ice cream, for serving

To make the crust, combine the flour, salt, and sugar in a food processor, electric mixer, or in a large bowl. Using the blade attachment of the food processor, the paddle attachment of electric mixer, or a pastry cutter, cut the cold butter and shortening into the dry ingredients until the mixture resembles a coarse meal. Add the cheese and mix to combine. If you are using a food processor, transfer the mix to a bowl. Sprinkle 6 tablespoons of the ice water over the mix, and stir quickly with a fork, until the mixture holds together but is not sticky, adding more ice water if necessary. Gather the dough into a ball and divide it in half. Wrap each half in plastic wrap and flatten into a 1-inch-thick disk. Refrigerate the dough for 20 minutes, or until firm enough to roll out.

To make the filling, combine the apples, lemon juice, vanilla, sugar, salt, and flour (1 tablespoon for a juicier pie, 2 tablespoons for a drier filling) in a large bowl. Toss to mix evenly.

On a lightly floured work surface, roll out one dough disk into an 11-inch circle, ¹/₄ inch thick. Set the rolling pin on top of the dough on the diagonal, and flip the dough edge (about one-third of the dough width) over the rolling pin. Holding the dough against the pin gently with one hand, pick up the pin and set the dough in a 9-inch tart pan, centering it as well as you can. With kitchen scissors, trim the dough to leave about a ¹/₂-inch overhang all the way around, saving the trimmings at room temperature for later crust repair. Put the filling into the crust and dot it with the butter. Roll out the remaining dough and set it atop the filling, trimming the edges even with the bottom dough. Press the dough edges together and roll or crimp them decoratively. Put the pie in the freezer for 15 minutes. (This "sets" the butter in the crust and prevents it from becoming greasy when it bakes.)

Preheat the oven to 425°. With a paring knife, cut 4 or 5 vents in the top crust. Whisk together the egg and water to make an egg wash. Brush the pie crust generously with the wash and sprinkle with sugar.

Bake the pie for 20 minutes, lower the oven temperature to 375°, and bake for 40 to 45 minutes more, until the filling is bubbly. Check to see if the apples are done by inserting a skewer or toothpick through one of the vent holes. Serve warm or at room temperature with ice cream.

Bing Cherry and Almond Tart

Makes one 11-inch tart
and serves 8 to 10

Bing cherries, those sweet and addictive early summer treats, are impossible to eat in moderation. As I sit on my porch pitting a case of them for the next day's special, my fingers dripping with the sticky black juices, it seems as if I eat one for every one I pit. Pitting cherries is no bowl of cherries, but when you share this tart with friends, you'll know it was worth the effort.

Prebaked 11-inch tart crust baked in tart pan with removable bottom (page 238)
3/4 cup unblanched almonds
4 cups pitted Bing cherries (about 1 1/2 pounds)
3/4 cup granulated sugar
1 1/4 cups unsalted butter
1 vanilla bean, split and scraped
2 cups confectioners' sugar
1 teaspoon salt
1 cup all-purpose flour
4 large eggs
1/4 teaspoon almond extract
Sweetened whipped cream for garnish

Prepare the tart crust as directed, and set it aside to cool. Reduce the oven temperature to 325°. Spread the almonds on a baking sheet and toast for 10 to 15 minutes, until fragrant. Remove from the oven and set aside. Leave the oven set at 325°. Toss the cherries with the granulated sugar in a bowl and set aside.

To prepare the filling, heat the butter with the vanilla bean in a sauté pan over medium heat until melted. Increase the heat to high and cook for about 8 minutes, until the butter is deep brown and very fragrant. Remove and discard the vanilla bean, and carefully transfer the butter to a metal container to cool.

Pulse together the confectioners' sugar, nuts, salt, and flour in a food processor or blender until the nuts are finely ground. Add the eggs and pulse until combined. Add the browned butter and almond extract and pulse until smooth. Pour the filling into the tart shell. Spread 2 cups of the cherries evenly over the filling. Bake for 20 to 30 minutes, until the filling is golden brown and the center is set. Cool the tart on a rack, then remove the pan sides and slide onto a serving plate.

To make a cherry sauce, place the remaining 2 cups cherries in a small saucepan over medium-high heat. Bring to a simmer and cook for about 5 minutes, until the liquid thickens slightly and the cherries are soft. Serve the tart at room temperature with whipped cream and warm cherry sauce.

Coconut Dream Pie with Gooey Chocolate-Coconut Sauce

Makes one 11-inch tart or 9-inch deep-dish pie and serves 10 to 12

Alert! This dessert is not for dieters! Being a coconut fanatic, Brigid has always been addicted to coconut cream pie, and this recipe gets an extra coconut flavor boost from the coconut milk and toasted coconut in the filling. The crust recipe is a great one for most tarts or pies, as it stays nice and crisp for a couple of days. She has given directions for making a tart here, but you could just as easily make a 9-inch deep-dish pie. Just roll the crust to the appropriate size and flute the edges before chilling and prebaking it.

If you really like coconut, you'll want to serve the pie with the Gooey Chocolate-Coconut Sauce. In that case, toast the coconut for the sauce along with the coconut for the pie filling (about 3 cups in all). The sauce is the most delicious, decadent sauce, the perfect thing for that late-afternoon sugar fix. This recipe makes more than you need for the pie, so there will be some left over for other desserts. It is also good on Coco-Nutty Cake (page 260) or even on a bowl of vanilla ice cream.

CRUST
2 cups all-purpose flour
$^{1}/_{4}$ teaspoon salt
1 tablespoon granulated sugar
$^{3}/_{4}$ cup cold unsalted butter, cut into small pieces
2 tablespoons plus 1 teaspoon water
$^{1}/_{4}$ teaspoon vanilla extract
1 large egg

COCONUT FILLING
$1^{1}/_{2}$ cups sweetened dried coconut flakes
1 (14-ounce) can coconut milk
$1^{1}/_{2}$ cups whole milk
$^{1}/_{2}$ vanilla bean, split and scraped
6 large egg yolks
$1^{1}/_{3}$ cups granulated sugar
$^{1}/_{4}$ cup cornstarch
Pinch of salt
6 tablespoons unsalted butter

GOOEY CHOCOLATE-COCONUT SAUCE
$1^{1}/_{3}$ cups sweetened dried coconut flakes
2 cups heavy whipping cream
$1^{1}/_{3}$ cups sugar
$^{1}/_{4}$ cup water
4 ounces semisweet chocolate, chopped
$^{3}/_{4}$ teaspoon almond extract
$^{1}/_{4}$ teaspoon salt

3 cups heavy whipping cream
$^{1}/_{4}$ cup confectioners' sugar

To make the crust, combine the flour, sugar, salt, and butter in food processor, electric mixer, or large mixing bowl. Using the blade attachment of the food processor, the paddle attachment of the electric mixer, or a pastry cutter, cut the cold butter into the flour until the mixture resembles a coarse meal. If you are using a processor, transfer the mixture to a bowl. Sprinkle the 2 tablespoons water and the vanilla over the mixture and mix with a fork until the dough clumps together. Gather the dough into a ball, wrap it in plastic wrap, and flatten into a 1-inch-thick disk. Refrigerate the dough for 30 minutes, until it is firm enough to roll out.

Have ready an 11-inch fluted tart pan with a removable bottom (or a 9-inch deep-dish pie pan). On a lightly floured surface, roll out the dough into a 13-inch circle. Set the rolling pin on top of the dough on the diagonal, and flip the dough edge (about one-third of the dough width) over the rolling pin. Holding the dough against the pin gently with one hand, pick up the pin and set the dough in the tart pan, centering it as well as you can. Trim the dough to leave about a $^{1}/_{2}$-inch overhang all the way around, saving the trimmings at room temperature for later crust repair work. Gently push the dough into the pan so that it fits snugly against the sides, then fold the overhang toward the inside, pressing the folded dough against the sides. With thumb and forefinger, gently pinch the dough so that the sides of the tart extend about $^{1}/_{4}$ inch above the edge of the pan, with an even thickness all the way up and around. Freeze the crust for 30 to 40 minutes, until it is hard. While the crust is chilling, preheat the oven to 350°.

When the crust is hard, line it with a piece of aluminum foil large enough to cover it, and fill with beans, rice, or pie weights. (Do not prick the crust!) Bake the crust for 35 minutes, then remove the weights and foil and bake for another 15 minutes, until the crust is golden brown and feels dry. If holes developed anywhere in the crust, they can easily be patched now by gently spackling with the leftover dough, but be careful not to break the tart sides while making repairs. Whisk the egg with 1 teaspoon of water to make an egg wash and brush all over the bottom and sides of the crust. Return the crust to the oven and bake for 5 minutes more, until the egg is set and dry. Set the crust aside on a rack to cool.

To make the filling, leave the oven set at 350°. Spread the coconut flakes on a baking sheet, place in the oven, and toast, stirring every 5 minutes to color evenly, until light brown. Depending on the thickness of the pan and the heat source of your oven, it will take 10 to 15 minutes. Measure out 1 cup of the coconut, and set the rest aside for topping.

Combine the coconut milk, milk, and vanilla bean in a heavy saucepan and bring to a boil. Remove from the heat and set aside. Whisk together the egg yolks and granulated sugar in a bowl until smooth, then whisk in the cornstarch and salt. Pour a small amount of the hot milk mixture into the yolks and whisk until smooth. Add the remaining milk mixture and whisk until smooth, then pour everything back into saucepan. Cook over medium-high heat, whisking constantly, until the mixture comes to a rapid boil. Lower the heat enough to keep the mixture at a low boil and cook for another 10 minutes, whisking constantly, until the mixture is very thick and pulls away from the sides of the pan when stirred. Strain the mixture through a fine-mesh sieve into a clean bowl and fold in the butter and the 1 cup toasted coconut. Pour the hot filling into the prepared crust and smooth the top with a spatula. Cover with plastic wrap, pressing the wrap directly onto the surface of the filling, and refrigerate the tart for about 2 hours, until cool. (Overnight is okay, too, if you want to make it ahead of time.)

To make the sauce, preheat the oven to 350°. Spread the coconut flakes on a baking sheet, place it in the oven, and toast, stirring every 5 minutes to color evenly, for 10 to 15 minutes, until light brown.

In a small, heavy saucepan, combine the toasted coconut and the cream, and bring to a boil. Remove from the heat and allow to steep for 15 minutes.

Stir the sugar and water in a saucepan, mixing until completed combined. Cook the mixture over high heat, without stirring, for about 7 minutes, until the mixture is a deep amber color. Brush the sides of the pan down with a clean pastry brush dampened with water, and continue brushing the sides if crystals form. Very carefully and slowly add the coconut-cream mixture, stirring with a wooden spoon (wear oven mitts, as the mixture will bubble up wildly). When all the cream has been added, stir the sauce until it is uniform, then add the chocolate, almond extract, and salt, and stir until the chocolate melts. Transfer the sauce to a metal container and set it on ice to cool, stirring occasionally.

To serve, warm the sauce over medium heat. Whip the cream with the confectioners' sugar until soft peaks form. Spread the whipped cream over the tart, then sprinkle with $1/2$ cup toasted coconut. Slice and serve on a pool of warm Gooey Chocolate-Coconut Sauce.

Chocolate-Hazelnut Truffle Tart

Makes one 11-inch tart and serves 10 to 12

I've discovered that by including the word truffle in the name of a Mustards dessert, I can sell a million of them. But we all know that a fancy name alone does not make a delicious dessert. This tart, I guarantee you, more than lives up to its name. The crust is simple, just a chocolate short-bread, which can be rolled out, cut, and baked as cookies, if you like. The filling is decadently rich, smooth, and creamy—downright truffle-riffic! If you want a nuttier texture in your tart, you can omit the straining step in the filling recipe.

CHOCOLATE SHORT CRUST
1 cup plus 2 tablespoons all-purpose flour
1/4 cup Dutch-process cocoa powder
1/2 cup confectioners' sugar
1/4 teaspoon salt
1/2 cup plus 2 tablespoons cold unsalted butter, cut into small cubes
1/4 teaspoon vanilla extract

TRUFFLE FILLING
1 1/3 cups hazelnuts
9 ounces bittersweet chocolate, chopped or broken into small pieces

1 cup heavy whipping cream
1/2 cup milk
1 large egg
1 large egg yolk
1/4 cup granulated sugar
1/4 teaspoon salt

Whipped cream for garnish
Fresh raspberries or raspberry purée for garnish

Have ready an 11-inch fluted tart pan with a removable bottom. To make the crust, combine all the ingredients except the vanilla in an electric mixer fitted with the paddle attachment. Mix on low speed until the dough comes together. Mix in the vanilla. Gather the dough into a ball, cover in plastic wrap, and flatten it into a thick disk. Refrigerate for 20 minutes, or until firm enough to roll out.

Roll out the dough into a 13-inch circle about 1/8 inch thick, and line the tart pan with the dough. If the dough breaks, press it together with your fingers, patching with extra pieces as necessary. Trim the dough to leave about a 1/2-inch overhang, saving the trimmings at room temperature for later crust repair. Gently push the dough into the pan so that it fits snugly against the sides, then fold the overhang toward the inside, pressing the folded dough against the sides. Along the inside of the tart pan, fold the dough edges over to a double thickness, and press the dough firmly against pan. Trim the dough flush with the pan rim, saving the excess dough for patching the crust again later. Gently prick the tart bottom all over with a fork and place the tart crust in the freezer for 30 to 40 minutes, until very hard. While the crust is chilling, preheat the oven to 375°. Bake the crust for about 15 minutes, until it is set and feels dry. Remove from the oven and if cracks have formed, carefully patch them with the reserved dough, gently spreading bits of it over the cracks. Cool the crust on a rack.

To make the truffle filling, lower the oven temperature to 350°. Spread the the hazelnuts on a baking sheet and toast in the oven for about 15 minutes, until they are fragrant and golden brown. Remove the nuts from the oven and, while still warm, rub off the skins with a kitchen towel. Grind the nuts in a blender or food processor to the consistency of peanut butter. Place the chocolate and hazelnut paste in a heatproof bowl. Put the cream and milk in a small saucepan and bring to a boil. Pour the hot milk mixture over the hazelnut paste and whisk until smooth. Strain the mixture through a fine-mesh sieve strainer and cool to room temperature. Whisk in the egg, egg yolk, sugar, and salt. Pour the filling into the tart shell. Bake for about 15 minutes, until the filling is set, about 15 minutes. Cool the tart on a rack. Remove the pan sides and cut the tart into 10 to 12 pieces.

To serve, place the pieces on a sheet pan and reheat them at 425° for 3 to 4 minutes. Garnish each serving with whipped cream and raspberries.

Double Berry Sorbet with Chocolate O's

Makes 1 ¹/₂ quarts & 24 cookies and serves 10 to 12

Raspberries and blackberries, with their intense, juicy flavors, make especially wonderful sorbets, and if you're lucky enough to live near wild blackberry bushes, this can be an economical dessert as well. The syrup, which will keep indefinitely in the refrigerator, can also be used to sweeten hot or iced tea and coffee drinks, as well as lemonade and cocktails. The cookie O's we serve with the sorbet are another version of the great American combination of peanut butter and chocolate—this time in the form of addictive, chocolatey butter cookies sandwiched with a creamy peanut butter filling. "Natural" peanut butter (which only contains peanuts and salt) is best for this recipe because the natural style tastes more like peanuts and less like fat, but the homogenized kind will work too. If you like your cookies crisp, serve them within an hour after assembly; as they sit the filling softens the cookies a bit.

SORBET
2 cups granulated sugar
2 cups water
3 cups fresh blackberries
2 cups fresh raspberries
Juice of 1 lemon
¹/₄ teaspoon salt

COOKIES
1 ¹/₂ cups unsalted butter, softened
³/₄ cup sugar
2 ¹/₂ cups flour
1 cup plus 2 tablespoons Dutch process cocoa powder
¹/₂ teaspoon salt

COOKIE FILLING
¹/₄ cup unsalted butter, softened
³/₄ cup peanut butter
Pinch of salt
1 ¹/₄ cup confectioners' sugar
2 tablespoons heavy cream, buttermilk, or plain yogurt

To make the simple syrup for the sorbet, combine the sugar and water in a saucepan and stir to dissolve. Bring to a boil, then remove from the heat. Chill before using.

Put the blackberries and raspberries in a blender or food processor and process until liquefied. Strain the purée through a fine-mesh strainer, and stir in 2¹/₂ cups of the syrup, the lemon juice, and the salt. Taste and add more simple syrup, if necessary. Freeze in an ice cream maker according to the manufacturer's instructions.

To make the cookies, cream the butter and sugar together on high speed until light and fluffy. Sift together the flour, cocoa powder, and salt, and add it to the butter mixture, mixing to combine. Divid the dough in half and roll each half into a log about 2 inches in diameter. Wrap the logs tightly in plastic wrap and freeze until firm enough to slice.

To make the filling, cream the butter, peanut butter, and salt together on high speed until very smooth. Add the confectioners' sugar and mix on low until the mixture comes together, then add the cream and beat until smooth. Refrigerate until ready to assemble the cookies (the filling is easier to work with if it is cold.)

Preheat the oven to 350°. To assemble the cookies, remove the logs from the freezer and cut them into ¹/₄-inch-thick rounds. Bake the rounds on a buttered or parchment-lined baking sheet until the cookies are set and slightly crackly on top, about 15 minutes. Cool cookies on racks.

To assemble the "sandwiches," turn half of the cookies over and scoop ¹/₂- to ³/₄-tablespoon balls of filling onto each overturned cookie. Top with the remaining cookies, gently squishing the filling until it is evenly sandwiched between the cookie rounds. The cookies can be stored at room temperature.

To serve, scoop the sorbet into serving bowls and place a cookie sandwich alongside.

Tangerine Sorbet with Blondies

Makes 1 quart and 36 cookies and serves 8 to 10

The perfect conclusion to a heavy or spicy meal, this tangerine sorbet is tart and pleasingly creamy, not icy. The key to its texture is the high ratio of simple syrup to fruit juice, which you offset with a healthy amount of lime juice. You will find tangerines in the grocery store from Thanksgiving to Easter, and there is an increasingly wide variety from which to choose. My favorites are the Satsuma (an early variety), Page, Lee, and Fairchild, all of which have that extra tang that defines good tangerine flavor. The sweetness may vary a bit, so adjust the amount of lime juice, syrup, and salt to taste. You will want to freeze this sorbet for at least 8 hours before serving, as it will be too soft to scoop otherwise. Don't let the Blondie dough sit around long if you want to end up with any actual cookies—if you're a cookie dough connoissuer, it is one of the finest to eat tartare.

SORBET

2 cups sugar

2 cups water

3 pounds tangerines

1/4 cup plus 3 tablespoons freshly squeezed lime juice

Pinch of salt

1 to 2 tablespoons Cointreau (optional)

COOKIES

1/2 cup pecan pieces

1/2 cup unsalted butter, at room temperature

6 tablespoons firmly packed light brown sugar

6 tablespoons granulated sugar

1 egg

1 teaspoon vanilla extract

1 cup plus 2 tablespoons all-purpose flour

1/4 teaspoon salt

1/2 teaspoon baking soda

6 ounces white chocolate pieces or chips

1/2 cup golden raisins

To make the simple syrup for the sorbet, combine the sugar and water in a saucepan and stir to dissolve. Bring to a boil, then remove from the heat. Chill before using.

Juice the tangerines and strain the juice through a fine-mesh sieve. You should have about 1 3/4 cups juice. Add 2 cups of the syrup and all the remaining ingredients and adjust the seasonings to taste. Freeze in an ice cream maker according to the manufacturer's instructions.

To make the cookies, spread the pecans on a baking sheet and toast for about 12 minutes, until fragrant and slightly darker. Remove and set aside.

In an electric mixer fitted with the paddle attachment, cream together the butter and sugars at high speed until light and fluffy. Add the egg and vanilla and mix on high speed until smooth. Add the flour, salt, and baking soda and mix only until combined. Stir in the pecan pieces, chocolate, and raisins. Cover and chill the dough for 30 to 40 minutes, until firm enough to roll into balls. Meanwhile, preheat the oven to 350°.

Scoop heaping tablespoons of dough onto parchment-lined or buttered baking sheets, and roll them into balls. Bake for 10 to 12 minutes, until the edges of the cookies are golden brown and the centers are set. Transfer the cookies to a rack to cool. (Cookies can be covered and stored at room temperature for 2 to 3 days.)

To serve, scoop the sorbet into serving bowls and place a cookie (or two) alongside.

Pear Sorbet with Cornmeal Sugar Cookies

Makes 1¹/₂ quarts and 36 cookies and serves 10 to 12

Because they are rich in pectin, pears make a deliciously smooth sorbet. You can use just about any variety for this recipe, although my favorites are Bartlett and Comice. Depending on the ripeness, you may have to adjust the lemon juice and/or syrup slightly.

Cornmeal Sugar Cookies are the perfect ice cream or sorbet cookie— they are crisp and crunchy and not too sweet. They are particularly nice with Caramel Ice Cream (page 247): Make giant ones and serve homemade ice cream sandwiches. The sparkly, crunchy crystal sugar makes these cookies extra special. Crystal sugar can be found in some gourmet or baking supply stores. The cookies are also a nice change from regular sugar cookies for holiday decorating. I like to cut out two Christmas trees (or any other shape), punch a smaller tree out of the center of one, put a dollop of raspberry jam in the center of the solid one, and top with the cut-out cookie. Press the two halves together gently, and bake until the jam bubbles and the edges are brown.

SORBET

2 cups sugar

2 cups water

4 pounds ripe pears (about 6 medium), peeled, quartered, cored, and thinly sliced

¹/₂ cup freshly squeezed lemon juice

¹/₄ cup water

COOKIES

1 cup plus 2 tablespoons all-purpose flour

1 cup fine cornmeal (not stone-ground)

³/₄ cup plus 2 tablespoons confectioners' sugar

¹/₂ teaspoon salt

¹/₂ teaspoon baking powder

¹/₂ cup cold unsalted butter, cut into cubes

1 egg

1 egg yolk

2 teaspoons vanilla extract

Crystal or granulated sugar for sprinkling on cookies

To make the simple syrup for the sorbet, combine the sugar and water in a saucepan and stir to dissolve. Bring to a boil, then remove from the heat. Chill before using.

Place the pears in a heavy, nonreactive saucepan along with ¹/₄ cup of the lemon juice and the water. Cover and cook over medium-high heat, stirring occasionally, for about 15 minutes, until the pears give off their juices. Reduce the heat to medium-low and cook, stirring occasionally, for 30 minutes more, or until pears are very soft and falling apart. Remove from the heat.

Purée the pears in a blender or food processor until very smooth, then strain through a fine-mesh sieve. (If desired, you can cool the pears before puréeing them. If you are using a blender and are careful not to get any seeds or skin in with the pears when you cook them, straining is not necessary.) Add 1 cup of the syrup and the remaining ¹/₄ cup lemon juice to the purée and mix well. Taste and add more lemon juice or syrup as needed. (Unused simple syrup can be stored in the refrigerator for at least 2 weeks and can be used to sweeten coffee or mixed drinks.) Cover and chill well. Freeze in an ice cream maker according to the manufacturer's instructions.

To make the cookies, put the flour, cornmeal, confectioners' sugar, salt, baking powder, and butter in an electric mixer fitted with the paddle attachment. On low speed, cut the butter into the dry ingredients until the mixture resembles a coarse meal. (You could also do this with a pastry cutter.) Add the egg, egg yolk, and vanilla and mix until the dough comes together. Wrap the dough in plastic wrap and chill for 20 to 30 minutes, until firm enough to roll out. Meanwhile, preheat the oven to 375°.

On a floured surface, roll out the dough ¹/₃ to ¹/₂ inch thick. Cut into desired shapes. Gather up the scraps, reroll, and cut out more cookies. Place on parchment-lined or buttered baking sheets and sprinkle the cookies with crystal sugar. Bake for 8 to 10 minutes, until the edges are golden brown. Transfer the cookies to a rack to cool. Cover and store at room temperature for 2 to 3 days.

To serve, scoop the sorbet into serving bowls and place a cookie (or two) alongside.

Milk Chocolate Malted Ice Cream

Makes 1 quart and serves 8 to 10

One summer, at the end of a long river trip in central Idaho, Brigid and her companions stopped in at a tiny cafe in a tiny town. Having spent the last few days sunburned and weary, sifting unsuccessfully through the wilted rations for something edible, and with nothing but warm beer to wash it down with anyway, they were more than ready for a juicy burger and a piece of pie. But a quick perusal of the menu revealed the holy grail of primal food satisfaction: the chocolate malted. Brigid says she'll never forget how that cool, creamy delight instantaneously restored her to full capacity, and it was that experience that inspired her to create this tribute to the curative properties of malt and milk chocolate.

Be sure to use a high-quality chocolate, such as Callebaut or Lindt, as the texture and flavor of the better brands will produce a superior ice cream. You can find malt powder in the cocoa section of your supermarket. Brigid recommends Horlick's, as it has no artificial additives and has a nice malty flavor.

1¹/₂ cups heavy whipping cream
5 ounces milk chocolate (see left)
2 ounces semisweet chocolate (see left)
2 cups milk
8 egg yolks
¹/₄ cup sugar
¹/₄ teaspoon salt
¹/₂ cup malt powder (see left)
¹/₄ cup Irish cream liqueur (optional)

Combine the cream and chocolates in the top of a double boiler or in a bowl set over simmering water. Stir occasionally until the chocolate has melted and the mixture is uniform. Set it aside.

Bring the milk to a boil in a heavy saucepan and remove from the heat. Whisk together the yolks, sugar, salt, and malt powder in a medium bowl until blended. Whisk in a small amount of the hot milk. Gradually whisk in the remaining milk, then return the mixture to the saucepan. Cook over medium-low heat, stirring constantly with a rubber spatula or wooden spoon for 5 to 8 minutes, until the custard has thickened enough to coat the spoon (about 170° on a candy thermometer). Remove the custard from the heat and whisk a small amount of it into the chocolate-cream mixture, then pour the chocolate-cream mixture into the custard, and whisk until thoroughly combined. Strain through a fine-mesh sieve and add the liqueur. Chill on ice or uncovered in the refrigerator. Cover when cool and continue to chill until cold. Freeze in an ice-cream maker according to the manufacturer's instructions.

Mint Julep Ice Cream

Makes 1 quart and serves 8 to 10

Few drinks are as ceremonial and Southern, not to mention downright fabulous, as the mint julep. I'm no bartender, but I still wanted to pay tribute at Mustards to the great mint julep tradition, so I came up with this ice cream. Now, purists would argue that Jack Daniel's is not a true bourbon (it's a sour mash whiskey made in Tennessee, not Bourbon County, Kentucky) and that it won't make a proper mint julep, but hey, this is California! If you want to be authentic, you can substitute a good-quality bourbon, such as Jim Beam or Maker's Mark. You can serve the mint julep ice cream by itself or accompanied by some cookies or some chocolate sauce. For true Southern decadence, serve with a big wedge of Chocolate Pecan Jack Daniel's Cake (page 254).

2 packed cups fresh mint leaves
1^1/$_2$ cups milk
1^1/$_4$ cups heavy whipping cream
6 egg yolks
^{3}/$_4$ cup sugar
Pinch of salt
^{1}/$_4$ cup Jack Daniel's whiskey
1 teaspoon vanilla extract

With the back of a large knife, bruise the mint leaves. Combine them with the milk and cream in a saucepan and bring to a boil on high heat. Remove from the heat and allow the mint to steep in the liquid for 20 to 30 minutes.

Strain the milk-mixture into another saucepan and discard the mint. Whisk together the yolks, sugar, and salt in a bowl. Add the hot milk a little at a time, whisking constantly. Return the mixture to the saucepan and cook over medium heat, stirring constantly, for 5 to 8 minutes, until it thickens enough to coat the back of a spoon (about 170°on a candy thermometer). Strain the custard through a fine-mesh sieve into a bowl, and stir in the whiskey and vanilla. Chill over ice or uncovered in the refrigerator. Cover when cool and continue to chill until cold. Freeze in an ice-cream maker according to the manufacturer's instructions.

Caramel Ice Cream

Makes 1 quart and serves 8 to 10

It is well worth the little extra effort it takes to caramelize the sugar. The result is a stupendous ice cream that makes a delicious accompaniment to any warm fruit or chocolate dessert, like the Strawberry-Rhubarb Cobbler (page 248). Or try it with just a little warm chocolate sauce on top. Yum!

1¹/₂ cups heavy whipping cream
¹/₂ vanilla bean, split and scraped
1¹/₂ cups sugar
6 tablespoons water
1¹/₂ cups milk
6 egg yolks
¹/₂ teaspoon salt
2 tablespoons bourbon or rum

Combine the heavy cream and vanilla bean in a small saucepan, bring to a boil, and remove from the heat but keep on hand. Combine the sugar and water in a saucepan, mixing until evenly combined. Brush the sides of the pan down with a clean pastry brush dipped in water to remove any sugar crystals, and continue brushing down the sides with a wet brush if crystals form. Cook the mixture over high heat, without stirring, for about 10 minutes, until it turns a deep amber.

Now, don some oven mitts. With the sugar still over the heat, very slowly add the reserved cream while stirring with a wooden spoon. (The mixture will bubble violently, so be careful!) When the caramel is of a uniform consistency (it will look like a light golden brown cream), stir in the milk and allow the pan to sit off the heat for 15 minutes.

Whisk the egg yolks and salt together in a bowl, then gradually add the hot caramel, whisking constantly. Strain the mixture through a fine-mesh sieve into a bowl, and stir in the liquor. Chill over ice or uncovered in the refrigerator, stirring occasionally. Cover when cool and continue to chill until cold. Freeze in an ice-cream maker according to the manufacturer's instructions.

Strawberry-Rhubarb Cobbler with Black Pepper Biscuits

Serves 6

This recipe calls for strawberries and rhubarb, but you can use any combination of berries or stone fruits. Strange as it may seem, black pepper has a special affinity for red fruits, particularly strawberries and raspberries. It somehow enhances their subtle spiciness. But peaches, plums, and blackberries are all delicious with the black pepper biscuits, too. Or you can substitute orange or lemon zest or aniseeds for the black pepper. For a special occasion, cut the biscuits into fun shapes with cookie cutters, and make the cobblers in individual gratin dishes. Although we say it's optional, you should be required to serve the cobbler with ice cream.

FILLING

4 cups stemmed and quartered fresh strawberries

4 cups rhubarb (1-inch pieces)

1 teaspoon vanilla extract

1½ cups granulated sugar

2 tablespoons freshly squeezed orange juice

2 tablespoons cornstarch

BISCUITS

1⅓ cups all-purpose flour

⅓ cup granulated sugar

1¼ teaspoons baking powder

1 teaspoon baking soda

¼ teaspoon salt

¾ teaspoon medium-coarse freshly cracked black pepper

¼ cup cold unsalted butter, cut into small cubes

½ cup buttermilk

1 large egg

1 teaspoon water

Crystal or granulated sugar for sprinkling on biscuits

Vanilla ice cream or Caramel Ice Cream (page 247) for serving (optional)

To make the filling, combine the strawberries, rhubarb, vanilla, sugar, orange juice, and cornstarch in a large bowl, mixing well. Spread the fruit out in an 8- to 10-inch baking dish with 2- to 3-inch sides and set aside. (Any shape dish will do.)

To make the biscuits, combine the flour, sugar, baking powder, baking soda, salt, and pepper in a bowl or in an electric mixer fitted with the paddle attachment. Scatter the butter over the top. With a pastry cutter, or with the mixer on low speed, cut the butter into the dry ingredients until the mixture resembles a coarse meal. Using a fork, stir in the buttermilk until a shaggy dough forms. Turn out the dough onto a floured work surface and knead gently for six to eight turns, until smooth. Do no overwork the dough or the biscuits will be tough. Roll out the dough about ½ thick. Using a 2½- to 3-inch biscuit or cookie cutter, cut out six biscuits. Reroll the scraps as necessary.

Whisk together the egg and water to make an egg wash. Arrange the biscuits on top of the fruit in the baking dish, brush the biscuits with the egg wash, and then sprinkle with sugar.

Bake the cobbler for 30 to 35 minutes, until the fruit is bubbly and the biscuits are golden brown. (For individual cobblers, cut the time to 20 minutes). Serve warm with ice cream.

Red Raspberry, White Peach, and Blueberry Cobbler with Cornmeal Brown Butter Biscuits

Serves 6

One summer, my ancient and venerable white peach tree blessed Mustards with several thousand pounds of the coveted fruit, prompting a no-holds-barred white peach blowout. Feeling a bit patriotic, Brigid came up with this juicy multicolored dessert for the Fourth of July. White peaches are not available everywhere, but you can use any ripe, flavorful peaches. The most important thing is to make this cobbler only when peaches and berries are in season (late June to late August) for maximum flavor and juiciness.

The browned butter adds a toasty flavor to the rich, tender biscuits and is deliciously complemented by the crunchy cornmeal. Substantial enough to stand up to the juiciest fruits without dissolving, the cornmeal biscuits are a nice change from the usual all-flour variety. This cobbler begs for a delicious scoop of vanilla ice cream.

CORNMEAL BISCUITS
5 tablespoons unsalted butter
1¼ cups all-purpose flour
¼ cup cornmeal (not stone-ground)
2 tablespoons sugar
2 teaspoons baking powder
¼ teaspoon salt
½ cup heavy whipping cream
2 teaspoons vanilla extract
2 large egg yolks

FILLING
2 large white or yellow peaches, sliced ½ inch thick
1 cup fresh raspberries or boysenberries
1 tablespoon freshly squeezed lemon juice
2 tablespoons cornstarch
½ cup sugar, or to taste
½ cup fresh blueberries
1 egg
1 teaspoon water
Granulated or crystal sugar for sprinkling on biscuits

Vanilla ice cream for serving

To make the biscuits, in a small sauté pan, cook the butter over medium-high heat for 5 to 7 minutes, until brown and very fragrant. Transfer the butter to a heatproof container and freeze for about 45 minutes, until hard. Combine the flour, cornmeal, sugar, baking powder, and salt in a bowl or in an electric mixer fitted with the paddle attachment.

When the butter is hard, cut it into cubes and add it to the dry ingredients (to loosen the butter, briefly heat the container on the stove or dip it into hot water). With a pastry cutter or with the mixer on low speed, cut the butter into the dry ingredients until the mixture resembles a coarse meal. Using a fork, stir together the cream, vanilla, and yolks together in a small bowl, then stir the mixture into the dry ingredients, mixing only enough to form a rough dough.

Turn out the dough onto a floured work surface and knead it gently six to eight folds, until smooth. Do not overwork the dough or the biscuits will be tough. Roll out the dough ½ inch thick. Using a 2½-inch to 3-inch biscuit or cookie cutter, cut out six biscuits. Reroll the scraps as necessary. Refrigerate the biscuits while preparing the fruit.

Preheat the oven to 375°. To make the filling, toss together the peaches, raspberries, lemon juice, cornstarch, and ½ cup of sugar in a large bowl. Taste and add more sugar if necessary. To assemble the cobbler, spread the mixed fruits evenly in a 9 x 9 x 2-inch baking pan (metal or glass). Scatter the blueberries over the top. Whisk together the egg and water to make an egg wash. Arrange the biscuits on top of the blueberries, brush the biscuits with the egg wash, and then sprinkle with sugar.

Bake the cobbler for about 35 minutes, until the biscuits are golden brown and the fruit is bubbly. Serve warm with vanilla ice cream.

Cinnamon-Oatmeal Strawberry Shortcakes

Serves 6

This is one for the quick-and-painless file—10 minutes to mix, 20 minutes to bake, and voilà—you are Superhost! The tasty sconelike shortcakes are perfect for soaking up the berry juices. The dough can be made ahead and refrigerated for up to 8 hours before baking, and the strawberries can be prepared ahead, too. Make a double batch of dough, and you can have fresh scones with butter and jam for breakfast the next day.

4 cups stemmed and quartered fresh strawberries
^{1}/$_2$ cup plus 2 tablespoons sugar
1^1/$_2$ cups all-purpose flour
1^1/$_2$ cups old-fashioned oats (not quick-cooking)
1^1/$_4$ teaspoons ground cinnamon
1 tablespoon baking powder
^{1}/$_4$ teaspoon salt
10 tablespoons cold unsalted butter, cut into cubes
^{1}/$_2$ cup heavy cream
3 large egg yolks
1 teaspoon vanilla extract
1 egg (optional)
1 teaspoon cream or water (optional)
Rolled oats and/or sugar for sprinkling on top (optional)
Whipped cream for garnish

Toss the strawberries with the ^{1}/$_2$ cup sugar in a bowl. Lightly crush the berries to release their juices and allow them to sit at room temperature while you prepare the shortcakes.

Preheat the oven to 425°. Combine the flour, oats, remaining 2 tablespoons sugar, cinnamon, baking powder, and salt in a large bowl. Toss in the butter and, with your fingertips or a pastry cutter, cut in the butter until the mixture resembles a coarse meal. Whisk together the cream, yolks, and vanilla in a small bowl. Using a fork, stir the mixture into the dry ingredients until a shaggy dough forms. Turn out the dough onto a floured work surface and knead gently for six to eight folds, until smooth. Do not overwork the dough, or the biscuits will be tough. Using your hands, gently pat the dough into a circle about ^{3}/$_4$ inch thick. Cut it into six wedges with a sharp knife. If you want a glaze, whisk together the egg and water or cream, and brush onto the tops of the wedges. Sprinkle with oats.

Place the wedges on a buttered or parchment-lined baking sheet. Bake for 20 to 25 minutes, until nicely browned and firm. Then let cool.

When cool, split the shortcakes horizontally. Cover the bottom halves with the sweetened strawberries, add a dollop of whipped cream, and replace the tops.

Chocolate Pecan Jack Daniel's Cake with Jack Daniel's Chocolate Sauce

Makes one 10-inch cake (10 to 12 normal servings or 6 really big ones)

I claim that this is the only dessert I'm able to make, not counting my tapioca pudding. Back in the early days of Mustards, when I had to perform impromptu pastry tasks, it was the first thing on the dessert menu, and aside from the onion rings and roasted garlic, it is the longest runner of all. You can use walnuts instead of pecans, or substitute rum or brandy for the Jack Daniel's, but the pecans have a special affinity for Jack Daniel's and give it that authentic Southern "it's-way-too-rich-but-I-can't-stop-eating-it" flavor. This great chocolate sauce recipe comes from the Fog City Diner Cookbook. It's the standard chocolate sauce at Mustards as well. A good basic sauce to have on hand, you can use it to dress up store-bought ice cream or cake when you're not in the mood to make some fancy dessert. Any type of booze will work, or you can leave it out altogether. Use a high-quality chocolate for optimum silkiness. We normally don't use all the garnishes I have listed, but just in case . . .

2 cups pecan pieces
6 tablespoons unsalted butter
6 ounces semisweet chocolate
$^{1}/_{4}$ cup Jack Daniel's whiskey
8 large eggs, separated
1 cup sugar
Tiny pinch of salt

JACK DANIEL'S CHOCOLATE SAUCE
8 ounces good-quality semisweet chocolate, chopped or broken into small pieces
$^{1}/_{2}$ cup unsalted butter
3 tablespoons Jack Daniel's whiskey
$^{3}/_{4}$ cup corn syrup
$^{3}/_{4}$ cup heavy whipping cream

OPTIONAL GARNISHES
Confectioners' sugar
Mint Julep Ice Cream (page 246)
Whipped cream, flavored with vanilla extract

Preheat the oven to 325°. Butter and flour a 10-inch springform pan.

Spread the pecans on a baking sheet and toast for about 12 minutes, until very fragrant. Let cool, then grind the nuts in a food processor or chop finely.

Combine the butter, chocolate, and whiskey in a large, heatproof bowl. Place over a saucepan of simmering water, and stir occasionally until melted and uniform. Remove from the heat.

Put the egg yolks and $^{3}/_{4}$ cup of the sugar in an electric mixer fitted with the whip attachment. Beat on high speed until very thick and pale. Stir the ground pecans into the chocolate mixture, then fold in the whipped yolks.

In a clean bowl, with a clean whip attachment, beat the egg whites on high speed until foamy. Slowly add the remaining $^{1}/_{4}$ cup sugar and the salt, and whip on high speed until soft peaks form. In three batches, quickly but gently fold the egg whites into the chocolate mixture, maintaining as much volume as possible. Pour the batter into the prepared pan and bake for 40 to 45 minutes, until the cake springs back when pressed gently in the center. Cool completely on a rack, then remove the sides of the pan.

To make the sauce, combine the chocolate, butter, whiskey, and corn syrup in a heatproof bowl and set over barely simmering water. Cook, stirring occasionally, until the chocolate and butter are melted. Remove from the heat and stir in the cream. Now, see if you can keep from eating it all before it's time to serve it!

To serve, cut the cake into the desired number of portions. Place each slice on a pool of warm chocolate sauce and dust liberally with confectioners' sugar. Place a big scoop of ice cream alongside and a dollop of whipped cream on top (why diet now?).

Blueberry Cornmeal Upside-Down Cake

**Makes one 9-inch cake
(serves 8 to 10)**

*A good old-fashioned cast-iron skillet
is the perfect baking pan for upside-
down cakes. No need to butter, flour,
or otherwise prepare the pan, cleanup
is a breeze on the stovetop, and the
cake benefits from the gentle, even
heat of the cast iron. This cake was
tested in an heirloom cast-iron skillet
that Brigid dug out of her mother's
basement. The pan said "8" on the
handle, but when she measured it
actually was 8 inches across the bottom and 9¹/₂ inches across the top. In
any case, measure your pan before
you start. It should have sides at least
2 inches high and should be 9 to 10
inches across. If you're using a wider
pan, check the cake a bit sooner as it
will bake more quickly in a larger
pan. You'll need 3 cups of blueberries
for the cake, and another 3 cups for
the sauce.*

CARAMELIZED BERRIES
¹/₄ cup unsalted butter
¹/₂ cup firmly packed light brown sugar
3 cups fresh or frozen blueberries

CAKE
³/₄ cup cornmeal
1¹/₂ cups all-purpose flour
2¹/₄ teaspoons baking powder
¹/₂ teaspoon salt
1 cup unsalted butter, softened
1¹/₂ cups granulated sugar
4 large eggs, at room temperature
1¹/₂ teaspoons vanilla extract
³/₄ cup sour cream

BLUEBERRY SAUCE
3 cups fresh or frozen blueberries
¹/₄ cup granulated sugar or to taste
2 teaspoons freshly-squeezed lemon juice

Whipped cream

To make the caramel, melt the butter in 8- to 10-inch cast-iron skillet over medium-high heat. Add the brown sugar and cook, stirring constantly, for 5 to 7 minutes, until the mixture is very thick and bubbly. Remove from the heat, distribute the blueberries evenly over the butter-sugar glaze, and set aside.

To make the cake, preheat the oven to 350°. Sift together the cornmeal, flour, baking powder, and salt. Cream the butter and sugar in an electric mixer fitted with the paddle attachment until very light and fluffy. Add the eggs one at a time, beating after each addition. Then add the vanilla and mix until smooth. On low speed, add the dry ingredients in three batches, alternating with the sour cream, and starting and ending with the dry ingredients. Beat only until combined. Spread the batter evenly over the blueberries in the skillet. Bake for 45 to 50 minutes, or until a toothpick inserted in center of the cake comes out clean. Allow the cake to cool for 15 minutes, then run a sharp knife around the inside edge of the skillet. Invert a large plate over the skillet and, using oven mitts, turn the skillet upside down to flip the cake over onto the plate. If the cake has cooled down too much, it may not release from the pan. If this happens, heat it for 2 or 3 minutes on the stovetop before attempting to turn it out.

To make the berry sauce, combine the blueberries and ¹/₄ cup sugar in a small saucepan and bring to a simmer over medium heat. Simmer the berries gently, stirring occasionally for about 10 min-utes, until they give off their juices and the skins are just beginning to burst. Remove from the heat and stir in the lemon juice. Taste and adjust the sugar, if necessary.

Serve the cake warm, with the blueberry sauce and whipped cream.

Brown Sugar Angel Cake with Whiskey Crème Anglaise

Serves 6

Brown sugar and molasses give this angel cake a robust flavor and beautiful golden brown color. A variety of serving options are possible for this versatile cake. If you want to dress it up, dust each slice with confectioners' sugar and serve with a generous helping of Whiskey Crème Anglaise and fresh raspberries. For a simpler approach, toast the slices and serve them with lightly crushed, sweetened strawberries and vanilla ice cream or whipped cream. In order to get the fluffiest and lightest angel cake, use only room-temperature egg whites from very fresh eggs, and make sure they are free of any trace of yolk.

The anglaise is a simple and versatile dessert sauce, suitable for everything from cakes and berries to bread pudding. It's also a good way to use up extra egg yolks. Other liquors can be used in place of the whiskey—Grand Marnier and Cointreau are nice substitutions—or you can leave out the liquor altogether. The crème anglaise will not keep for more than 4 or 5 days, so you may only want to make half a batch.

1¹/₂ cups firmly packed light brown sugar
1¹/₃ cups cake flour
¹/₄ cup molasses (not blackstrap variety)
1 teaspoon vanilla extract
1³/₄ cups egg whites (about 12 large egg whites)
³/₄ teaspoon salt
1 teaspoon cream of tartar

WHISKEY CRÈME ANGLAISE
2 cups half-and-half
¹/₂ vanilla bean, split and scraped
5 large egg yolks
¹/₂ cup sugar
2 tablespoons whiskey or other liquor
Pinch of salt

Confectioners' sugar (optional)
Fresh raspberries for garnish (optional)

Preheat the oven to 350°. Have ready a 10-inch tube pan.

Sift ³/₄ cup of the brown sugar and the cake flour together two times into a bowl. Stir together molasses and vanilla in a large bowl. Combine the egg whites, salt, and cream of tartar in an electric mixer fitted with the whip attachment. Beat on high speed until foamy. Gradually add the remaining ³/₄ cup brown sugar (no need to sift it) and whip until firm, moist peaks form. Using a spatula, transfer the egg white mixture to the bowl with the molasses and mix gently to combine. Sprinkle half of the flour mixture over the whites and fold it in, then repeat with the remaining flour. Spoon the batter into the tube pan, then firmly rap the pan once on the counter to remove any air bubbles. Bake for 40 to 45 minutes, until a toothpick or skewer inserted into the center of the cake comes out clean. Remove the pan from the oven and invert it on a rack or slide it over a long-necked bottle to cool.

To make the anglaise, combine the half-and-half and the vanilla bean in a saucepan. Bring to a boil and remove from the heat. Allow the bean to steep for 20 minutes.

In a bowl, whisk the yolks and sugar together until smooth, then gradually whisk in the hot half-and-half. Return the mixture to the saucepan and cook over medium heat, stirring constantly, for 5 to 7 minutes, until the sauce is thick enough to coat the back of a spoon (about 170° if you're using a candy thermometer). Strain the sauce through a fine-mesh sieve. Add the liquor and salt. Chill it on ice or in the refrigerator.

When the cake is completely cool, run a knife around the sides of the pan, and gently twist the center tube to remove the cake. Cut the cake into slices with a sharp serrated knife. Place each slice in a pool of the crème anglaise, dust with confectioners' sugar, and garnish with raspberries.

Peach Melba Cakes

Makes one 10-inch tube cake

This cake was inspired by the famous peach-and-raspberry combination Escoffier created for the Australian opera singer Nellie Melba. In the Mustards version, sweet, juicy peaches are baked into individual golden butter cakes and sauced with tangy raspberries—a fruit-and-cake match made in heaven. You can use flavorful freestone peaches that are firm but ripe. If they have thick, fuzzy skins, you should peel them. (This is easily accomplished by blanching them briefly in boiling water to which you have added a bit of lemon juice, then plunging them into ice water. The skins should then slip right off.) I recommend superfine sugar for the cakes, but granulated sugar will do. The cakes can be made early in the day, then reheated as described below.

1¼ cups all-purpose flour
1½ teaspoons baking powder
¾ teaspoon salt
6 tablespoons unsalted butter, softened
¾ cup superfine sugar
1½ teaspoons vanilla extract
3 large egg yolks
¾ cup sour cream
3 large, firm but ripe peaches, halved and pitted
6 tablespoons light brown sugar

4 cups raspberries
½ to 1 cup granulated sugar
1 teaspoon freshly squeezed lemon juice

Whipped cream, for garnish

Preheat the oven to 350°. Butter and flour six 4-inch ramekins (they should each hold about 1¼ cups). Place the ramekins on a baking sheet and set them aside. Sift together the flour, baking powder, and salt. Cream the butter and superfine sugar in an electric mixer fitted with the paddle attachment, until light and fluffy. Add the vanilla and beat until smooth. With the motor running, add the egg yolks one at a time, beating after each addition, and beat until smooth. On low speed, add the dry ingredients in three batches, alternately with the sour cream and starting and ending with the dry ingredients. Beat only until combined. Finish mixing by hand with a spatula. Divide the batter among the ramekins, and level the cake batter with a small spatula or butter knife. Set a peach half, cut side up, into the center of each ramekin atop the batter. Sprinkle each cake with 1 tablespoon of the brown sugar. Bake the cakes for 30 to 35 minutes, until the cakes are golden brown around edges and a toothpick or skewer inserted into the center of the cake comes out clean. The cake batter will bake up around the peaches without completely covering them up. Allow the cakes to cool in the ramekins on a rack.

While the cakes are baking, combine the berries with the ½ cup sugar and the lemon juice, and gently crush the raspberries with a fork to release the juices. Allow the raspberries to macerate at room temperature for at least 30 minutes, then taste and add sugar as necessary. The raspberries can sit at room temperature for up to 1 hour, or you can refrigerate them until they are needed.

To serve, increase the oven temperature to 450°. Return the cakes to the oven for 3 to 4 minutes, then run a paring knife around the edges of the ramekins and turn out the cakes. Turn them right side up on serving plates, and surround each with a helping of raspberries. Top with a dollop of whipped cream.

Coco-Nutty Cake

Makes one 10-inch tube cake
and serves 10 to 12

This is a cake for that cake stand buried in your grandma's attic. A giant, white behemoth of a dessert, it is perfect for a special event, though Brigid has relatives who swear by it for breakfast. It is equally delicious filled with raspberry or blackberry jam. Be sure to sift the cake flour before measuring it, as cake flour tends to get very lumpy and compacted in the box. If you make a vertical stripe of frosting on the edge of the cake before you split it into layers, it will help you to reassemble the cake, which can be a tricky proposition with 3 or 4 layers. After you've split the cake and spread the layers with filling, just line up the stripes.

A versatile treat to have on hand, lemon curd takes only minutes to make and keeps for up to 2 weeks in the refrigerator. For a simple and delicious dessert, serve a dollop of it with mixed summer berries or atop a slice of angelfood or pound cake. You will find dozens of uses for this tangy delight—you may even want to make a double batch!

LEMON OR LIME CURD

1 cup sugar

2 whole eggs

2 egg yolks

$1/3$ cup freshly squeezed lemon or lime juice

6 tablespoons unsalted butter, cut up

1 teaspoon grated lemon or lime zest

CAKE

2 cups sweetened coconut flakes plus
   $1/2$ cup for garnish (optional)

$3^{1}/_{2}$ cups sifted cake flour

5 teaspoons baking powder

$1/4$ teaspoon freshly grated nutmeg

$1/2$ teaspoons salt

$3/4$ cup unsalted butter, at room temperature

$2^{1}/_{3}$ cups sugar

1 vanilla bean, seeds only, or 4 teaspoons vanilla extract

2 cups coconut milk

1 cup egg whites (about 8 large egg whites)

2 tablespoons dark rum

FLUFFY WHITE FROSTING

$3/4$ cup egg whites (about 6 large egg whites)

$1/2$ teaspoon cream of tartar

$1^{3}/_{4}$ cups sugar

$1/4$ cup water

2 teaspoons vanilla extract

To make the curd, whisk together the sugar, eggs, and egg yolks in a heavy, nonreactive saucepan. Add the citrus juice, butter, and zest, place over medium heat, and cook, whisking constantly, for 10 to 15 minutes, until very thick. Do not allow the curd to boil. Strain the curd through a medium-mesh sieve into a bowl and cover with plastic wrap, pressing it directly onto the surface. Refrigerate until cold.

Preheat the oven to 350°. Butter and flour a 10-inch tube pan. To make the cake, spread 2 cups coconut flakes on a baking sheet, place in the oven, and toast, stirring every 5 minutes, for 10 to 15 minutes, until golden brown. Set aside.

To make the cake, sift together the flour, baking powder, nutmeg, and salt into a large bowl. Combine the butter, 2 cups of the sugar, and vanilla in an electric mixer fitted with the paddle attachment. Cream on high speed until light and fluffy. On low speed, add the dry ingredients in three batches, alternately with the $1^{1}/_{2}$ cups coconut milk, and starting and ending with the dry ingredients. Beat only until combined. Stir in the 2 cups of coconut flakes and transfer the batter to a large bowl. In another clean bowl, with a clean whip attachment, beat the egg whites on high speed until foamy. Slowly add the remaining $1/3$ cup sugar and whip until soft peaks form. In two batches, quickly but gently fold the egg whites into the coconut batter. Pour the batter into the prepared pan.

Bake the cake until a toothpick or skewer inserted into the center of the cake comes out clean, about 1 hour. Cool the cake in the pan for 10 minutes, then turn it out onto a rack to cool completely.

When the cake is completely cooled, use a serrated knife to split it into three or four layers. Combine the remaining $\frac{1}{2}$ cup coconut milk and the rum in a small bowl, and brush the top of each layer with the mixture. Spread the bottom two or three layers with jam or curd and stack the cake back together.

To make the frosting, place the egg whites and cream of tarter in an electric mixer fitted with the whip attachment. Combine the sugar and water in a small saucepan, mixing until evenly combined. Brush the sides of the pan with a clean, wet pastry brush if crystals form. Attach a candy thermometer to the pan and turn the heat on high. Cook, without stirring, for 10 to 12 minutes, until the mixture registers 230° on the thermometer, at which time you should start whipping the egg whites on high speed and let the sugar continue to cook until it registers 240°. The whites should form firm peaks before you add the sugar, so remove the sugar from the heat if it is ready before the whites to medium-low speed and pour the sugar into the whites in a very thin stream. After all sugar has been added, turn the mixer to high and whip until the mixture is cool, and the frosting is glossy, thick, and very white. Mix in the vanilla.

Frost the sides and top of cake with the white frosting and sprinkle with the remaining $\frac{1}{2}$ cup coconut. Display your masterpiece on a large cake stand.

Glossary

Asian Ingredients

Take a stroll down your favorite supermarket's Asian foods aisle, and you will be surprised by the variety and quality of ingredients available today. Of course, if you have an Asian grocery nearby, it is a better place to shop. A few ingredients called for in these recipes may take a little extra effort to find, but you'll learn a lot in the searching process. Look at labels, and pass up those products that contain MSG.

CURRY PASTE: A good-quality Indian curry paste, such as Patak's, is a time-saving way to add an exotic element to salads and to fish or chicken dishes. When you buy a curry paste, the hard part of making a curry dish-the toasting, expert mixing, and cooking of the spices with oils and garlic-is bottled for you to use as you please. Check the labels for items like MSG that you don't need. There are also Thai-style curry pastes on the market. Beware if you have a shellfish allergy, as they usually contain dried shrimp.

FISH SAUCE: Made from salted, fermented fish, this zinger of a flavor enhancer is produced in different Southeast Asian countries under different names. The two most common varieties are the Vietnamese nuoc mam and the Thai nam pla. Used in the proper sparing amounts, fish sauce can add a whole new dimension to sauces and marinades. We prefer the brand with the crab on the label.

LEMONGRASS: From looking at it, you'd never know that this Southeast Asian herb has such subtle, lemony flavors. It resembles a very tough, overgrown scallion, but peel away the tough outer leaves of the stalk and you will find the bulblike base, which can be shredded or minced for use in various recipes. In a pinch, you can substitute the grated zest of 1 lemon for 1 tablespoon minced lemongrass.

MIRIN: This sweetened Japanese rice cooking wine is often used in marinades. If you can't find it, add a bit of sugar to sake, bring it to a boil to cook off the alcohol, and reduce it to a light syrup consistency.

SOY SAUCE/TAMARI SOY SAUCE: Although most of the soy sauce you find in the supermarket is the same fermented soybean-and-wheat concoction that you splash on in your favorite Chinese restaurant, countless varieties are made, ranging from light and thin to dark and syrupy. Check out different types, particularly if you have access to an Asian market. Tamari soy sauce is a Japanese product, generally brewed without wheat. It is thicker and mellower than other soy sauces, qualities that make it a great condiment. Also keep your eye out for *ketjap manis,* a sweet Indonesian soy-based condiment that is marvelous in marinades.

Bread

Great artisanal bakeries are popping up all over the country. They bake a taste of the past, in the form of hearty French- and Italian-style breads. When a recipe calls for a "rustic country bread," look for a sturdy, crunchy-crusted loaf with an interesting texture that will hold up to grilling, saucing, and spreading.

Bread crumbs can be made from just about any kind of bread, but if you have tasty bread, you will have tasty bread crumbs. To make bread crumbs, arrange slices or chunks of bread on a baking sheet and toast t 375° until golden and dry, then grate on the large holes of a grater or pulse in a food processor. To make a delicious garnish for pasta or baked vegetable dishes, toss bread crumbs with a mixture of equal parts olive oil and melted butter, sprinkle with salt and pepper, and return to the 375° oven for 6 to 7 minutes, until golden brown.

Chiles and Peppers

DRIED CHILES: Always look for supple, freshly dried, not-too-dusty chiles. If you see fine dust in the bottom of the bag, it's an indication that the chiles have small worms or moths and that their insides will have been eaten, leaving just the tough outer skin. Some common dried chiles are the California, New Mexico, ancho, árbol, guajillo, and pasilla negro. Chipotles are smoked, dried jalapeños. The dried red chipotles are called morita: the brown ones, as far as I've been able to discover, are just called chipotles. I prefer the red chipotles, but whichever one you find will work. (Canned dried chipotles are also available, sometimes in adobo, a thick, tomato-based sauce.) Store whole dried chiles in well-sealed plastic bags in the freezer if they're not used frequently.

Dried chiles need to be rehydrated and puréed before you can cook with them. To prepare them, first remove the stems and seeds. (If you keep the seeds in, your purée will be hotter. Some say the hotter the better, but I don't always agree.) Briefly toast the chiles. If you have a gas range, just grab them with some tongs and wave them over a flame for 1 or 2 seconds per side, until fragrant. Otherwise, stick them in a 350° oven for 2 or 3 minutes. Soak the toasted chiles in warm water to cover for 5 to 10 minutes, until pliable. When the chiles are soft, they can be puréed in a blender or food processor and strained. When placed in a clean container and refrigerated, puréed chiles will keep for up to 2 weeks.

FRESH CHILES: Commonly used fresh chile varieties, such as the jalapeño and serrano, can be found in most supermarket produce sections. In California, we have our own little idiosyncrasy regarding the large, dark green stuffing chile that we call the pasilla. In other parts of the country this chile is called a poblano, so look for it under that name. When buying chiles, look for freshly cut stem ends and a smooth, unwrinkled skin. Large, smooth lobes make for easier charring and peeling, if that's your plan. Small, odd-shaped, curved chiles are best for chopping.

Fresh chiles are often roasted and peeled before use. To roast them, hold them over an open flame of a gas stove or wood fire, or place them in a heavy, flat pan over an electric element. Turn them as needed to char and blister the skins evenly. I have also broiled them in the oven. When the skins are nicely blackened, put the chiles in a covered bowl or in a plastic bag and let them cool. When cool, the skins will easily slip off. Yes, a wood or charcoal fire produces the best flavor by far, and roasting chiles this way is a good way to use up those perfect coals after you've finished cooking dinner.

All chile varieties will vary in heat from crop to crop and season to season, so check your chiles for the desired heat before using 5 or 6 extra serranos in a recipe. The heat is found in the seed and in the seed-holding membrane. Remove both to tame the spiciness of your recipe.

PEPPERS: Sweet red bell peppers and fall pimientos are some of my favorite foods, which is probably why you find them in so many of my recipes. For best flavor, both should be roasted and peeled, which is done in the same manner as fresh chiles (see above). Try this: Roast the peppers until the skins just begin to blacken, cover, and steam for a few minutes. Peel away the charred skin and douse with a good bit of extra virgin olive oil. Sprinkle on some coarse gray salt, and serve on a thickish slab of rustic country bread for a wonderful, quick meal.

Dairy Products

BUTTER: Real butter has a flavor and texture that cannot be duplicated by any vegetable-based, hydrogenated, artificially stabilized product. In other words, everything is better with butter. We used unsalted butter in all the recipes in this book, which allows you to add salt at your discretion. Using unsalted butter is essential when it comes to making Brigid's desserts. Butter is salted as a means of preservation, so unsalted butter is more perishable. It's a good idea to store unsalted butter in the freezer if you use only a little at a time.

CHEESE: Search out local artisanal cheese makers. Finding them and using their cheeses will help preserve an important

source of good food. For a few classic cheeses, such as Italian Parmigiano-Reggiano, Swiss Emmentaler, or Norwegian Jarlsburg, no domestic substitutes exist. But for most, there are domestic varieties that are just as good. Maytag Blue is one I especially like, and I love the domestic goat cheeses. Some cheeses can provide big flavor in small amounts, like an Italian Asiago, a delicious fresh goat cheese from Laura Chenel. Buy small amounts of the more expensive cheeses and wrap them in parchment or waxed paper, then in plastic wrap or in airtight plastic storage bags, and refrigerate. For the best flavor and texture, allow cheese to come to room temperature before serving,

CREAM: Heavy whipping cream, once the staple of restaurant sauce making, has fallen out of favor with the general public and modern chefs. As with any rich and extravagant food, however, the operative word should be "moderation," that is, a little goes a long way. It takes only a small addition of cream to make a potato or squash soup noticeably richer and more elegant, or a pasta sauce a little more substantial. The higher the butterfat content of the cream, the richer the texture will be, so check out the health food or gourmet stores for cream from small dairies that produce old-fashioned, rather than "ultrapasteurized," cream. It is usually worth the extra expense.

CRÈME FRAÎCHE: If fresh cream were not pasteurized, bacteria would naturally thicken it at room temperature, giving you crème fraîche, a thick and voluptuous cream. Since nearly all dairy products in the United States are pasteurized, we can only make crème fraîche here by introducing a live culture into cream: combine 2 tablespoons of buttermilk, which contains active cultures, with 1 cup of heavy whipping cream and allow it to stand, covered, at room temperature for 24 hours, and it should thicken nicely. After it has thickened, stir it up and store it in the refrigerator. Crème fraîche is a delicious addition to fresh fruit, soups, or Mexican dishes, and can be flavored with herbs, citrus juice or zest, sugar, or spices. If you don't have time to make crème fraîche, and you can't find it at the store, you can substitute sour cream, but only if you're using it in a preparation that will not be cooked. Sour cream will curdle when heated, but crème fraiche will not.

Fish

It has been a long time since fishermen regularly arrived at our back door with great-looking, freshly caught bluefin tuna, king salmon, or halibut to sell. Things have gotten more formal, but as our local fish purveyors' businesses have grown, so have our options on seafood. Everything from soft-shell crabs from Maryland to Alaskan salmon is now possible. Availability changes constantly, though, so I don't like to put seafood on the printed menu. I know that as soon as a fish or shellfish item appears, it will become impossible to get or much too expensive. So we check with our seafood suppliers first thing every morning, then decide on the seafood specials to offer for the day.

SOME FISH COOKING BASICS: It's not possible to be exact about cooking times, as heat of fire, distance from fire, and thickness of fish all make a difference. The rule of thumb, however, is 8 to 10 minutes total time per inch of thickness to cook fish through. Cut the time a little if you like your fish a bit less done. When grilling fish fillets, I leave the skin on the fish, as this keeps it from breaking up on the grill, making it easier to handle. The fish should be scaled, though. After the fish is cooked, the skin will peel off easily, or, if you prefer, you can just leave it on.

Anyone interested in learning more about seafood should search out a copy of James Peterson's *Fish & Shellfish*.

CHILEAN SEA BASS: Despite the name, this is not a sea bass at all, but a mero or Patagonian toothfish. It's oily and dense, comes from very deep waters, and is always frozen, or so I've been told by people whom I trust. It's in short supply, so it may be hard to find. West Coast white sea bass or halibut are okay substitutions, but Florida grouper or monkfish, the latter one of my favorite fish, would be a better choice.

HALIBUT: Among our chefs there seems to be a split, with some on the side of local halibut and others on the side of Alaskan halibut. The Alaskan season starts in March or April and runs through September, and the California season depends on the water temperature: if it's cold, they're not here. Sole, flounder, cod, and haddock can be substituted.

SALMON: In many areas around the world, including the West Coast of the United States, Atlantic salmon is farmed, a species that is almost extinct in the wild. Norway, Scotland, Chile, and Canada are among the largest producers. For some wonderful salmon eating, there is West Coast Pacific salmon, which is also farmed. But nothing can beat the taste of wild salmon. The season for king or Chinook salmon runs from May 1 to September 30, with many restrictions on fishing in specific areas throughout the period. Some chefs feel that the king salmon from the Copper River in Alaska is the best eating salmon of all, but these fish have a very short season and are in very high demand, so it can be difficult to find them. Sockeye salmon is another choice fish. It also has a very limited season, often just a single day. Silver or coho salmon is illegal if from southern Oregon and Washington, but okay if from Canada and Alaska. Finally, there are the pinks and the chums that are mostly for the canning industry.

STURGEON: Farmed sturgeon is readily available in California. Now and then we get wild sturgeon from the Chehalis River in Washington or from the Columbia River on the border between Oregon and Washington. Both sources provide outstanding fish. Swordfish, monkfish, and shark are good substitutes for sturgeon.

TROUT: Although red trout and catfish are available on a regular basis, I usually find these fish disappointing, as the meat tends to taste muddy from the overcrowded ponds in which they are farmed. Several Idaho trout farms produce tasty fish, however, I do love to go to the California Trout Hatchery in Calistoga, where you can fish two days a week in the summer. It's almost as if the trout are trained to grab your hook. I've always found these fish to be delicious.

TUNA: We use ahi tuna, which is the Hawaiian name for yellowfin, bluefin, or bigeye tuna, and tombo, which is the Hawaiian name for albacore. Tombo has a much lower fat content than the ahi, which makes people think it is dry. Cook it to medium-rare and serve it in a moist, juicy presentation, and it will be delightful. Commonly you hear about sashimi-grade tuna, which is presumed to be the highest quality, suitable for raw preparations, and grill-grade tuna, which is thought to be of lesser quality. These terms are somewhat arbitrary, however. They may mean something in Japan, but here, sashimi grade only seems to indicate fresher fish with maybe a higher oil content. Mahimahi, swordfish, and jacks would also be nice in recipes calling for tuna.

Shellfish

CALAMARI: To clean calamari (small squid), pull the tentacles away from the body with a twisting motion, so that the sac of the viscera inside the body comes out in one piece. Cut the tentacles away just above the eyes, or beak, and discard the insides (the tentacles are delicious, so don't throw them away). Rinse out the body, removing the piece of clear cartilage inside, and peel off the spotted outer membrane.

CLAMS: Manila clams are cultivated versus farmed and are mostly from Washington. They are best, to my taste, in the fall and winter months.

DUNGENESS CRABS: This is our West Coast delight. The season for Alaska and Washington opens in October, and the Northern California and Oregon seasons are in full swing usually by November 15. Alaska's season goes the longest, shutting down in August. The crabs average 2 to 2½ pounds each, with jumbo ones running up to 4 pounds each. You can figure that one crab will feed two average eaters, although if you're just serving cracked crab, cocktail sauce, and drawn butter, figure on one crab per person.

If you are using just crabmeat and not serving it in the shell, our favorite crab is the Maine rock crab.

MUSSELS: Basically, three varieties of mussel are available on the market. First, there are the Prince Edward Island mussels from Nova Scotia. These are rope grown and have no beard and no grit. Mediterranean mussels, the seed for which originated in the Mediterranean Sea, are farmed next to the Prince Edwards in Nova Scotia, and in Mexico and Washington. Wild black mussels are harvested on the Eastern seacoast of the United States and Canada. Pacific mussels are not harvested commercially.

When buying mussels, be sure the shells are tightly closed, indicating that they are alive. To prepare for cooking, cut or pull off the beard and rinse well. After cooking, discard any that have not opened up.

SOFT-SHELL CRABS: These are in season May through September. Someone once told me that they begin molting after the first full moon in May. That sounds great but I can't find it in any of my three thousand cookbooks and food references, so maybe it is nothing more than a romantic marketing ploy. A soft-shell crab is a crab that has just molted and is in a brand-new, still soft, edible shell. Most of these delicate shellfish come from the Chesapeake Bay in Maryland-at least it is the most famous for them-but they are harvested from Florida and Louisiana waters as well.

Garlic and Leeks

Ready-chopped garlic, available in the produce section, may look like a great convenience, but it is almost always bitter. Instead, buy fresh, whole garlic heads, and prepare them for use yourself. Gently whack whole, unpeeled garlic cloves with the side of a large knife to loosen the skin, then trim off the root end and remove the peel. If the germ in the center of the clove has started to sprout, remove it. This little green stem, which is the beginning of a new garlic plant, will give the clove a bitter taste. Late-season garlic can be quite strong. At the end of the year, we often blanch the garlic briefly to help tame the end-of-season bitterness (drop the peeled cloves in boiling water for 1 or 2 minutes, then drain and chill them to stop the cooking). The red variety is often less bitter. Unless otherwise specified, peel garlic (and shallots and onions) before using.

LEEKS tend to hold a lot of grit, so always clean them carefully. Cut off the root ends, remove any tough outer leaves, and trim off the tops, leaving 1 to 2 inches of the light green parts. Cut the leeks in half lengthwise (or in rings, if the recipe calls for that), then wash thoroughly under cold running water.

SPRING GARLIC, also know as green garlic, is the immature bulb of a garlic plant, harvested in early spring before the garlic peel has firmed and dried. It is milder and sweeter in flavor than mature garlic, so you can use almost all of it, as you do leeks or scallions, and it can be substituted for scallions or garlic cloves. If you can't find it or if it's not the right season, you may want to try garlic chives, a flat, garlicky-tasting chive variety. You may find ivory or yellow garlic chives in some areas, particularly in Asian markets. These have been "blanched" (covered up) during growing to stop the photosynthesis and greening of the herb. When we thin our garlic crop, we pull spring garlic out of our garden and use it in the kitchen. Many garlic growers here in California are marketing spring garlic as well, sometimes as early as January.

Herbs

Fresh herbs give dishes a special bright, sweet flavor that dried herbs can't match. You can find fresh herbs in the produce section of most supermarkets, or you can buy a few little herb plants from the nursery (chives, mint, and rosemary are particularly easy to grow) and keep them in pots, indoors or out. Chop fresh herbs with a very sharp knife or scissors. A dull blade will bruise and discolor the leaves. Buy only small amounts and store unused herbs wrapped in a damp paper towel in the refrigerator.

Some herbs, such as epazote, are harder to find than others. Epazote is a musky, pointy-leaved herb used in Latin American cooking, particularly in Mexico, where it is commonly added to dishes (it helps to reduce their gaseous effects). It can be found in Latin markets in its fresh and dried forms, and, because it grows like a weed, in gardens and vacant lots around California. Epazote has a pungent flavor, like a cross between oregano, basil, and cilantro, and since it can't be found everywhere, you may have to substitute with those herbs accordingly. See mail-order sources on page 269, too.

Dried herbs are not as bad as I once thought. Some herbs, such as Mexican oregano, are only available here dried. And when my garden is full of blooming thyme, I do like to dry it, as it seems to me to be at the peak of its flavor at that point. Most herbs are better fresh, however, and some simply don't take well to drying. Basil, for example, is best fresh, and you're better off making pesto with your excess rather than drying it to use throughout the winter.

Pepper

For many years, all I would use was white pepper. But over time I have grown up, and now I really love Tellicherry black pepper, and that's all I use. It *must* be freshly ground, however. If I don't want to use the pepper mill, I will grind up a tablespoon or so before I begin to cook, to use for the dishes of the upcoming meal. It really makes a difference.

Salt

Salt may be the most important ingredient in the kitchen, as you need at least a pinch of it in just about every dish you cook. It's such a common ingredient that most people don't give it a second thought. But it can make or break your dish: too much, too little, the wrong kind. So taste as you're cooking, and give some consideration to the salt you're buying. Read the labels carefully, as salts often contain preservatives and "free-pouring" agents, and you should avoid these products. We used pure coarse kosher salt or fine or coarse sea salt for all of the recipes in this book, all of which should be easy to get.

Many unusual types of salt are available, and believe it or not, they all taste slightly different and frequently have different applications. Gray sea salt, which comes from France, is slightly gray and has coarse crystals. I use it most often crushed over vine-ripened tomatoes, or sprinkled gingerly over roasted red meat or on meats as they come off the grill, to melt in as the food goes to the table. (I very lightly salt the meat prior to cooking, too.) When I travel, salts are one of the things I search out. A lot of interesting salts are out there: Hawaiian red salt for roasting fish, Japanese sea salts that are very finely ground and are excellent with grilled rare tuna and salmon, and several varieties of gray sea salt. Fleur de Sel, which comes from Brittany, has coarse, hard, gray crystals. Maldon sea salt from England is a flake salt and dissolves excellently.

Spices

Buy small amounts of whole spices to toast and grind as you need them. A health food store that sells spices in bulk is an invaluable source, or try Penzey's if you have to mail order (see Sources). By selling the spices in bulk, these suppliers can forego the expense of packaging and offer fresher, better-quality products. Buy whole nutmeg and grate it on that little raspy section of the grater you never use! Buy whole cloves, allspice berries, cumin, fennel seeds, and aniseeds, and grind them in a coffee or spice grinder. You'll be astonished at the strength of flavor present in freshly ground spices as compared to the preground variety. To bring out the flavor of cumin and fennel seeds, before grinding them, toast them briefly in a dry skillet over high heat, tossing frequently, until they are fragrant. Another good tool is a mortar and pestle, which can be used for making pastes of garlic and herbs such as pesto, as well as for grinding spices.

Mushrooms

Shiitakes, creminis, portobellos and other formerly exotic mushroom varieties are now being successfully cultivated in the United States. Porcini (fall and late spring), morels (spring), and chanterelles (fall to early winter, with some areas getting summer ones) are less common wild varieties that you might find in your local gourmet shop or farmers' market in season. Gently brush fresh mushrooms free of dirt, and stem woody-stemmed varieties such as the shiitake. If you're using a lot of mushrooms, save the stems for making mushroom stock. Avoid washing mushrooms in water if possible. They act like sponges and will dilute the flavor of your finished dishes.

You can often find good-quality dried mushrooms in the produce or spice setion of your supermarket. Soak them in liquid for 30 minutes or so to rehydrate before using in risotto, pasta, or meat dishes. The dried mushroom soaking liquid can be used in place of stock in recipes, but avoid using the grit from the mushrooms that will settle to the bottom of your soaking container. Either strain the liquid first, or carefully pour off liquid from the top. Roughly, 2 ounces of dried mushrooms will equal about 1⅓ cups fresh.

Nuts

Choose fresh, raw nuts and toast them in small amounts as needed. Store nuts, tightly wrapped, in the freezer, as they will turn rancid in a warm kitchen.

Oils

OLIVE OIL plays a major role in the kitchen at Mustards, and it's good to have on hand for most home cooking oil needs. Extra virgin olive oil is the lowest-acid and fruitiest variety, made from the first cold pressing of the finest olives. It is best in cold preparations such as salads, since its flavor diminishes as it is heated. For sautéing and most other cooking preparations, I recommend pure olive oil. Good-quality olive oils are made in California, Spain, Greece, and Italy. You'll want to try different brands to determine which one has the taste you like best.

PEANUT OIL has a high smoke point, making it ideal for deep-frying. It is also best for Asian-inspired dishes and other recipes incompatible with the flavor of olive oil, unless you're worried about an allergy, of course. The Asian brands often have a distinct peanut flavor that can contribute to the complexity of a dish. A combination of canola oil or safflower oil also works well for high-temperature cooking. Sesame oil is a delicious flavoring for Asian dishes, and is available in mild and roasted varieties. Most American oils are mild and virtually flavorless, and I would again recommend trying different brands to find one with a flavor you like.

Salad Greens

Arugula, frisée, kale, red and green oak leaf, and many other varieties of lettuce are turning up in supermarkets everywhere. Most lettuces are easy to grow and can be cut several times from the same plants. Look for greens that are perky and brightly colored. Clean them by submerging them in cold water, then dry them in a salad spinner or by whirling them in a clean, dry kitchen towel or pillowcase (outside!). To store, place the greens in a plastic bag or in a bowl covered with a damp towel and refrigerate. Only buy what you need and use as soon as possible.

Tomatoes

Summer garden tomatoes are one of life's greatest pleasures. They are incomparable in flavor, texture, and juiciness. Making a recipe using fresh tomatoes in the dead of winter is a waste in terms of flavor, aesthetics, and money. I'd go so far as to say you'd be better off with canned tomatoes. Several brands of organic canned tomatoes on the market will work nicely in winter and early spring, when good fresh tomatoes are impossible to get. These are good for cooked dishes only, though. In season, visit farmers' markets to find what are called heirloom tomatoes. These are old varieties that, because they do not ship well, have been passed over by large commercial growers, but that generally have wonderful flavor, color, and aroma. Look for such varieties as Brandywine, German Johnson, Marvel Stripe, Golden Jubilee, and Husky Gold. If you can't find heirlooms, almost any ripe garden tomato will work. Smell the tomatoes: they should smell like tomatoes, not a hothouse!

PEELING TOMATOES: Cut an X into the skin on the blossom end of the tomato, then cut out the core. Dip the tomato into boiling water for 5 to 10 seconds, until the skin has loosened. Scoop it out and plunge it into ice water to chill it immediately. The skin should slip off easily.

Vinegars

Made from a variety of fermented liquids, such as wine, cider, and other fruit juices, vinegar is an indispensable kitchen staple. Have a few basic kinds on hand: cider vinegar, red and white wine vinegars, Japanese or Chinese rice vinegar, Spanish aged sherry vinegar, and, of course, Italian balsamic vinegar. All have endless uses and will keep for months if stored in a cool, dark place. When buying rice vinegars, always purchase the unseasoned variety. Seasoned rice vinegar is too sweet and salty, and some brands contain MSG. It is fun to search out artisanal vinegars and to make your own. You can spend hundreds of dollars on an aged balsamic, which is not absolutely necessary but always delicious. It is something we goofy chefs do.

BLANCHING: Many recipes call for blanching vegetables, sometimes to loosen the skin so that you can peel it off (as with tomatoes), sometimes to cook partially (if the item is to be finished as part of another dish), and sometimes to cook fully (often for foods that are going into a salad). To blanch, start with a large pot of rapidly boiling salted water, then add the vegetables, stirring if needed. When cooked to the desired doneness, put the food in ice water to "shock" it and prevent it from cooking further. Precise times for blanching are not generally possible, as there are too many variables: how much water you boiled, how much food went into the pot, how cold it was, and how large the chunks are. It's easiest to check for doneness by sampling.

SWEATING: The first step in many recipes calls for "sweating" onions and garlic. Sweating means to cook foods carefully over medium heat so that they do not take on any color, yet are tender throughout. Usually 5 to 7 minutes will do it. Sweating will eliminate the sharp taste of raw onions and garlics.

Sources

The Bakers' Catalogue
P.O. Box 876
Norwich, Vermont 05055
800-827-6836
GRAY SEA SALT

Bridge Kitchenware
214 East 52nd Street
New York, NY 10022
212-688-4220
KITCHEN EQUIPMENT

Guittard Chocolate Company
10 Guittard Road
P.O. Box 4308
Burlingame, CA 94010
800-468-2462
QUALITY CHOCOLATE

King Arthur Flour Baker's Catalog
P.O. Box 876
Norwich, VT 05055
800-827-6836
BAKING EQUIPMENT, NIELSEN-MASSEY
VANILLA, GRAY SALT, CRYSTAL SUGAR

J. B. Prince
29 West 38th Street
New York, NY 10018
212-302-8611
GIGANTIC SELECTION OF KITCHEN
EQUIPMENT

La Palma Mexicatessen
2824 24th Street
San Francisco, CA 94110
415-826-4334
MEXICAN SEASONINGS

Laura Chenel Chevre
4310 Fremont Drive
Sonoma, CA 95476
707-996-4477
AGED AND FRESH GOAT CHEESES

Penzey's, Ltd.
P.O. Box 1448
Waukesha, WI 53187
414-574-0277
SPICES

Scharffen Berger Chocolate
250 South Maple Avenue (Unit F)
South San Francisco, CA 94080
800-930-4528
QUALITY CHOCOLATE

Vella Cheese Company
315 Second Street East
Sonoma, CA 95476
707-938-3232
800-848-0505
RAW MILK WHITE CHEDDAR, FRESH
AND AGED JACK, FONTINA, FRESH AND
AGED ASIAGO

CP's Book List

Bayless, Rick, Deann Groen Bayless, and JeanMarie Brownson. *Rick Bayless's Mexican Kitchen*. New York, NY: Scribner, 1996.

Cunningham, Marion. *The Fannie Farmer Cookbook*. New York, NY: Knopf, 1996.

Field, Carol. *The Italian Baker*. New York, NY: Harper & Row, 1985.

Greenspan, Dorie. *Baking with Julia*. New York, NY: William Morrow and Company, Inc., 1996.

Hazen, Janet. *Mustard: Making Your Own Gourmet Mustards*. San Francisco, CA: Chronicle Books, 1993.

Herbst, Sharon Tyler. *The Food Lover's Companion*. Hauppauge, NY: Barron's, 1990.

Jordan, Michele Anna. *The Good Cook's Book of Mustard*. Reading, MA: Addison-Wesley, 1994.

Roberts-Dominguez, Jan. *The Mustard Book*. New York, NY: Macmillan Publishing Co., 1993.

Sax, Richard. *Classic Home Desserts*. Shelburne, VT: Chapters, 1994.

Scherber, Amy and Toy Kim Dupree. *Amy's Bread*. New York, NY: William Morrow and Company Inc., 1996.

Thorne, John. *Simple Cooking*. New York, NY: Penguin, 1989.

Thorne, John with Matt Lewis Thorne. *Outlaw Cook*. New York, NY: Farrar, Straus & Giroux, 1992.

Thorne, John with Matt Lewis Thorne. *The Serious Pig*. New York, NY: North Point Press, 1996.

Index